The Evolving Relations China, the EU and the USA

This book closely scrutinizes the individual and collective roles played by China, the EU and the USA in contemporary world politics.

Examining the three actors' respective strategic and policy positions on and behaviour towards the flux of the contemporary global order, the analysis focuses on three major issues and challenges: foreign and security policy; economics and trade; and climate change and energy. Discussing their relative power, as well as their interests, beliefs and positions on a set of decisive issues, this book explores bilateral relations between the three powers and the ways in which they may interact trilaterally in a broader global context to shape international politics.

Written by a stellar line-up of experts from the fields of politics and international relations, *The Evolving Relationship between China, the EU and the USA* will be of huge interest to students and scholars from within these fields, as well as policy-makers and practitioners more generally.

Jing Men is Baillet Latour Chair of EU-China Relations and Director of the EU-China Research Centre in the Department of EU International Relations and Diplomacy Studies of the College of Europe in Bruges, Belgium.

Simon Schunz is a Professor in the Department of EU International Relations and Diplomacy Studies of the College of Europe in Bruges, the Academic Coordinator of the joint College of Europe–The Fletcher School of Law and Diplomacy 'Master of Arts in Transatlantic Affairs' (MATA) and an Associate Research Fellow at UNU-CRIS, Bruges, Belgium.

Duncan Freeman is Research Fellow at the EU-China Research Centre in the Department of EU International Relations and Diplomacy Studies of the College of Europe, Bruges, Belgium.

Routledge Studies on Comparative Asian Politics

Books in this series will cover such areas as political institutions and systems, political economy, political culture, political thought, political psychology, public administration, law, and political histories of Asia. The studies may deal with Asia as a whole, a single country, or a group of countries in Asia. Those studies that have a clear comparative edge are especially welcome.

The series is edited by Shiping Hua, the Calvin and Helen Lang Distinguished Chair in Asian Studies, Director of the Asian Studies Program and Professor of Political Science at the University of Louisville, USA.

Social Cohesion in Asia
Historical Origins, Contemporary Shapes and Future Dynamics
Edited by Aurel Croissant and Peter Walkenhorst

The Evolving Relationship between China, the EU and the USA
A New Global Order?
Edited by Jing Men, Simon Schunz and Duncan Freeman

For more information about this series, please visit: https://www.routledge.com

The Evolving Relationship between China, the EU and the USA

A New Global Order?

Edited by
Jing Men, Simon Schunz and Duncan Freeman

LONDON AND NEW YORK

First published 2020
by Routledge
2 Park Square, Milton Park, Abingdon, Oxon OX14 4RN

and by Routledge
52 Vanderbilt Avenue, New York, NY 10017

Routledge is an imprint of the Taylor & Francis Group, an informa business

First issued in paperback 2021

British Library Cataloguing-in-Publication Data
A catalogue record for this book is available from the British Library

Library of Congress Cataloging-in-Publication Data
A catalog record has been requested for this book

ISBN: 978-0-367-13388-7 (hbk)
ISBN: 978-1-03-208277-6 (pbk)
ISBN: 978-0-429-02620-1 (ebk)

Typeset in Times New Roman
by codeMantra

Contents

Figures

Tables

Contributors

Yan Bo is Professor in the School of International Relations and Public Affairs, Fudan University. Her research interests are related to global environmental governance and international organizations. She is the author of many journal articles and of *The Trilateral Relations among China, the US, the EU in Global Climate Governance* (2012) and *International Negotiations and Domestic Politics: The Case of the US and Kyoto Protocol* (2007). She is also the editor of *Environment Issues and International Relations* (2009) and the Chinese translator of *Rules for the World: International Organization in World Politics* (2010).

Isidoro Campioni-Noack is currently a coordination officer at the International Organization for Migration (IOM) – UN Migration in Cairo, Egypt. He holds a Bachelor's degree in International Studies from Leiden University, specializing in the region of North America. He worked as a research assistant to Professor Giles Scott-Smith on topics related to transatlantic relations and was a research intern at the United Nations University Institute on Comparative Regional Integration Studies (UNU-CRIS) in Bruges, Belgium before taking up his current position.

Ciwan Maksut Can is a PhD candidate at Fudan University's School of International Relations and Public Administrations in Shanghai, where he has focused on International Relations Theory, China-EU Relations and Chinese Diplomacy and Security Studies. He is former Visiting Young Scholar at Uppsala University's Department of Government in Sweden. He holds an MA in International Relations from the University of Stellenbosch in South Africa and a BA in International Relations from Lillehammer University College in Norway. He was awarded the 'best paper' award at Fudan University's China-EU workshop in April 2017. He also has a background as an advisor for the Center for International and Strategic Analysis in Norway from 2014 to 2016.

Ding Chun is Professor, Jean Monnet Chair, Director of Centre for European Studies as well as of the Dutch Study Centre, Fudan University, China. He also holds positions including Chief Expert of the Centre for

China-EU People-to-People Exchange Studies of Chinese Ministry of Education, Vice-President of the Chinese Association of European Studies and of the Chinese Society for EU Studies, Councillor of the Chinese Society of World Economics, and Vice-President of the Chinese Association of Social Security World Study Branch. He is specialized and engaged in research and teaching of European integration, European economy, social welfare issues, and so forth. He is a senior researcher in the Institute of European integration studies (ZEI) at Bonn University, Germany; Member of the International Academic Board at the Centre for European Research at the University of Gothenburg, Sweden; Academic Board Member at the Centre for European Studies at Sichuan University, China; Member of the World Economic Forum's Global Agenda of the Council of Europe.

Duncan Freeman is Research Fellow at the EU-China Research Centre of the College of Europe. He was Research Fellow and has taught and carried out research on China's economic and policy development in addition to EU-China relations at the Brussels Diplomatic Academy and Brussels Academy for China and European Studies, both at the Vrije Universiteit Brussel (VUB). He has an MSc in Chinese Politics from the School of Oriental and African Studies, London, a Postgraduate Diploma in Economic Principles from the University of London and a PhD completed at the VUB. Recent book chapters and articles include 'Redistributing the EU-China Economic Relationship: The Role of Domestic Change' in China, in T. Christiansen et al. (eds.), *Asia Europe Journal, special issue on EU-China,* June, 2017, 'Bilateral and Domestic Dimensions in China's Approach to ODI Governance' in J. Men, and A. Linck (eds.), *Reform and Governance in the EU and China*, Routledge, 2017; and 'Industrial Policy and Climate Change Strategy: Comparing China, the EU's Path to the Paris Agreement (COP21)', with C. Goron, in M. Telo et al. (eds.), The *EU-China Partnership: Bridging Institutional and Ideational Differences between Two Unprecedented Global Actors*, Routledge, 2017; China and Renewables: The Priority of Economics over Geopolitics in D. Scholten ed, The Geopolitics of Renewables, Springer, 2018; Negotiating an Uncertain World: Economic and Political Dimensions of the CAI, in J. Chaisse ed, China-European Union Investment Relationships: Towards a New Leadership in Global Investment Governance?, Edward Elgar, 2018.

Sieglinde Gstöhl is Director of the Department of EU International Relations and Diplomacy Studies at the College of Europe in Bruges. She has been Professor at the College since 2005. From 1999 to 2005 she was Assistant Professor of International Relations at Humboldt University of Berlin. She holds a PhD and an MA in International Relations from the Graduate Institute of International and Development Studies in Geneva as well as a degree in Public Affairs from the University of St. Gallen. She was, inter alia, a research fellow at the Liechtenstein Institute, Bendern, and at the Center for International Affairs at Harvard University, Cambridge, MA. Her recent publications include *The European Neighbourhood Policy in a Comparative Perspective: Models, Challenges, Lessons* (ed., Routledge, 2016); *Theorizing the European Neighbourhood Policy* (ed. with S. Schunz, Routledge, 2017); and *The Trade Policy of the European Union* (with D. De Bièvre, 2018); and the Proliferation of Priveleged Partnerships between the European Union and its Neighbours (ed. with D. Phinnemore, Routledge, 2019).

Alan K. Henrikson is the Lee E. Dirks Professor of Diplomatic History Emeritus and founding Director of Diplomatic Studies at The Fletcher School of Law and Diplomacy, Tufts University. During the academic year 2010–2011 he was Fulbright Schuman Professor of US-EU Relations at the College of Europe in Bruges. In the spring of 2003 he taught as Fulbright/Diplomatic Academy Visiting Professor of International Relations at the Diplomatische Akademie in Vienna. He has also taught as Lloyd I. Miller Visiting Professor of Diplomatic History and Scholar-in-Residence at the U.S. Department of State in Washington and as United Nations Development Programme (UNDP) Visiting Professor of Diplomatic History at the China Foreign Affairs University in Beijing. Recent publications of his include 'Historical Forms of US-European Cooperation: Combination or "Only" Coordination?', *European Foreign Affairs Review* (2016) and 'United States Contemporary Diplomacy: Implementing a Foreign Policy of "Engagement"' in *Diplomacy in a Globalizing World: Theories and Practices* (2013, 2017).

Madeleine O. Hosli is Professor of International Relations at Leiden University and a Jean Monnet Chair ad personam. After a postdoctoral fellowship at the University of Michigan, Ann Arbor, she was an Assistant Professor at the Free University Amsterdam before being appointed as Associate and then Full Professor at Leiden University (2007). She has held visiting positions at the University of Zurich, the Graduate Institute of International Studies and Development (Geneva), the European Institute of Public Administration (Maastricht) and the University of Michigan (Ann Arbor). Between 2017 and 2019, she combined her professorship with the Directorship of the United Nations Institute of Regional Integration Studies (UNU-CRIS) in Bruges, Belgium. She is author of *The Euro: A Concise Introduction to European Monetary Integration* (2005) and a co-editor of *Decision-making in the European Union before and after the Lisbon Treaty* (with Amy Verdun, Amie Kreppel and Bêla Plechanovová; Routledge 2015). She has published widely in international peer-reviewed journals, including *International Organization, the International Studies Quarterly*, the Review of *International Organizations, the Journal of European Public Policy, European Union Politics* and the *Journal of Common Market Studies*. Her main research interests are in international political economy, international organizations, conflict resolution and European integration.

Rory Johnson is the Grant Acquisition Officer at UNU-CRIS. After completing a Bachelor of Arts (BA) in History at Durham University, he obtained a master's degree in International Relations (cum laude) from Leiden University. During his time at Leiden, he co-founded and subsequently became a lead editor and contributor for the student-run online journal the *Leiden International Review*.

Jing Men is the Baillet Latour Chair of European Union-China Relations and the Director of the EU-China Research Centre in the Department of EU International Relations and Diplomacy Studies, College of Europe. She obtained a PhD in Political Science at the Vrije Universiteit Brussel. Her research and teaching focus on EU-China relations and Chinese foreign policy. She is the founder of the electronic journal *EU-China Observer*, launched in 2009, which publishes research articles and policy analysis on EU-China relations. Together with other professors, she founded the EU-China Collaborative Research Network (CRN) under the University Association of Contemporary European Studies (UACES), which is a widely extended network for people who share the common interests on the research of EU-China relations. She publishes widely on EU-China relations and Chinese foreign policy in books and journals. Her most recent publications include *The EU and China: Reform and Governance*, Abingdon, Routledge, 2017 (edited together with Annika Linck); 'European perspective regarding the evolving security architecture in East Asia', in Stefan Fröhlich and Howard Loewen (eds.), *Asian Security Architecture*, a special issue of *Zeitschrift für Außen- und Sicherheitspolitik* (Journal of Foreign and Security Policy), 2017, pp. 145–163; 'China's Belt & Road Initiative and Its Opportunities and Challenges to EU-China Relations', in M. Telo et al. (eds.), *The EU-China Partnership: Bridging Institutional & Ideational Differences between two Unprecedented Global Actors*, Abingdon, Routledge, 2017, pp. 55–63; 'EU-China Security Relations', in Hoo Tiang Boon (ed.), *Chinese Foreign Policy Under Xi*, Abingdon, Routledge, 2017, pp. 62–73.

Sophie Meunier is Senior Research Scholar in the Woodrow Wilson School of Public and International Affairs at Princeton University and Director of the EU Program at Princeton. She is the author of *Trading Voices: The European Union in International Commercial Negotiations* (2005) and *The French Challenge: Adapting to Globalization* (2001), winner of the 2002 France-Ameriques book award. She is also the co-editor of several books on Europe and globalization, most recently *The Politics of Interest Representation in the Global Age* (Cambridge University Press, 2014) and *Speaking with a Single Voice: The EU as an Effective Actor in Global Governance?* (Routledge, 2015). Her current work deals with the politics of Foreign Direct Investment in Europe, notably the politics of hosting Chinese investment in Europe. She is Chevalier des Palmes Academiques in France.

Francesco Saverio Montesano is a PhD candidate at the Copernicus Institute of Sustainable Development, Utrecht University, The Netherlands. He previously was Senior Research Assistant to the Baillet Latour Chair of EU-China Relations in the Department of EU International Relations and Diplomacy Studies at the College of Europe, Bruges, and Research Assistant at the Netherlands Institute of International Relations 'Clingendael' in The Hague. He also carried out research at the EU in the World unit of the Centre for European Policy Studies (CEPS) in Brussels. He holds an MSc in Global Politics from the London School of Economics and a BA in Political Science from LUISS University in Rome. His main research interests include International Relations theory, EU and Chinese foreign policy, EU-China relations, global security policy global sustainability governance.

Miranda A. Schreurs (PhD, University of Michigan) is Professor of Environment and Climate Policy at the Bavarian School of Public Policy, Technical University of Munich. Her research focuses on climate change, low-carbon energy transitions and environmental movements. She is currently Vice-Chair of the European Environment and Sustainable Development Advisory Councils and co-chairs the National Committee to Monitor the Nuclear Waste Management Site Location Search in Germany. She was also a member of the Ethics Committee for a Secure Energy Future set up by Chancellor Angela Merkel in 2011 in reaction to the Fukushima nuclear accident.

Simon Schunz is a Professor at the Department of EU International Relations and Diplomacy Studies of the College of Europe in Bruges, the Academic Coordinator of the joint College of Europe–The Fletcher School of Law and Diplomacy programme 'Master of Arts in Transatlantic Affairs' (MATA) and an Associate Research Fellow at the United Nations University Institute on Comparative Regional Integration Studies (UNU-CRIS) in Bruges. He previously worked inter alia for the European Commission and the University of Leuven (KU Leuven), where he was awarded his doctorate and also continues to lecture. His research interests include European Union foreign policy and external relations, especially EU external climate, environmental, cultural and science policies and the EU's relations with major powers, in particular the United States. His recent publications include 'Between Cooperation and Competition: Major Powers in Shared Neighbourhoods', *Contemporary Politics*, vol. 24, no. 1, 2018 (with Sieglinde Gstöhl and Luk Van Langenhove); *The European Union's Evolving External Engagement – Towards New Sectoral Diplomacies?* Abingdon, Routledge, 2018 (with Chad Damro and Sieglinde Gstöhl); and 'The Prospects for Transatlantic Leadership in an Evolving Multipolar World', *European Foreign Affairs Review*, vol. 21, no. 3, 2016.

Xavier D. Soto is a PhD candidate at Fudan University's School of International Relations and Public Administration in Shanghai, where he has focused on Chinese diplomacy and security studies, as well as international relations theory. He holds a master's degree in China Studies from the Center for Asia and African Studies (CEAA) at El Colegio de México (COLMEX), where he studied the process of modernization of the People's Liberation Army during Hu Jintao's administration. He also holds a master's degree in Chinese-English Translation and Interpreting, from Beijing Language and Culture University. He has published articles, book chapters and book reviews in Mexico, Taiwan and in the United States, dealing with topics like the process of economic integration in Latin America; the process of modernization of the People's Republic of China's maritime, aerospace and energy security capabilities; Chinese military assistance to Latin American countries; and nationalism in Mexico and Northeast Asia.

Lunting Wu is a PhD fellow at the Berlin Graduate School for Global and Transnational Studies (BGTS) at the Freie Universität Berlin. He holds a BA degree (first class honours) from the Macau University of Science and Technology and a MA in International Relations and Affairs (*magna cum laude*) from the University of Lisbon. He was a Government Affairs Assistant at the European Union Chamber of Commerce in Shanghai, China, and a research intern and later visiting scholar at the United Nations Institute of Comparative Regional Integration Studies (UNU-CRIS). Lunting Wu has also worked as a research assistant on a H2020 project at the University of Lisbon, Portugal.

Abbreviations and acronyms

AIIB	Asian Infrastructure Investment Bank
ASEAN	Association of East Asian Nations
BRI	Belt and Road Initiative
CBDRRC	Common but Differentiated Responsibilities and Respective Capabilities
CETA	EU-Canada Comprehensive Economic and Trade Agreement
CO_2	Carbon dioxide
ETS	Emission Trading System
EU	European Union
EUR	Euro (€)
EV	Electric Vehicle
FDI	Foreign Direct Investment
FTA	Free Trade Agreement
GATS	General Agreement on Trade in Services
GATT	General Agreement on Tariffs and Trade
GDP	Gross Domestic Product
GHG	Greenhouse gases
IAEA	International Atomic Energy Agency
ibid.	Ibidem
IFC	International Finance Corporation
IPCC	Intergovernmental Panel on Climate Change
IR	International Relations
IRENA	International Renewable Energy Agency
ISDS	Investor-to-State Dispute Settlement
JCPOA	Joint Comprehensive Plan of Action
KORUS	United States-Korea Free Trade Agreement
MES	Market Economy Status
NAFTA	North American Free Trade Agreement
NATO	North Atlantic Treaty Organization
NDC	Nationally Determined Contribution (Paris Agreement)
NGO	Non-Governmental Organization
OECD	Organization for Economic Cooperation and Development
PLA	PRC People's Liberation Army

PRC	People's Republic of China
RCEP	Regional Comprehensive Economic Partnership
RMB	PRC *Renminbi*
SCO	Shanghai Cooperation Organization
TDM	Transnational Dispute Management
TiSA	Trade in Services Agreement
TPP	Trans-Pacific Partnership Agreement
TRIPs	Agreement on Trade-related Aspects of Intellectual Property Rights
TTIP	Transatlantic Trade and Investment Partnership
UK	United Kingdom
UN	United Nations
UNCLOS	UN Convention on the Law of the Sea
UNESCO	UN Educational, Scientific and Cultural Organization
UNFCCC	UN Framework Convention on Climate Change
UNPKO	UN Peacekeeping Operations
US	United States
USD	US Dollar (US$)
WTO	World Trade Organization
WWII	World War II

Part I

Introduction

1 Introduction

Jing Men, Simon Schunz and Duncan Freeman

Introduction: global politics in flux

Ever since the dawn of the millennium, global politics has been very much 'in flux' (Posen 2012; Lieber 2016). Power shifts are underway that point to a relative decline of Western players, especially the United States (US) and the European Union (EU), vis-à-vis emerging actors such as China, whose growing, especially economic clout has led to demands for a greater say in global politics (Quinn 2011; Subramanian 2011; Walt 2011; White 2013; Chen 2016). Although the debate about the 'decline of the West, rise of the rest' is far from settled (Zakaria 2009; Lieber 2012; Nye 2012), it is undeniable that global politics is becoming more multipolar across a variety of issue areas, with the centre of gravity increasingly shifting from the Atlantic to the Asia-Pacific. While the precise contours of a new global order that is to substitute the Western, transatlantic model of liberal institutionalism have yet to take shape, it seems highly likely that its parameters will be strongly determined by the interactions, whether cooperative or confrontational, of major powers.

This edited volume sets out to contribute to the debate on the prospects of a novel global order by focusing on the individual and collective agency of a set of such major powers, based on the premise that they are among the ones who will decisively shape future global structures. It focuses on three players that are already key to contemporary global politics given their overall economic, political and security primacy and bound to remain central to it in the future: one player which has been dominating the post-WWII international system (the US), a second actor that has (re-)'risen' in the last couple of decades (China) and a third one whose constitutive parts dominated global politics in the 19th and early 20th centuries and which has become a global actor in its own right since the fall of the Iron Curtain but is now struggling to keep up with global developments (the EU). The volume discusses these actors' relative power and their interests, beliefs and positions on a small set of decisive issues as well as the foreign policy strategies – grounded in domestic politics – they deploy both vis-à-vis each other and towards major global political challenges. In so doing, it examines their bilateral relations, but also – where applicable – the way they interact trilaterally in a broader global context to shape global politics.

This introductory chapter prepares the ground for the various contributions to this volume by outlining its rationale, including the choice of key themes, and briefly foreshadowing its contents.

Examining the evolving relationship between China, the EU and the US

In a global political context that is in flux, key actors are equally in the process of re-constructing their roles and strategies so as to enhance their chances of impacting global structures on issues considered relevant. China, the EU and the US are no exception to this rule.

Each of them has only recently engaged in revisions of its strategic outlook on the changing global context. China has in many respects been well served by the structure of international relations of the post-Mao period after it adopted a policy of 'reform and opening' under Deng Xiaoping in the late 1970s. Although dominated by and designed for Western powers, especially after the fall of the Soviet Union, the system permitted China the space to pursue its focus on economic development and cautious global engagement under Deng's slogan of 'keeping a low profile and biding our time'. Nevertheless, China has been forced to address its increasing global importance, for instance through the use of the formulation of its 'peaceful rise' under President Hu Jintao. Global developments, especially shifts in economic power in the past decade following the economic crisis that began in 2008, and the advent of a new leadership under Xi Jinping, have prompted new policies and formulations that raise questions over their intent. As a primary beneficiary of economic globalisation, China has reiterated its commitment to the globalised economy, while asserting that reform is necessary (Xi 2017). At the same time China under Xi has declared with greater clarity its intention to occupy a role at the centre of the global system. While declaring its support for the existing order, its policies such as the Belt and Road Initiative, which is said to consist of policy coordination, infrastructure connectivity, unimpeded trade, financial integration and people-to-people exchanges, but which is also claimed to provide global public goods and even global governance, and concepts advanced such as the 'community of a shared destiny for mankind' offer an ambiguous at best token of China's actual commitment to global institutions that it argues require democratisation. China's official strategic doctrine remains largely defensive, but its rise evinced through increased economic, technological and military power poses unresolved questions in its relations with other actors.

In the case of the EU, a thorough analysis of the implications of multipolarity for the conduct of its foreign policy (EEAS 2015) resulted in a strategic re-orientation that is embodied in the 2016 EU Global Strategy (High Representative 2016). Contrary to its past desire to 'upload' its own model to the global stage, strive for 'effective multilateralism' (European Council 2003) and shape 'what is considered as normal' – in line with its image as a 'normative power' (Manners 2002) – the EU has become a more 'modest' global player in reaction to changing global geopolitics and in the wake of the financial and economic crises. The central concept of its Global Strategy is arguably the notion of 'principled pragmatism', which in practice translates into an approach intended to 'partner selectively with players whose cooperation is necessary to deliver global public goods and address common challenges' (High Representative 2016: 12). Having such a strategy of 'issue-specific partnering' and actually implementing it are two different steps in the foreign policy cycle, however (Brighi & Hill 2012), which is why the Union's de facto adaptation to the new global context must remain subject to empirical scrutiny for the time being.

Finally, US foreign policy had undergone a pragmatic shift during the Obama era (2009–2017), which paired an attempt to 'lead from behind' on security issues with a 'globalist approach' relying on multilateralism on economic and other issues such as climate change (Tocci & Alcaro 2014: 370; White House 2015). Under President Trump, the US then moved towards a perception of multipolarity as a primarily competitive scenario. The Trump administration's 2017 National Security Strategy translates the President's 'America First' agenda into a foreign policy guided by 'principled realism', which combines sovereignty concerns and hard power display with opposition to multilateralism (White House 2017). Just like the EU's foreign policy, Trump's strategic rhetoric and external action may not always be congruent, requiring empirical scrutiny.

As each of these players is trying to (re)define its place in a global context that is rapidly changing (partially in reaction to their own doings), their bi- and trilateral relationship(s) are also evolving. Where the EU-US relationship was arguably of central significance for much of the post-WWII period, it has increasingly come under pressure, notably by the rise of the BRICS including China (Tocci & Alcaro 2014). The resilience of transatlantic relations, and that of the institutions created by the US and Europe at the global and regional levels to pursue their interests and shared values – from the United Nations (UN) to the Bretton Woods institutions and the security architecture built around the North Atlantic Treaty Organization (NATO) – is increasingly put to the test. Since at least the 2000s, and in reaction to this pressure, both the EU and the US have therefore inter alia intensified their bilateral relations with major emerging economies. China has taken a very prominent place in this regard.

EU-China relations evolve around an intricate dialogue structure that was developed in the wake of the 2003 EU-China 'Comprehensive Strategic Partnership', which has been broadened and deepened ever since, notably in line with the EU-China 2020 'Strategic Agenda for Cooperation' (EU-China 2013). The EU's strategy has from the start acknowledged China as a competitor, but also saw it as a potential collaborator in global politics.

In March 2019, a Commission communication on 'EU-China – A strategic outlook' assessed the EU's relations with China as follows (European Commission 2019: 1):

> China is, simultaneously, in different policy areas, a cooperation partner with whom the EU has closely aligned objectives, a negotiating partner with whom the EU needs to find a balance of interests, an economic competitor in the pursuit of technological leadership, and a systemic rival promoting alternative models of governance. This requires a flexible and pragmatic whole-of-EU approach enabling a principled defence of interests and values.

This points to an ambiguous relationship involving delicate balancing acts as the EU and the China move into the 2020s, heavily conditioned by the global role of the US.

Turning to the US' relations with China, the Obama era witnessed an intensification of relations. Obama's self-depiction as the 'US first Pacific President' and his country's 'pivot to Asia' also meant a certain rapprochement with China, which remained however simultaneously a competitor that had to be 'rebalanced' (Davidson 2014; Silove 2016). The Trump administration's assessment of China is then again a wholly different one: as US President, Trump has repeatedly denounced what in his view constitute unfair trade practices by China. His 2017 National Security Strategy goes as far as considering China as one among several 'rival powers … aggressively undermining American interests around the globe' (White House 2017: preface).

From China's perspective, the relationships with the EU and the US constitute important elements of its view of the global system, but they are far from being seen in equal terms. The relationship with the US has long been the prevalent concern of China. The US, as the primary global power, dominates China's economic and security concerns. China has sought to avoid direct conflict and confrontation and insists that a cooperative relationship is possible, based on the formulation of a 'new type of great power relationship' advanced by Xi Jinping. The EU is seen as having less potential for a conflictual relationship than the US, primarily due to its lack of direct security presence in East Asia. The EU is considered to be an economic partner, although this also brings potential for both cooperation and friction.

After coming to power, Xi Jinping promoted the concept of a 'new type of great power relationship' with Washington and received Trump in Beijing. The Chinese government asserts that cooperation with the US is necessary for China's development. At the same time, the Chinese government actively promotes its political system, economic model and culture in contrast to the US while seeking to revitalise its national dream of power and prosperity within the current international order. Therefore, its leadership is eager to maintain a stable and workable partnership with the US and emphasises shared interests between the two sides. The first two decades of the 21st century are regarded as 'a period of important strategic opportunity' for China, but with the US designating China as a strategic rival and escalation of a US-China economic war that has been looming since the beginning of the Trump presidency, the Chinese government is concerned that Sino-US relations will be defined by confrontation.

While China considers the EU an important international player, its importance is not comparable with that of the US. Therefore, the Sino-EU partnership is always influenced by the Sino-US relationship. For instance, in 2003 the Comprehensive Strategic Partnership between the EU and China was created partly in reaction to US unilateral action in Iraq against the opposition of major EU member states. In 2005, the EU proposal to lift its arms embargo against China was abandoned to a large degree due to the pressure from the US. For its part, prompted by the election of President Trump and the increasing conflict in the relationship with the US, China has sought to find common ground with the EU, notably on global governance matters such as trade and climate change, but significant differences remain, evidenced by the EU, at least partially, defining China as a 'systemic rival' in 2019.

Taking their current strategic and policy positions on and behaviour towards the aforementioned fluidity and each other as a starting point, this edited volume intends to closely scrutinise the individual and collective roles played by China, the EU and the US as the three corners of what can be referred to as a 'global triangle' in contemporary world politics. It does so by focusing on three major issues representing key challenges for each of them and for global politics on the whole: foreign and security policy, economics and trade and climate change and energy. The choice of these issues seems intuitive, as they cover essential areas of global politics related to key needs common to all of humanity: security, prosperity and the planet's material living conditions. Each of them constitutes a field of global governance in which major powers have particular responsibility for providing leadership – assuming that the joint management of security, of economic globalisation so as to guarantee citizens' prosperity and well-being, and the stewardship of global resources are indeed in their collective interest.

Each of these issue areas is examined in a doubly 'de-centred' fashion (Fisher-Onar & Nicolaïdis 2013) that does not privilege either the perspective of one of the three analysed players or that of traditional Western International Relations (IR). Rather, it attempts to give each actor's perspective equal weight while remaining committed to conceptual and theoretical pluralism. First, when it comes to decentring in the sense of a plurality of actor perspectives, this volume examines the 'triangle' from the point of view of each of its corners, that is, for each policy domain the triangle is analysed – in three different chapters – through a prism focusing on China, the EU and the US, respectively. Each chapter is written by one or more scholars with expertise on one of the three players, and who in most cases also hail(s) from that country/region. This pluralism of perspectives is intended as a step towards an analysis that perceives the future of the global order as a largely 'open terrain' that – while building on existing institutions and practices – might be shaped by new ideas and practices emanating from each of the three players or evolve through their continued interaction.

Second, decentring is pursued by opting for an agnostic approach to the choice of conceptual-theoretical lenses through which to study the China-EU-US relationship and its contribution to global order. The choice was entirely left to the contributing authors, in line with a commitment to 'analytical eclecticism', that is, 'an intellectual stance that supports efforts to complement, engage, and selectively utilize theoretical constructs embedded in contending research traditions to build … argument[s] that bear on substantive problems of interest to both scholars and practitioners' (Sil & Katzenstein 2010: 411). The concluding chapter provides an overview of the ways in which the authors took up this analytical challenge across different chapters, employing concepts and theories from mainstream IR and Foreign Policy Analysis (FPA), but also other perspectives such as those of International Political Economy (IPE), to make sense of the link between the tri-partite relationship and a rapidly evolving global order.

This commitment to a multiplicity of perspectives is reflected in the guiding themes chosen for this volume and has a bearing for the contributions it aims to make.

Guiding themes and key contributions of this volume

With its 3 × 3 matrix organised around chapters on each of the three key actors – China, the EU and the US – focusing on three essential cases – foreign and security policy, economics and trade and climate change and energy – this edited volume addresses several guiding themes: first, each chapter discusses the *position* of the player it focuses on in the issue-specific relationship between the three actors as well as, second, *that player's view on the tri-partite relationship*, before, third and most importantly, focusing on the question of *whether, how and to what extent the relations between these three players can or already do contribute to a form of global order* in the examined policy domain. Although this volume deliberately wishes to avoid succumbing to a 'presentism bias' by overly focusing on the present-day context, and notably the changes brought about since the beginning of the Trump Presidency, it does emphasise the current state of the relations between the three actors, but places it into its historical context while developing an understanding of possible future evolutions.

By empirically mapping out the evolving strategies of the three powers and their bi-/tri-/multilateral relations and conceptually reflecting on the nature of their relations and their impact on the contemporary and future global order, this volume intends to contribute to debates in IR and FPA on the dynamics of change and agency in world politics (e.g., Posen 2012). Current works in IR tend to view this change very much in function of US hegemonic decline (e.g., Walt 2011; Nye 2015) and/or the 'rise of the rest' (e.g., Zakaria 2009; Kupchan 2013; Allison 2017). Foreign policy analyses have tended to focus on each of the three actors and their role in global politics (e.g., on the EU: Keukeleire & Delreux 2014; on the US: Brooks & Wohlforth 2016; on China: Su 2019). Their bilateral relations have equally received increasing attention over recent years, albeit to different degrees: where the study of transatlantic relations has been proliferating ever since the Cold War period (see, for instance, Simoni 2013), China-EU relations have been gradually emerging as a field of study only in the last couple of decades (e.g., Christiansen et al. 2019); similarly, China-US relations have more recently picked up speed to generate a quickly growing strand in the IR and FPA literature (e.g., Allison 2017). In this context, the concept of 'power transition' from the US to China has increasingly become a subject of analysis (e.g., Layne 2018; Urio 2019).

Despite this growing body of literature relevant to understanding and explaining the variegated interactions between China, the EU and the US in global politics, their triangular relationship and its contribution to global order remains largely understudied and has so far mostly been the subject of think tank publications (e.g., Barkin 2019; Garcia Herrero 2019). With its multi-perspective and pluralist approach, this edited volume aims to make a first contribution to filling this gap in empirical and conceptual-theoretical terms, while providing findings of relevance beyond academia. Its insights should fuel the debate on major powers' interactions and responsibilities in global politics and – as such – appeal to scholars, students and policymakers engaged in the study and practice of global politics, notably in the issue areas covered by this volume.

The next section foreshadows the key contents of this volume.

Overview of this volume

This volume is divided into five parts. Part I comprises, alongside this introduction, a second chapter focusing on 'A New Order or No Order? The EU-China-US Relationship and its Impact on Global Order' and authored by *Madeleine O. Hosli, Isidoro Campioni-Noack, Rory Johnson and Lunting Wu*, which conceptually and empirically sets the scenery for the three parts that follow.

Part II is dedicated to foreign and security policy. In their chapter focusing on China, *Ciwan M. Can and Xavier D. Soto* take a broad perspective of security to trace China's new role as a major power and its transition from a follower of international, transatlantic-made rules and practices to an indispensable rule-maker. Focusing on the EU, *Francesco Saverio Montesano* argues that while the US appears to be veering away from proactive global security engagement, China has been stepping up its outreach and 'rule-making' ambitions in an increasingly assertive fashion. In this context, the EU could further seize opportunities to take on greater global responsibilities. Last, *Alan K. Henrikson* discusses the US transatlantic and transpacific relationships with respect to three major regional security problems – the nuclear ambitions of Iran, contention in the South China Sea and escalation on the Korean peninsula – to demonstrate that the US is *not* capable of managing international 'disorder' on its own. He argues that the construct of a US-EU-China 'triangle', owing to the large economic size and growing interdependence of the three despite their competition, could help give political shape to a necessarily more complicated and inclusive configuration, involving smaller countries, in support of global order.

Part III of this edited volume focuses on the issues of economics and trade. *Ding Chun* analyses the current trade and investment relationships between China, the EU and the US from the perspective of China. He argues that these relationships are primarily the result of the structure of trade and investment rooted in the development stages of China, a developing economy, and the EU and US, advanced industrial and service economies, based on comparative advantage. Current imbalances that derive from these factors result in frictions in the economic relationships between China and the EU and the US, but economic cooperation through trade and investment flows will predominate in the long term. In her chapter examining trade relations between the three players from the EU's strategic perspective, *Sieglinde Gstöhl* shows how changes in relative power, in the institutional framework of the World Trade Organization and to a lesser extent in ideas help explain the transformation of the international trade structure into a tripolar one. This has repercussions for the EU's trade strategy. Focusing on the US, *Sophie Meunier* contends that US President Trump's 'America First' agenda has turned into actual policy especially in the areas of international trade and investment, challenging the post-war multilateral trade order. She examines the likelihood of the apparent US retreat from global trade governance resulting in the EU or China individually or jointly taking over the management of the global trade and investment system.

Part IV delves into the closely intertwined domains of climate change and energy. In her chapter dedicated to China's perspective, *Bo Yan* discusses the historical evolution of the triangular relationship between China, the EU and the US in the context of global climate negotiations under UN auspices. She finds that different combinations of bilateral relations in the overarching trilateral relationship have produced varying outcomes when it comes to the global climate order. The most favourable – but rarely realised – scenario, a 'ménage à trois', involves three sets of positive bilateral relations. Where this scenario allowed for negotiating the 2015 Paris Agreement, its durability has been called into question by the election of Donald Trump as US President. Yan argues that it is now up to China and the EU to sustain the Paris Agreement global climate architecture. In his chapter focusing on the EU, *Duncan Freeman* starts from the observation that much of the optimism regarding the effectiveness of the Paris Agreement, even in the face of the threat of US withdrawal, is based on the belief that technology and economics will bring about decarbonisation of economies. This belief must however be questioned, as China, the EU and the US all increasingly let national interests prevail in their economic and industrial policies, possibly hampering the necessary diffusion of clean energy technologies. Finally, *Miranda Schreurs* in her chapter focusing on the US investigates how the sceptical views held by American policy-makers about climate science and climate change as an economic opportunity determine their foreign policy positions and stand in stark contrast to the ideas of Chinese and EU policy-makers. This opposition in turn makes a durable trilateral cooperation on climate change much less likely as long as the US domestic ideational context at the federal level does not evolve.

In the final part, Part V, the editors of this volume – *Jing Men, Simon Schunz and Duncan Freeman* – provide a set of conclusions that – while not providing a single answer to the question of how global order is changing in function of the evolving relationship between China, the EU and the US – identifies a set of major trends on the evolution of global order in function of the trilateral EU-China-US relationship.

References

Allison, G. (2017) *Destined for War: Can America and China Escape Thucydides's Trap?* Boston: Houghton Mifflin Harcourt.

Barkin, N. (2019) 'The U.S. Is Losing Europe in Its Battle with China', *The Atlantic*, 4 June. Available at: www.theatlantic.com/international/archive/2019/06/united-states-needs-europe-against-china/590887/.

Brighi, E. & C. Hill (2012) 'Implementation and Behaviour', in S. Smith, T. Dunne & A. Hadfield (eds.), *Foreign Policy: Theories, Actors, Cases*, Oxford: Oxford University Press, 147–167.

Brooks, S.G. & W.C. Wohlforth (2016) *America Abroad: The United States' Global Role in the 21st Century*, Oxford: Oxford University Press.

Chen, Z. (2016) 'China, the European Union and the Fragile World Order', *Journal of Common Market Studies* 54(4), 775–792.

Christiansen, T., E. Kirchner & U. Wissenberg (2019) *The European Union and China*, Basingstoke: Palgrave Macmillan.

Davidson, J. (2014) 'The U.S. "Pivot to Asia"', *American Journal of Chinese Studies*, 21(special issue), 77–82.

EEAS (2015) *The European Union in a Changing Global Environment – A More Connected, Contested and Complex World*, Brussels, 25 June.

EU-China (2013) *EU-China 2020 Strategic Agenda for Cooperation*, 23 November.

European Commission (2019) *EU-China – A strategic outlook*, JOIN(2019) 5 final, Strasbourg, 12 March.

European Council (2003) *A Secure Europe in a Better World: European Security Strategy*, Brussels, 12 December.

Fisher-Onar, N. & K. Nicolaïdis (2013) 'The Decentring Agenda: Europe as a post-Colonial Power', *Cooperation and Conflict* 48(2), 283–303.

Garcia Herrero, A. (2019) *Europe in the Midst of China-US Strategic Economic Competition: What Are the European Union's Options*? Working Paper, Brussels, Bruegel.

High Representative of the EU (2016) *Shared Vision, Common Action: A Stronger Europe*, Brussels, June.

Keukeleire, S. & T. Delreux (2014) *The Foreign Policy of the European Union*, Basingstoke: Palgrave.

Kupchan, C.A. (2013) *No One's World: The West, the Rising Rest, and the Coming Global Turn*, Oxford: Oxford University Press.

Layne, C. (2018) 'The US–Chinese Power Shift and the End of the Pax Americana', *International Affairs* 94(1): 89–111.

Lieber, R.J. (2012) *Power and Willpower in The American Future: Why The United States Is Not Destined to Decline*, Cambridge: Cambridge University Press.

——— (2016) *Retreat and Its Consequences: American Foreign Policy and the Problem of World Order*, Cambridge: Cambridge University Press.

Manners, I. (2002) 'Normative Power Europe: A Contradiction in Terms?' *Journal of Common Market Studies* 40(2), 235–258.

Nye, J.S. (2012) 'The Twenty-First Century Will Not Be a 'Post-American' World', *International Studies Quarterly* 56(1), 215–217.

——— (2015) *Is the American Century Over?* New York: Polity Press.

Posen, B.R. (2012) 'From Unipolarity to Multipolarity: Transition in Sight?' in G.J. Ikenberry, M. Mastanduno & W.C. Wohlforth (eds.), *International Relations Theory and the Consequences of Unipolarity*, Cambridge: Cambridge University Press, 317–341.

Quinn, A. (2011), 'The Art of Declining Politely: Obama's Prudent Presidency and the Waning of American Power', *International Affairs* 87(4), 803–824.

Sil, R. & P. Katzenstein (2010) 'Analytic Eclecticism in the Study of World Politics: Reconfiguring Problems and Mechanisms across Research Traditions', *Perspectives on Politics* 8(2), 411–431.

Silove, N. (2016) 'The Pivot before the Pivot: US Strategy to Preserve the Power Balance in Asia', *International Security* 40(4), 45–88.

Simoni, S. (2013) *Understanding Transatlantic Relations: Whither the West?* London: Routledge.

Su, G. (2019) '2018: World Changes and Chinese Diplomacy' (2018: Sijie bianju yu Zhongguo waijiao), *Contemporary World (Dangdai Shijie):* 1, 4–9.

Subramanian, A. (2011) 'The Inevitable Superpower: Why China's Dominance Is a Sure Thing', *Foreign Affairs* 90: 66.

Tocci, N. & R. Alcaro (2014) 'Rethinking Transatlantic Relations in a Multipolar Era', *International Politics* 51(3), 366–389.

Urio, P. (2019) 'China and the New World Order – Why and How China's Foreign Policy Has Put an End to the World America Made', in P. Urio (ed.), *China 1949–2019, From Poverty to World Power*, Berlin: Springer, 195–320.

Walt, S.M. (2011) 'The End of the American Era', *The National Interest*, November–December, 6–16.

White, H. (2013) *The China Choice: Why We Should Share Power*, Oxford: Oxford University Press.

White House (2015) *National Security Strategy*, Washington, February. Available at: http://nssarchive.us/national-security-strategy-2015/.

——— (2017) *National Security Strategy of the United States of America*, Washington, December. Available at: http://nssarchive.us/national-security-strategy-2017/.

Xi, J. (2017) *Work Together to Build a Community of Shared Future for Mankind*, 18 January.

Zakaria, F. (2009) *The Post-American World and the Rise of the Rest*, London: Penguin Books.

2 A new order or no order? The EU-China-US relationship and its impact on global order

Madeleine O. Hosli, Isidoro Campioni-Noack, Rory Johnson and Lunting Wu

Introduction

It is a historical truism that global power parities are constantly in flux, and that the rise and decline of power may have significant implications for the evolution of world order. At a time when the US seems to be losing both the willingness and the capacity to assume hegemonic leadership, other emerging powers may strive to fill the void. During the course of such a struggle, conflicts or wars may occur, as envisioned by the early proponents of power transition theory (Organski & Kugler 1980). Alternatively, peace may be maintained, as power could be more diffused among actors and is also constrained by the pre-existing relationships between nations and international organizations.

What characterizes today's world order is that it is highly institutionalized and multi-layered, covering multiple issue areas, implying that world leadership should require an institutionalized context that provides stability and continuity, and that leadership is always 'issue-specific, and different terms of power and leadership are required in different situations' (Nabers 2010: 56).

This chapter analyses the importance of EU-US-China tripartite relations and the three players' interactions with each other in shaping the emerging world order. While other powers are also gaining or maintaining significant power in global relations – among them India, Japan, Brazil and Mexico – this chapter will focus on the three 'giants' that are at the heart of this volume. To give direction to this scenario, this chapter will first offer a brief overview of the current state of relations between these three players, with a focus on three broad areas of discussion: trade and investment, foreign and security policy and energy and climate change. It will highlight current examples both of cooperation and competition in this trilateral relationship. Drawing upon a few key cases, tentative propositions are made as to whether the existing US leadership may soon be replaced by a new multipolar global order or by a more 'disordered' multipolar global system.

Analytical framework

The classic definition of power by Robert Dahl is that 'A can get B to do something that B would not otherwise do' (1957: 203). Dahl also acknowledged that the concept of power must be defined according to operational criteria, which may alter its meaning. A distinction can be drawn between power as influence and power as material capabilities. This chapter mainly adopts the latter as the conceptual foundation upon which the discussion will be developed.

According to (neo-) realist thinking, the distribution of power in the anarchic context of the international system determines who controls the system and whose self-interests are reflected or promoted through the system (e.g., Gilpin 1981; Mearsheimer 2004). From this perspective, the global power constellation provides significant implications for this system. Substantial studies have been undertaken to determine how power relations may influence the system. Among the ensuing theories, 'power transition theory' and 'co-leadership theory' present key insights for this chapter.

Organski put forward the idea of power transitions when he posited that 'an even distribution of political, economic, and military capabilities between contending groups of states is likely to increase the probability of war' and that 'peace is preserved best when there is an imbalance of national capabilities between disadvantaged and advantaged nations' (Organski & Kugler 1980: 19). Echoing Organski's views, Gilpin introduced the idea of prestige – the acknowledgement or reputation of a state's power by other states – and contended that 'a weakening of the hierarchy of prestige and increased ambiguity in interpreting it are frequently the prelude to eras of conflict and struggle' (Gilpin 1981: 31). He also argued that as differential growth among nations shifts the distribution of power, leading to a 'disjuncture between the existing governance of the system and the redistribution of power', a hegemonic conflict is eventually inevitable, corresponding to what Modelski called the '*long cycle* of world politics' (Gilpin 1981: 186). As per Modelski, the dominant world power that has previously emerged from a conflict and has since established a new world order attracts competitors that gradually drain its own pre-eminent authority, moving the system to multipolarity and to what resembles an oligopolistic competition, until the dissolution of the system 'towards its original point of departure, that of minimal order and a Babel of conflicting and mutually unintelligible voices' (Modelski 1978: 217).

(Neo-)liberal thinkers are generally less pessimistic, seeing economic ties as potential foundations for peace and stability (for early work on this topic, e.g. Keohane and Nye 1977, 1987). First, greater security and economic interdependence increase the benefits of peace and cooperation, while at the same time the existence of weapons of mass destruction has elevated the expected costs of warfare. By comparison, deterrence theory, largely used during the Cold War and based on realist thought, assumed that the (mutual) threat of the use of nuclear capacity would deter hegemonic powers in the future from attacking one another and, with this, keep a global 'balance' and remove the threat of war (for a critical assessment of the theory, see Zagare 2008). However, although a hegemon may be in decline, the existing regimes built by and around it still have a great 'inertia effect' on the world order and often continue to serve as a platform for global policy coordination and provision of information (Keohane 1984; Krasner 1982). Furthermore, international organizations are able to 'affect preferences of future governments by creating constraints on their freedom of action' (Keohane 1984: 120). Finally, even if there is an ultimate dispersion of concentrated power, ascending powers do not necessarily become dissatisfied challengers since they grew within the system. Instead, they would rather opt for a hedging strategy of eschewing direct confrontation vis-à-vis the dominant power while 'preparing for favourable conditions [...] to shape an emerging world in the long term' (Schweller & Pu 2011: 66). The dominant power, by contrast, frustrated by free-riding within the system, will grow less willing and able to provide public goods covering every specific issue area. Based on these assumptions, it could be expected that a new co-leadership world order between several great powers may form, due to their primacy in the economic, political and security domains.

This chapter will Keohane 1984: provide an overview of the interactions among these three actors in a changing world. By evaluating specific examples of this tripartite cooperation or co-leadership as well as some potential areas of competition, conclusions will be drawn.

Contextualizing China, the US and the EU as global powers

Order in international relations (IR) is often facilitated by common understandings and cooperation arising from interactions between the concerned parties. Until relatively recently, the majority of economic transactions, and therefore global prosperity in general, were concentrated in the so-called 'Western or Atlantic world', comprising of North America and Western Europe. Prior to beginning its economic reforms in the late 1970s, China's economy was no match for the great power of the US free market-based liberal model that arguably decided the outcome of the Cold War. However, over the past four decades an 'economic miracle' has occurred in China, the speed and scale of which has overall been staggering. In 2013, China overtook the US in terms of Gross Domestic Product (GDP) on the basis of power purchasing parity (PPP), thus becoming the world's largest economy. In 2016, its GDP stood at $21.4 trillion (calculating by PPP), $2.8 trillion more than the US and with growth rates clearly ahead of both the US and the EU (The World Bank 2017). Such achievements resulted from China's integration into the world economy and domestic adaptations that gradually endowed China with economic great power status and, in spite of rivalries among powerful nations, brought it more closely in line with the 'traditional' Western global forces of the US and the EU.

China's rapid economic rise occurring in conjunction with growing levels of global interconnectivity has meant that widespread economic interactions between the EU, US and China are now unavoidable. While other actors are highly important as well (Japan, Brazil, India, to name a few), this chapter will focus on this tripartite engagement. The questions posed are whether this interaction has encouraged formal economic and political cooperation or competition and if the US and the EU have approached this process in different ways. After first looking at examples of growing cooperation between China, the US and the EU, situations of heightened competition are taken into consideration.

Cooperation

Accounting for 20.2 per cent of the total EU imports in 2016, China is the EU's largest source of imports and the second largest recipient of EU exports after the US (European Commission 2017a). Additionally, in 2016 alone, Chinese foreign direct investment (FDI) in Europe amounted to around EUR 35 billion (Seaman et al. 2017). Clearly, the two economies are highly interconnected. Proponents of market integration theory suggest that it is primarily because of this that a broader willingness to nurture political relations through dialogues and bilateral agreements has arisen – an essentially neo-liberal argument.

Sino-European diplomatic relations have made significant progress since they were first officially established in 1975. Both China and the EU now make efforts to pursue an open dialogue, meeting annually for strategic talks on topics such as foreign and security policy, trade and cooperation. The number of channels for dialogue has also steadily increased, with the most high-profile one being the annual EU-China Summit. The China-EU High-Level Strategic Dialogue is also held on an annual basis to address issues of common interest. There is cooperation in many specific areas, such as the China-EU Roadmap on Energy Cooperation (2016–2020). Both sides also demonstrated their commitment to medium-term bilateral relations with the launch of the 'EU-China 2020 Strategic Agenda for Cooperation'. Ongoing negotiations over an investment agreement between the two parties are seen by the EU as a central component of such efforts.

In 2014, in what was dubbed as a 'landmark' occasion, President Xi Jinping became the first-ever incumbent Chinese leader to visit the EU's headquarters in Brussels as part of an 11-day tour of Europe. This event lent further weight to the argument that Sino-European relations had moved well beyond the economic realm to inhabit the political one as well. Such diplomatic achievements have been backed up by the discourse of leaders on both sides, who have indicated that there is indeed a reinforced relationship. In June 2017, during the 12th EU-China Business Summit, Commission President Jean-Claude Juncker stated that 'our partnership [with China] today is more important than ever before' (Juncker 2017). The EU has also been exploring cooperation with China on the Belt and Road Initiative (BRI), especially in the field of jointly promoting connectivity. Also in June 2017, during a press conference with US President Trump in Paris, French President Macron, when asked about Xi Jinping, said 'there are differences, but a joint willingness to sort them out' (White House 2017). In January 2018, EU Ambassador to China Schweisgut confirmed President Juncker's speech, stating that the EU was developing its connectivity blueprint and would like to connect it with the BRI. This is not to say that EU leaders have not criticized aspects of Chinese policies and vice versa. There still are indeed deep concerns on a number of issues on the part of the EU, but tentative efforts and high-level diplomatic relations on the whole appear to be progressing.

Recently, a new avenue for cooperation has emerged around the increasingly pressing issue of climate change. Being the world's largest emitter of greenhouse gases, the decision by China to ratify the 2015 Paris Agreement was seen as a pivotal development. Despite initial concerns, the US withdrawal from the agreement announced by President Trump in June 2017 has in fact served to strengthen the alliance between the EU and China on this issue. At the time of Trump's withdrawal announcement, the EU's climate commissioner Miguel Arias Cañete stated that the EU and China would join 'forces to forge ahead on the implementation of the Paris Agreement and accelerate the global transition to clean energy' (Boffey & Neslen 2017). This pronouncement was backed up by a concurrent statement made by Chinese Premier Li Keqiang that China would 'continue to steadfastly implement the commitment of the Paris climate deal and join hands with all parties to tackle climate change' (Oko 2017). The EU has previously offered substantial financial assistance and expertise to help China overcome the significant obstacles it will face in order to realize its green energy objectives through their existing cooperation on energy and climate change.

To meet carbon-reduction targets, drastic changes will need to be made, and these will impact on all aspects of production, supply and consumption. To realize this, an overhaul of global consumption practices as we know them will have to occur, and the EU and China now have an opportunity to collaborate in leading this process. If new low- or zero-carbon technologies are determinedly pursued, Chinese and European businesses may acquire a competitive advantage over their American counterparts in the mid- to long-term, which will have an influence on the global economic order.[1] In this way, the incentive for cooperation has broken out of the field of trade alone and expanded into the domain of science and innovation.

Turning to EU-US relations, despite some recent setbacks, these two remain closely interlinked in many ways. The US and the EU both adhere to basic free market principles to a much greater extent than China, which is still characterized by heavy state intervention in the economy or 'socialism with Chinese characteristics'. Consequently, commentators perceive US-EU economic interactions as occurring within a common 'rule-based trading system' (European Commission 2017a). When competition does arise, it is therefore deemed to take place under relatively 'fairer' circumstances, although this long-standing perception has lately been increasingly challenged by the Trump administration. Indeed, both the EU and the US economies are often seen as a unit, falling under the category of 'the West' and the EU-US trading relationship remains one of the defining features of the global economy. It is the largest bilateral trade relationship in the world, accounting for more than 30 per cent of global trade in goods and 40 per cent of global trade in services, and the US and the EU also remain each other's largest trading partners (European Commission 2017a).

The EU-US relationship goes beyond the realm of economics to a much greater extent than either a Sino-American or Sino-European relationship arguably ever could. The Western European states that continue to exert stronger influence over the EU share more of a common political, social and economic historical trajectory and philosophical outlook with the US than with China. Soft power indicators such as cultural similarities further strengthen such bonds. Finally, in the realm of foreign and security policy, a large proportion of EU member states are also members of the North Atlantic Treaty Organization (NATO) which, with respect to its military capabilities, is by far the most pre-eminent intergovernmental military alliance today. In fact, the combined military spending of all NATO members accounts for over 70 per cent of the global total and NATO institutions such as the Cooperative Cyber Defence Centre of Excellence offer concrete examples of how this international body facilitates multinational cooperation in the field of security, binding the two sides of the Atlantic.

When it comes to Sino-US cooperation, progress made in 2018 on the Korean Peninsula may serve as an opportunity. Both countries share a common interest in the denuclearization of North Korea. Pyongyang's nuclear weapons and missiles represent a threat to Beijing's regional interests and a possible conflict would result in the demise of the Democratic People's Republic of Korea, which could trigger a refugee crisis and might weaken China's regional influence should a unified Korea come under Washington's influence (Haass 2018). Meanwhile, the US 'has no appetite for a war that would prove costly by every measure' (ibid.: para. 10). Hence, these two major powers are incentivized to use diplomacy to solve this regional crisis and to steer the future of the Korean Peninsula to their favour.

Exponents of co-leadership theory (Hånggi 1999) have described the relationship between the US, China and the EU as representing a so-called 'global triangle' due to their economic, political and security primacy and their collective shift towards an interdependence management model approach to issues pertaining to global public goods. However, the very use of the term 'triangle' in this instance is somewhat misleading because it is not formally institutionalized, as Washington, Brussels and Beijing – with 'Brussels' being multilateral in itself – overwhelmingly prefer to deal with each other bilaterally. Furthermore, in several respects entrenched tensions exist between these three power entities which have a debilitating effect upon their ability to shape and direct changes in the global order in a manner agreed in common. Apart from these three powers, other important components of the international system also shape the emerging world order, notably the rest of the BRICS countries (Brazil, Russia, India and South Africa) and non-state actors. Adherents of power transition theory state that it is much more likely that we will see rising levels of competition rather than cooperation in the coming years. The next part of this chapter will assess some of the examples that those of this opinion may turn to in justifying their fears.

Competition

From a realist perspective, states will remain constantly vigilant of other states threatening their survival regardless of any increased economic interdependence. Gilpin envisaged that 'as the power of a state increases, it seeks to extend its territorial control, its political influence, and/or its domination of the international economy' (1981: 106). China's economic ascent drives the outward expansion of its interests, both economic and military, which poses a potential threat to the dominant state which, in order to arrest its own decline, is likely to choose to confront China directly. Taking the economic sphere as an example, the reason why dialogue channels are of such importance is because increased economic interdependency brings with it both greater opportunities for collaboration (according to neo-liberal thinking) and greater risks of confrontation (a perspective based on realist thought). When it comes to economic interactions with China, it is necessary to highlight three main factors that may destabilize such a triangular relationship, namely China's investment in sensitive domestic sectors in both the EU and the US, their entrenched trade deficits with China and Chinese foreign debt holdings. What's more, US-China tensions over the South China Sea and the disagreement between Brussels and Washington on multiple issues add to the complexity of this tripartite relationship.

Despite the positive steps taken between China and the EU, there continue to be several barriers to greater cooperation between these two powers. First, the EU and China remain in sharp disagreement over certain key trade policies. There is a continuing impasse surrounding the issue of tariffs against Chinese steel 'dumping' as well as over questions of differences in the protection and enforcement of intellectual property rights. The EU is also worried about the lack of reciprocity in the field of trade and investment in areas such as China's non-tariff barriers and public procurement policies and also its restrictions on foreign investment. At the same time, China is frustrated by the fact that its Market Economy Status under the terms of its World Trade Organization (WTO) accession is being refused by the EU. A second area of contention is that of human rights and disagreements over their interpretation. The EU has attempted to extend its human rights model on the Chinese through channels such as the annual EU-China Human Rights Dialogue. The discussion that is occurring is seen as a positive step by both sides, but the outcomes are minimal. The lack of leverage that the EU appears able to assert in this area is cited by – mainly Western – sceptics as a reason to doubt the capacity that the two parties will ever have to truly find a mutually agreeable solution. Chinese policymakers have also not shied away from setting EU members against each other. A typical example is the '16+1' group that was formed between China and 16 Central and Eastern European countries in 2011. Some of these countries have been offered significant unilateral investment promises, which may distort their priorities when negotiating multilaterally with the rest of their EU counterparts over the EU's future China strategy.

Looking in greater detail at the issue of FDI, in 2016 China's stock of outbound direct investment in the EU increased by 77 per cent from 2015, to a total of EUR 35 billion (USD 37.3 billion) (ibid.). Chinese enterprises have mainly been targeting infrastructure, the energy sector as well as the high-technology sector; from the Piraeus Port of Athens to the Hinkley Point Nuclear Plant in the UK, even to German high-tech firms like Kuka. Some European leaders have become increasingly concerned about Chinese intrusion into these sensitive economic domains. Additionally, China's capacity to actually successfully implement its contracted projects was put in doubt when a Chinese company withdrew from the construction of the Polish A2 motorway linking Warsaw to the German border (Bao 2011). During the European Council summit in June 2017, Germany, France and Italy put forward a proposal on a screening mechanism for investment from outside the EU, only to be blocked later by countries that benefitted most from receiving Chinese investment, such as Portugal, Greece and the Czech Republic (Cerulus & Hanke 2017). In his State of the Union address, President Juncker proposed a framework of vetting FDI, claiming that 'we (the EU) are not naïve free traders' (European Commission 2017b). Although the possible impact from such a screening mechanism remains unclear, it would put some constraints on China's ability to advance its BRI in the EU. Examples have already manifested themselves. The Belgrade-Budapest railway, deemed as a landmark BRI project, is still pending due to an EU investigation 'into whether it violated EU laws on public tender processes' (Poggetti 2017).

Both the US and the EU run large trade deficits with China, for a total amount of USD 347 billion and EUR 175 million, respectively, in 2017. There is ambiguity as to whether running such a large trade deficit is indeed problematic. However, the trade deficit issue has undoubtedly served as a powerful rhetorical tool for populist and nationalist political forces that associate it with domestic unemployment and economic slowdown. Even French President Macron, a supporter of free market liberalism, has criticized the EU's trade deficit with China stating 'I am for free trade ... but I am not for naivety' (Emmott & Rose 2017). Until recently US-China relations had been kept relatively amenable albeit with precautionary measures being followed. The Obama administration opted for a passive-aggressive foreign policy towards China with its 'Pivot to Asia'. From 2009, it made concerted efforts to strengthen its strategic partnerships among South East Asian countries such as Vietnam, the Philippines and Singapore, in an attempt to check and constrain the growing Chinese hegemony in this region. However, perhaps partly instructed by the maxim to 'keep your friends close, but your enemies closer', Obama complemented this with an active engagement with the Chinese leadership.

This stands in marked contrast to the stance adopted by Trump. Even during his election campaign, he belligerently attacked what he deemed to be the unfair trading relationship that the US currently has with China, calling it the 'greatest theft in the history of the world' (Stracqualursi 2017) and even threatened to start a trade war. At the start of his presidency, Trump at first gave indications that he may actually be open to the idea of following up on Obama's efforts to nurture a positive relationship with China. However, this ceasefire was short-lived and has been superseded once again by open criticisms made against China for taking away jobs from the US and pursuing unscrupulous trading methods.

On 22 March 2018, President Trump invoked Section 301 of the Trade Act 1974 with the intention to raise tariffs on a wide range of imports from China, following a seven-month inquiry into China's alleged intellectual property theft and forced technology transfers (Diamond 2018). Before signing the memorandum, Trump was reported to have lamented 'the US' multi-hundred billion dollar trade deficit with China' (ibid.). At the time of writing, the US and China have implemented three rounds of tariffs on each other, with $250 billion of US tariffs applied exclusively to China and $110 billion of retaliatory China tariffs applied exclusively to the US, without even considering the newly levied duties on steel and aluminium as a result of a Section 232 investigation (Wong & Koty 2018). As a consequence, US-China trade tensions have since become highly strained, and the outcome of this conflict is unclear. US animosity towards, and ongoing competition with, its second-largest trading partner have already destabilized the stock market, and may unleash a wave of international protectionism which could have worldwide repercussions, and could severely undermine global economic growth.

Looking at the third, significant, potential destabilizing factor, i.e. foreign debt holdings, as of August 2017, China's holdings of US government debt stood at $1.2 trillion, equal to 28 per cent of the entire overseas US government debt holdings (Amadeo 2017). Estimates suggest that a further 25 per cent of China's foreign reserves are held in euro-denominated assets. Although it is as much against China's interests to call in these debt holdings as it is against anyone else's, some commentators have pronounced that this current arrangement places the EU and the US in a compromising situation. Coinciding with the US-China trade disputes, Beijing reduced US debt holdings by $4.4 billion in June 2018. Should China further sell off US bonds, it would be debilitating for the US economy, since the increase of the supply of US bonds may bring about the fall of fixed income prices as well as a rise in yields, making it more expensive for American companies and citizens to borrow.

With few incentives to cooperate, a growing militarization of the South China Sea heightens the risk of competition between the US and China. As part of the ongoing efforts to secure their presence and assert influence in this geostrategic region, China's Ministry of Defence announced in 2015 that it was switching its military status in the region from solely defensive to both offensive and defensive (Fields 2015). Through dredging and land reclamations China is turning reefs and atolls into military bases and airstrips, posing potential threats to some ASEAN nations. In January 2018, the US Department of Defence shifted its military strategic focus from counter-terrorism to facing revisionist powers, including China. As this strategic geopolitical area becomes more militarized, the need for decisive, clear and controlled management from both sides becomes all the more acute. Increased saturation only heightens the risk that an unwanted and ill-advised confrontation may occur. Mitigating the tension was an agreement reached between China and the US in 2015 on Confidence-Building Measures, which encompasses the Notification of Major Military Activities Agreement and the Rules of Behaviour Memorandum of Understanding, among other endeavours.

The lack of policy coherence of the current US administration is not only a case for concern for China but is affecting relations with the EU as well. Transatlantic relations have deteriorated following the election of Donald Trump. Following the 2017 G7 and NATO summits, Angela Merkel stated that 'the times in which we could rely fully on others', referring to the US, 'they are somewhat over' (Henley 2017). The two traditional allies are disagreeing on various topics. Aside from pulling the US out of the Paris climate agreement, there are other actions taken by President Trump which have caused antagonism, including his decision to withdraw the US from the Iran nuclear deal and from the UN Human Rights Council, and to openly question the integrity of the EU by speaking in support of Brexit. Furthermore, his blunt and direct stance with regard to financial pledges to NATO has led to disillusionment among its Western European members.

Continuity or volatility?

The discussion above demonstrates the complexity of the relationships between these three powers. It seems that both (neo-)realist and (neo-)liberal arguments can provide partial explanations for the existing and shifting balance of influence between these three global powers, in the framework of a multipolar world order. Of course, other approaches – including the various strands of constructivism – could further explain how each power views the other, whether they see them as a 'friend' or an 'enemy', and how intersubjective interpretations can affect how developments in shifting power balances are interpreted. Based on the examples given of cooperation and competition between these three powers – embedded into a global power structure that comprises many other units – this section aims to draw out some implications in order to shed light on the question as to whether a new order is likely to emerge or increasing levels of disorder will ensue.

At the beginning of his presidency in 2009, Obama opened two days of high-level talks with China by stating that 'the relationship between the United States and China is the most important bilateral relationship of the 21st century' (Associated Press 2009). Although it is true that the US derives the largest share (21 per cent) of its imports from China, 9.3 per cent of US exports also go to China, making it the third largest trade partner of the US after Canada and Mexico. China's economic rise to power has brought it unprecedentedly close to the US in recent times, but when compared to the attitudes of the EU towards China there are much greater levels of reluctance and suspicion in the face of this process. The recent trajectory of US-China relations seems to be defined much more by discontinuity and fluidity than continuity.

During Obama's administration, a 'pivot' towards East Asia was adopted. Various partnerships were made in order to both try and maintain a position of dominance over China but also to facilitate engagement with the region as a whole. Obama demonstrated an understanding that the US must be wary of the rise of emerging economies and their impacts on the new world order. Despite these precautions and the latent distrust between the two nations, Obama made concerted efforts to promote partnership and cooperation in order for the two to survive as global powers together. Trump on the other hand seems happy to settle for 'no order' instead of a 'negotiated order'. As Trump pursues his protectionist policies, the 'America first' ideology, he is distancing both the EU and China from the US. This raises the likelihood that China will try to push its multipolar global order model through the soft power diplomatic channels which it has strived to cultivate and enhance.

The antagonistic decisions taken by the Trump administration are also placing increasing strain on, and threatening, the integrity of EU-US relations, an established cornerstone of the current global order. The European Council continues to denounce protectionist agendas, with overt references to Trump's policies, and has stated that 'trade relations with China should be strengthened' (Casarini 2017). The EU can seek to overcome language and cultural barriers by looking for similarities in policy between China and the EU, which go beyond the realms of just trade. Both countries have expressed support for multilateralism and international agreements, most obviously, the Paris Agreement. China, for its part, has also made concerted efforts to outwardly demonstrate its respect and support for the EU integration project. Therefore, we can see how China could be perceived as a more favourable ally and partner for the EU in the future and how a new global order could feasibly arise as a result.

With attempts at bilateral diplomacy already hitting obstacles, trilateral or multilateral engagement will be even harder to pursue. However, we should pay attention to the role that international forums and international institutions, including the United Nations, could play in this regard. The United Nations Security Council (UNSC), for example, could offer one established mechanism for continued dialogue among China, the US and the EU (notably France after Brexit), plus Russia. At UNSC meetings there are plenty of opportunities to conduct both formal and informal negotiations and discussions among the current permanent members of the UNSC. These interactions and the greater understandings that they can facilitate arguably remain a key component of international diplomacy in the current constellation of global power relations. The G20 is another platform in which these three global powers can engage with each other. Immediately after the US departure from the Paris Agreement, European Commission President Juncker claimed at a press meeting following the 19th EU-China Summit in June 2017 that

> we [the EU] were happy to see that China is agreeing to our unhappiness about the American climate decision. This is helpful, this is responsible, and this is about inviting both, China and the European Union, to proceed with the implementation of the Paris Agreement.
>
> (European Commission 2017c)

The G20 may play an important role in the evolving pattern of world order, particularly when the EU and China aim to cooperate on some issue areas without the US.

Finally, when considering the issue of continuity and discontinuity and changing global orders, we should think about the level of flexibility that each of these three powers has in this regard. For the US and China global power shifts seem to present much more of a zero-sum game and questions of national pride and self-interest restrict their options and room for manoeuvre. Their two visions of an ideal global order are not only different but also in direct competition with each other. The EU, by contrast, is of strategic importance for both the US and China. While the EU's support is crucial for China to implement its flagship connectivity project, it is equally vital for the US in the realms of security, trade and on other issues. This could grant the EU some flexibility and leverage to engage with both powers. This reality must also be taken into consideration when trying to understand the relationships between the three. Some mainstream IR theories, as shown above, can explain part of the developments in global affairs as witnessed in practice. None of them, however, will be capable of explaining the relations between these three 'global giants' uniquely, and any explanation will always need to draw on a combination of their respective insights and predictions.

Conclusion

The purpose of this chapter was to analyse how the current EU-China-US interactions may possibly shape the global order, acknowledging that the relations between these three major entities are embedded into a global power structure that encompasses many more actors. This chapter makes several propositions in this regard.

First, when considering the primary field in which increasingly closer interaction has taken place, that of economics, it has been suggested that there are key indicators today showing how Sino-European relations have built upon economic interactions to also foster a bilateral political dialogue. In this sense, (neo-)liberal and constructivist predictions seem to be able to capture parts of these developments. High-level summits now occur on an annual basis and a further significant step forward was taken when both China and the EU agreed to form a binding alliance to support the multilateral Paris Agreement in the face of the US withdrawal. However, despite frequent contacts between the two sides, there remain distinct obstacles. On the one hand, disparity between their respective domestic political and legal standards cannot be ignored. The two have, and advocate for, very different political systems. On the other hand, the EU has also pushed China to adopt some of its human rights standards with little success so far.

The cultural similarities between the EU and the US in terms of shared values and views, in contrast to the difference between China and either of these two powers, not only facilitate trade and political relations but also raise the opportunity cost of breaking this order. This may explain the high levels of tolerance and patience EU member states and leaders have already been able to display in the face of President Trump's unclear agenda regarding issues such as the future of NATO and, after Brexit, even the integrity of the EU itself. There is an underlying opportunity cost of forsaking a deeply entrenched relationship while it still continues to bring stability. Any pivot means a leap into the unknown for both powers.

It is the issue of foreign investment in sensitive sectors, 'unfair' trade and foreign debt holdings that has arguably become a leading destabilizing factor when it comes to Sino-American-EU relations. The scale of US debt that China holds, combined with their consistently asymmetric trade balance, has led to distrust and apprehension as the US increasingly feels that its no longer superior economy is being placed in a compromising and precarious position. The so-called 'pivot to Asia' looked to engage with China itself while simultaneously strengthening bonds with the US' traditional allies situated in China's geopolitical neighbourhood. This engagement included increasing the American military presence in countries such as Japan, South Korea, Singapore and the Philippines.

Increased military saturation, especially within the South China Sea, necessitates more careful management to minimize confrontation and avoid unnecessary antagonism. This has been starkly absent since the election of Donald Trump. Despite a brief initial tempering in attitude, Trump has quickly reverted to what may be called 'belligerent' or 'bombastic' rhetoric when it comes to his approach to Chinese relations. Again, economic issues have been central to this rhetoric. However, caution against defining a nation such as the US through the lens of one specific presidential administration is warranted. Both the transience of presidential tenure must be remembered and the fact that the power of any one individual in a globalized world, even the President of the United States, always faces checks and balances from greater overarching forces.

For now, at least China knows that it cannot challenge the US hegemony in the military sense – the traditional way that global orders have been overthrown according to predictions encompassed in some power transition models based on realist thought – but it is making increasing efforts to overcome this shortcoming. The historian Niall Ferguson was already writing over ten years ago about the 'descent of the West' and 'a reorientation of the world' (Ferguson 2006). If historical precedent is anything to go by, we should be apprehensive that a shift in global power balances is far more likely to be characterized by tension, distrust, conflict and disorder than by order. Indeed, from his neorealist IR perspective, John Mearsheimer envisaged that 'the United States and China are likely to engage in an intense security competition with considerable potential for war' (Mearsheimer 2004). (Neo-)liberals would approach such interpretations more cautiously and also see increasing economic ties between these two powers – notwithstanding the significant political and economic tensions – as a potential foundation for a more interdependent, peaceful structure of co-existence in the future. In addition to this, approaches based on neo-liberal thought would attribute a much greater role to international institutions in the maintenance of global stability.

An overriding problem is that it remains as difficult as ever to discern the true intentions of today's decision-makers, let alone predict what these might be in ten or twenty years' time. Varying responses and reactions to China's ongoing BRI are demonstrative of how policy objectives can be interpreted in multifarious ways. Ostensibly, China projects the argument that this project first and foremost aspires to increase global trade, and therefore overall prosperity, across wide swathes of Eurasia and even parts of East Africa. At the World Economic Forum in Davos, in January 2017, Xi Jinping reiterated the message that China seeks to champion free trade. However, sceptics within the EU and beyond see this project as a significant threat, the true intentions of which are to slowly subsume the whole of Eurasia under Chinese hegemony. This demonstrates that the realist paradigm of interpreting economic gains of another power as a threat to one's own security in the long term is very much prevalent in current interpretations of global affairs. What is clear from examples like this is that we must strive even harder to look for quantifiable indicators when trying to make informed judgements about the situation around us and how this may impact on our future.

It seems fair to assert that on an individual basis, China, the US and the EU all desire order. However, as each one tries to impose its own interpretation of order onto one global model, the end result could well be disorder. This is not to say though that disorder is inevitable. In a few crucial ways, the international order today is fundamentally different from its historical predecessors. First, the development of nuclear weapons would make any war between these three great powers much costlier to the point of global oblivion. Deterrence theory as presented in the realist tradition is founded on the principle that awareness on all sides of their common overwhelming destructive capabilities is what also makes the prospect of conflict between the global superpowers much less likely. The process of globalization has also meant that the system increasingly offers benefits to all, albeit in varying amounts, rather than just a selected geographical region. There is a much greater opportunity cost now for any nation that tries to overhaul the integrated and rule-based Western order. This order has a remarkable capacity to accommodate rising powers as it is preferable to try and assert pressure and make adaptations from within it than to directly compete against it. Although the US and its Western European allies were instrumental in creating this order, this does not mean that they will forever fully control its future trajectory. This may well be the main uncertainty that dominates US-China-EU relations today.

Note

1 See also the chapters by Bo, Freeman and Schreurs in this volume.

References

Amadeo, K. (2017) 'U.S. Debt to China: How Much Does It Own?' *The Balance*. Available at: www.thebalance.com/u-s-debt-to-china-how-much-does-it-own-3306355.

Associated Press (2009) *Obama: U.S.-China Ties Shape 21st Century*. Available at: www.cbsnews.com/news/obama-us-china-ties-shape-21st-century/.

Bao, C. (2011) 'COVEC Stops Polish Highway Construction', *China Daily*. Available at: www.chinadaily.com.cn/bizchina/2011-06/18/content_12728120.htm.

Boffey, D. & A. Neslen (2017) 'China and EU Strengthen Promise to Paris Deal with US Poised to Step Away', *The Guardian*, 13 May. Available at: www.theguardian.com/environment/2017/may/31/china-eu-climate-lead-paris-agreement.

Casarini, N. (2017) 'How Trump is Reconnecting Europe with China', *RealClearWorld*. Available at: www.realclearworld.com/articles/2017/05/04/how_trump_is_reconnecting_europe_with_china.html.

Cerulus, L. & J. Hanke (2017) 'Enter the Dragon: Chinese Investment in Crisis-Hit Countries Gives Beijing Influence at the European Union's Top Table', *Politico*. Available at: www.politico.eu/article/china-and-the-troika-portugal-foreign-investment-screening-takeovers-europe/.

Dahl, R. (1957) 'The Concept of Power', *Behavioral Science* 2(3), 201–215.

Delegation of the European Union to China (2016) *China and the EU*. Available at: https://eeas.europa.eu/delegations/china_en/15394/China per cent20and per cent20the per cent20EU.

Diamond, J. (2018) 'Trump Hits China with Tariffs, Heightening Concerns of Global Trade War', *CNN.* Available at: https://edition.cnn.com/2018/03/22/politics/donald-trump-china-tariffs-trade-war/index.html.

Emmott, R. & M. Rose (2017) 'At EU Summit, Macron Pleads for Limits to Foreign Takeovers', *Reuters.* Available at: https://uk.reuters.com/article/us-eu-summit-macron/at-eu-summit-macron-pleads-for-limits-to-foreign-takeovers-idUKKBN19D2HY.

European Commission (2017a) *A Balanced and Progressive Trade Policy to Harness Globalisation.* Available at: https://ec.europa.eu/commission/priorities/balanced-and-progressive-trade-policy-harness-globalisation_en.

——— (2017b) 'State of the Union 2017- Trade Package: European Commission Proposes Framework for Screening of Foreign Direct Investments', Press Release. Available at: http://europa.eu/rapid/press-release_IP-17-3183_en.htm.

——— (2017c) *EU-China Summit: Moving Forward with Our Global Partnership.* Available at: http://europa.eu/rapid/press-release_IP-17-1524_en.htm.

Ferguson, N. (2006) *The War of the World: Twentieth-Century Conflict and the Descent of the West*, London: Penguin Press.

Fields, L. (2015) 'China Goes on the Offensive in the South China Sea', *Vice News.* Available at: https://news.vice.com/article/china-goes-on-the-offensive-in-the-south-china-sea.

Gilpin, R. (1981) *War and Change in World Politics*, Cambridge: Cambridge University Press.

Hånggi, H. (1999) 'ASEM and the Construction of the New Triad', *Journal of the Asia Pacific Economy* 4(1), 56–80.

Haass, R. (2018) 'A North Korean Opportunity for America and China', *Council on Foreign Relations.* Available at: www.cfr.org/article/north-korean-opportunity-america-and-china.

Henley, J. (2017) 'Angela Merkel: EU Cannot Completely Rely on US and Britain Any More', *The Guardian*, 28 May. Available at: www.theguardian.com/world/2017/may/28/merkel-says-eu-cannot-completely-rely-on-us-and-britain-any-more-g7-talks.

Juncker, J.-C. (2017) *Speech by President Jean-Claude Juncker at the 12th EU-China Business Summit.* Available at: http://europa.eu/rapid/press-release_SPEECH-17-1526_en.htm.

Keohane, R. and J. S. Nye (1977). *Power and Interdependence: World Politics in Transition.* Boston: Little and Brown.

Keohane, R. and J.S. Nye (1987) 'Power and Interdependence Revisited', *International Organization*, 41(4), 725–753.

Krasner, S.D. (1982), Structural Causes and Regime Consequences: Regimes as Intervening Variables, *International Organization*, 36(2), 185–205.

Keohane, R. (1984) *After Hegemony*, Princeton: Princeton University Press.

Mearsheimer, J. (2004) *Why China's Rise Will Not Be Peaceful.* Available at: http://mearsheimer.uchicago.edu/pdfs/A0034b.pdf.

Modelski, G. (1978) 'The Long Cycle of Global Politics and the Nation-State', *Comparative Studies in Society and History* 20(2), April, Cambridge University Press, 214–235.

Nabers, D. (2010) 'Power, Leadership and Hegemony in International Politics', in D. Flemes (ed.), *Regional Leadership in the Global System*, Surrey: Ashgate Publishing Company, 51–69.

Oko, M. (2017) 'Global Leaders Deliver Message of Resolve Following Trump's Decision to Abandon Paris Agreement', *World Resources Institute.* Available at: www.wri.org/blog/2017/06/global-leaders-deliver-message-resolve-following-trump's-decision-abandon-paris-0.

Organski, A.F.K. & J. Kugler (1980) *The War Ledger.* Chicago: University of Chicago.

Poggetti, L. (2017) 'China's Charm Offensive in Eastern Europe Challenges EU Cohesion', *The Diplomat,* 24 November.

Schweller, R.L. & X. Pu (2011) 'After Unipolarity: China's Visions of International Order in an Era of U.S. Decline', *International Security* 36(1), 41–72.

Seaman, J., M. Huotari & M. Otero-Iglesias (eds.) (2017) *Chinese Investment in Europe. A Country-Level Approach, ETNC Report,* French Institute of International Relations (Ifri), Elcano Royal Institute, Mercator Institute for China Studies.

Stracqualursi, V. (2017) '10 Times Trump Attacked China and its Trade Relations with the US', *ABC News.* Available at: http://abcnews.go.com/Politics/10-times-trump-attacked-china-trade-relations-us/story?id=46572567.

Wong, D. & A.C. Koty (2018) 'The US-China Trade War: A Timeline', *China Briefing,* 14 December.

The World Bank (2017) World Bank Country Profiles; US, China and EU. Available at: www.worldbank.org.

White House (2017) *Remarks by President Trump and President Macron of France in Joint Press Conference.* Available at: www.whitehouse.gov/briefings-statements/remarks-president-trump-president-macron-france-joint-press-conference-jul-13/.

Zagare, F.C. (2008) Classical deterrence theory: A critical assessment, *International Interactions,* 21(4), 365–387, 1998 (published online 9 January 2008).

Part II

Foreign and security policy

3 China, the EU, the US, and global governance

Ciwan M. Can and Xavier D. Soto

Introduction

China's economic revitalization has been followed by an increasing role and influence on issues related to international security, as its significant involvement in the Iranian and North Korean nuclear crises, United Nations Peacekeeping Operations (UNPKO), and the fight against climate change and other regional and global traditional and non-traditional security issues reveal. China has shifted the focus of its foreign policy from emphasizing the principle of 'concealing one's capabilities and biding one's time' during the early years of its modernization, to stressing the principle of 'making a modest contribution' (Wang & Song 2016: 3), and more recently, as President Xi Jinping has emphasized, to taking a place at the centre stage of international politics and striving for the achievement of a 'community of common destiny for humankind' (Mardell 2017).

There is a growing literature on the 'China threat', and theories of 'hegemonic transition' and the 'Thucydides trap', which argue that war is a most likely outcome when a rising power displaces a ruling power, have been applied to predict the impact China's continuous revitalization will have on international relations (Allison 2017). Whether China's continuous revitalization will lead to an intense security competition and great power struggle with the US, a great power war between them, or whether China's revitalization is a threat to the liberal international order in general, have become central topics in the study of international relations.

According to Chen, world order can be defined as a set of sustainable arrangements in the international system to allow political entities, and the peoples within them, to enjoy a meaningful level of peace, welfare, and justice (Chen 2016a: 776). Kissinger further argues that the arrangements of world order are based on two fundamental components: (i) a balance of power and (ii) a consensus on the legitimacy of the existing arrangements (Kissinger 2014: 26). Since China's rise has been achieved within the existing arrangements, it should not be difficult to understand that China has an interest in safeguarding them. There is a consensus among policy-makers in China that in order to modernize in the age of globalization, it is important for China to integrate itself with the rest of the world and to maintain the world order (Wang & James 2009: 11). This has been asserted by Chinese leaders several times on different occasions. In his national New Year speech in 2018, for instance, President Xi Jinping stated that China 'always will be a builder of world peace, contributor of global development, and keeper of international order' (Xinhua 2017b). Also, China's Ambassador to the EU stated that by 'the middle of this century', China will be turned into a 'great modern country that is strong, prosperous, democratic, culturally advanced, harmonious, and beautiful' and that for this end, it is of crucial importance for China to have a 'peaceful and stable world, and to work with others with an open mind' (Ming 2018).

However, it is also clear that China, together with partners from the developing world, perceives several aspects of the existing arrangements of the international order as instruments of Western dominance, and with the shift in the global distribution of power wants to make more inclusive and egalitarian these arrangements that currently marginalize the interests of those countries that were absent during their creation after WWII. At a study session of the politburo of the Chinese Communist Party's Central Committee (CPCC) in 2016, President Xi Jinping underlined that as the 'international balance of power has shifted and global challenges are increasing, global governance system reform has emerged as a trend of the times', and that China must take the 'chance and ride the wave to make the international order more reasonable and just to protect the common interests of China and other developing countries' (Xinhua 2016).

The main argument of this chapter is that China has a fundamental interest in maintaining the existing arrangements of world order and that at the same time is engaged in order-reforming activities, seeking to enhance the legitimacy of the existing arrangements of the international system at a time of global power shift (Chen 2016a: 780). Furthermore, following Chen (2016b), we argue that China follows two basic strategies in its order-reforming activities: 'reform from inside' and 'reform from outside'. Focussing on international security, this chapter argues that China's revitalization will have a fundamental impact on the future of global security governance, and that the future relationship, both bilaterally and multilaterally, between China, the US, and the EU, on international security will be of key importance in this regard.

This chapter is organized as follows. First, it deals with China's bilateral relationship with the US and with the EU on international security, respectively. Second, it looks at the US-EU relationship from a Chinese perspective, and how the dynamics in the transatlantic relationship impact the perception China has of these major actors in its own foreign and security policy. Third, it discusses the triangular relationship between China, the US, and the EU, and how this relationship impacts the evolution of global governance. Finally, the concluding section argues that in an era of US withdrawal from its traditional global leadership role, the China-EU relationship, which is one of the most comprehensive partnerships between two major powers, has the potential to become the most potent force for preventing the fragmentation of the global governance architecture.

China-US

In the early years of the post-Cold War era, China had a minor strategic importance in US foreign policy. However, with the steady revitalization of China, Washington's approach alternated between policies of containment and engagement. The first Clinton administration's China policy is perceived from the Chinese perspective to be one in which the US often attempted to intervene in China's domestic affairs, such as by linking human rights to economic issues, denying the People's Republic of China (PRC) the Most Favoured Nation (MFN) status, and getting involved into the 1995–1996 Taiwan Strait crisis.

Although President Clinton softened his approach during his second term, such as the pledge by both sides to build a constructive strategic partnership looking forward to the 21st century (Zhao 2012: 371), the following US administration under President George W. Bush soon constructed China as a strategic competitor whose influence had to be balanced by strengthening the US-Japan alliance. President Bush also reinforced the US commitment to Taiwan, approving the largest arms sales package ever, including a number of F-16 fighters. The bilateral relationship worsened with capture of a US spy plane by the People's Liberation Army (PLA) in the South China Sea in April 2001 but improved again after the terrorist attacks of 11 September 2001 when China agreed to cooperate with the US on a number of security issues, i.e. on sharing intelligence during the 2001 military intervention in Afghanistan and working together with the US on the North Korean nuclear issue (Wu 2010a: 3940). Washington reciprocated granting Beijing permanent normal trading relations (PNTR) status, supporting the PRC's membership to the World Trade Organization (WTO) (Lanteigne 2009: 100), and curbing Chen Shuibian's pro-independence policy in Taiwan; however, another arms sales package to the island was approved during the last months of the Bush administration (Zhao 2012: 371).

As the Obama administration intended to repair the US international image after the previous administration's mishandling of the financial crisis and the unilateral invasion of Iraq, which had gone against the desires of a majority of the international community, the US proposed the establishment of a positive, cooperative, and comprehensive relationship with China, in order to jointly address the challenges posed by the economic and financial crisis and other traditional and non-traditional security issues. It was seen by the Chinese side as a positive development in the relationship when Washington delayed not only President Obama's meeting with the exiled Dalai Lama in October 2009 but also the announcement of any arms sales to Taiwan (which was made in October 2011). China was recognized as a strategic partner and a joint statement was signed in November 2009, acknowledging the need for paying attention to each other's core interests in order to improve the bilateral relationship (U.S.-China Joint Statement 2009). However, these positive developments raised a series of unrealistic expectations about the possibilities for cooperation. For instance, the idea of a Sino-US duopoly at the roof of a hierarchical system of global governance was floated by several US scholars and was widely discussed in the media from 2008 to 2010 (Jin 2016: 89). The argument that the two countries economic interdependence had increased to such an extent that it would be easy to cooperate in solving all kinds of international economic issues was also popular at the time (Zhao 2012: 372). Differences soon began to appear in 2010 as the US leadership saw with anxiety China's increasing defence spending and influence in international politics. This resulted from the country's emergence from the 2008 global financial crisis as the largest foreign reserve holder, and the world's second largest economy (after September 2010), positioning itself at the centre of the G20, and acting as the defender of the interests of the developing world (Wu 2010b: 158; Jin 2016: 89).

By announcing the 'pivot' strategy, through which the US sought to bolster its bilateral security alliances with Japan, South Korea, and the Philippines (Wu 2012b: 49), the US intensified the strategic distrust in the relationship. For the Chinese leadership, the pivot strategy clearly had the aim of containing China's revitalization (Xiang 2012). This strategy would be complemented in the economic field with the Trans-Pacific Partnership Agreement, which was never implemented. The US also increasingly applied political pressure on China by attempting to interfere in China's domestic affairs, such as in the South China Sea, on the issue of human rights, Tibet, currency management, and Taiwan, among others.

As President Xi Jinping took office in 2012, China aimed at creating a stable and healthy bilateral relationship with the US, by attempting to overcome historical, ideological, and political differences between the two countries. President Xi proposed the concept of a 'New Model for Major Power Relations' (NMMPR) with the US, based on the principles of non-aggression, non-confrontation, mutual respect, and mutually beneficial cooperation. The objective was to build strategic trust in the relationship and to avoid the notion of the Thucydides trap (Jin & Huang 2015: 38), which had already gained an increasing foothold in the US perspective on the relationship following China's test of an anti-satellite system back in 2007 (Lanteigne 2009: 100–101). By that time, China had also started to prioritize the development of its military capabilities. For example, 'The Diversified Employment of China's Armed Forces' (SCIOPRC 2013) stated the objective of developing power projection capabilities, including blue water platforms (i.e. aircraft carriers, submarines), and air force capabilities. The development and modernization of China's military capabilities is part of its defensive strategy of 'counter-intervention', also called A2/AD in the West. Today, China has the world's largest navy with two aircraft carriers, and a third one under construction. However, its increasing military capabilities 'are not meant to be for offensive purposes', but simply to 'protect its rights and interests', as emphasized by Li Jie, an analyst at the Chinese Naval Research Institute in Beijing (Myers, 2018).

The concept of the NMMPR is furthermore intended to fully integrate China into the liberal democratic world order and to safeguard its territorial sovereignty, political regime, and social stability, without threatening other countries in the pursuit of their own security. President Obama was at first receptive to the concept when President Xi proposed it to him during his visit to the US in June 2013 (Jin 2016: 90), but it soon became clear that the US was reluctant to develop such a relationship with China. By the end of the Obama administration the bilateral relationship ambiguously remained one of cooperation on shared interests in issues related to non-traditional security, such as anti-terrorism and climate change, but with strategic competition in the East China Sea and the South China Sea. Differences especially persisted on cybersecurity, human rights, Taiwan, Tibet, Iran, North Korea, trade, foreign direct investment, and currency exchange, among others (Lieberthal & Wang 2012: 27–29; Jin & Huang 2015: 38).

The transition towards the Trump administration in June 2017 was unexpectedly smooth. President Xi visited the US in April 2017, and President Trump responded with a visit to China in April 2017. Soon, a Comprehensive Dialogue was established (which includes the Diplomatic and Security Dialogue, the Comprehensive Economic Dialogue, the Law Enforcement and Cybersecurity Dialogue, and the Social and Cultural Dialogue). The US Secretary of Defence James Mattis visited China in June 2018 and extended an invitation to Minister of Defence Wei Fenghe to visit the US in an effort to improve military-to-military communication. Both sides agreed on expanding cooperation in the fields of nuclear non-proliferation, drugs control, cybercrime, military-to-military trust building, counterterrorism, the North Korean nuclear issue, freedom of navigation, and non-weaponization of the South China Sea, promoting stability and development in Afghanistan, and pushing forward the cooperation between Afghanistan and Pakistan. However, President Trump soon changed the course of US policy by labelling China as a revisionist great power (The White House 2017: 25) and initiated a trade war, producing great uncertainty about the future of the bilateral relationship and creating suspicion in China about the US strategic aims. So far, China has responded to Washington's economic and political pressures with a tit-for-tat strategy, and at the same time urged for the solution of the current tensions through diplomatic means.

Overall, more than 40 years of relations have created a wealth of mechanisms through which cooperation between the two countries could be enhanced, such as a high degree of economic interdependence, an extensive social network, 93 dialogues at the deputy ministerial level and above, and a pragmatic approach to cooperation on dealing with both traditional and non-traditional threats (Jin 2016: 96). China has undoubtedly reaped abundant benefits from its cooperation with the US and its integration into the liberal world order. However, competition between the two countries persists. Based on a traditional realist perspective, Washington concluded that – as it was impossible to know Beijing's intentions with certainty – the best strategy to follow would be getting ready to safeguard its interests and dominant position in the world in case confrontations emerge. These elements made evident to China the importance of taking into consideration Washington's security concerns, avoiding overreacting to US containment measures, and the need to reassure the US about China's constructive intentions.

Accordingly, the aforementioned document on 'The Diversified Employment of China's Armed Forces' asserts:

> It is China's unshakable national commitment and strategic choice to take the road of peaceful development. China unswervingly pursues an independent foreign policy of peace and a national defence policy that is defensive in nature. China opposes any form of hegemonism and does not interfere in the internal affairs of other countries.
>
> (SCIOPRC 2013)

The document also advocates 'a new security concept featuring mutual trust, mutual benefit, equality and coordination, and pursues comprehensive security, common security and cooperative security' (ibid.). Although *any form of hegemonism* refers not only to China's future intentions but also to the US current international behaviour, the document specifies the principles of China's cooperation in security affairs. It also states the objectives of the PLA in terms of security cooperation, i.e.

> the establishment of just and effective collective security mechanisms and military confidence-building mechanisms. Bearing in mind the concepts of openness, pragmatism and cooperation, China's armed forces increase their interactions and cooperation with other armed forces, and intensify cooperation on confidence-building measures in border areas.
>
> (Ibid.)

The concepts of openness, pragmatism, and cooperation suggest that when normative or ideological positions make it difficult to reach an agreement, a practical attitude should be adopted in order to get positive results.

The objectives of the new security concept are further defined in China's Policies on Asia-Pacific Security Cooperation (2017) and complemented with the new goal of sustainable security. Common security is defined as 'respecting and ensuring the security of each and every country involved' (SCIOPRC 2017), and to avoid seeking absolute security for oneself at the expense of the security of others. Comprehensive security means approaching traditional and non-traditional threats in a 'multipronged and holistic approach, and enhancing regional security governance in a coordinated way' (ibid.). Cooperative security is defined as 'promoting the security of both individual countries and the region as a whole through dialogue and cooperation' (ibid.). Finally, sustainable security is based on the principle that sustainable development is the foundation of sustainable security, therefore, it advocates improving people's lives and narrowing the wealth gap.

Although both the 2015 White Paper on China's Military Strategy and the recent US National Defence Strategy identify each other as a security threat (SCIOPRC 2015; The White House 2017), communications remain open through bilateral and multilateral mechanisms. Currently, China's military and security cooperation with the US centres on confidence-building measures and is implemented through a series of defence dialogues, military exchanges, and cooperation mechanisms. The main objectives of these measures are to prevent the emergence of conflicts due to a bad communication or misunderstandings, to push forward the institutionalization of codes of conduct during air and maritime encounters, and to cooperate on dealing with new non-traditional security threats.

However, China-US security cooperation goes beyond their bilateral relations and is similarly crucial within the framework of international institutions in which they are members, most importantly the United Nations. The transnational nature of the emerging non-traditional security threats requires greater cooperation between nations whose interactions are institutionalized by formal and informal rules and managed by international and global institutions. Chinese participation within the UN is evidence of its interest in increasing its provision of common goods to the international community as a responsible great power. China is one of the biggest troop and police contributors to peacekeeping missions among the five members of the UN Security Council. The Chinese Navy has coordinated with the US and other countries since 2012 on the protection of the sea lines of communication (SoC). Regarding non-proliferation and disarmament, China has put emphasis on implementing the Treaty on the Non-proliferation of Nuclear Weapons, promoting the resolution of the North Korean nuclear issue together with the US by peaceful means, upholding the Joint Comprehensive Plan of Action (JCPOA) with Iran, and advocating the establishment of a South East Asia Nuclear Weapons Free Zone. China has also cooperated in several UN missions on the combat against transnational crimes. In 2002, China also established a dialogue with North Atlantic Treaty Organization (NATO) to discuss activities to be conducted in Central Asia.

In sum, the bilateral relationship between China and the US has increasingly been perceived from the US side as one of strategic competition. From the Chinese perspective, it became clear with the 'pivot' strategy, and more recently with the 'free and open Indo-Pacific' strategy, that the US seeks to contain the revitalization of China. With this aim, the US also seeks to revive the Quadrilateral Security Dialogue cooperation with Australia, India, and Japan. China, on the other hand, perceives its relationship with the US as one of key importance and pushes for the NMMPR as a model for great power cooperation in a world in which global challenges require effective cooperation between major players. However, US power politics has also prompted China to respond to US policies with similar measures, such as retaliating against US trade policies and developing military counter-intervention capabilities in the region. Nevertheless, four decades of relations have also laid the foundation for dialogues to build confidence and trust between China and the US and important cooperation is sustained through several multilateral initiatives and institutions, such as the JCPOA (which Trump unilaterally withdrew from), the Six-Party Talks, and several UN-initiated activities, such as the fight against transnational crime and protection of SoC, among others.

China-EU

China's relations with the EU can be dated back to 1975 when the Sino-EU (then the EC) relationship was established. However, the most recent significant aspect of the EU relationship in Chinese foreign and security policy can be dated back to 2003, with the forging of the Comprehensive Strategic Partnership amid shared concerns of increased US unilateralism following the intervention in Iraq (Chen 2013: 176). That same year, China released its first White Paper on EU Policy, which was also the first White Paper related to a foreign counterpart that the Chinese government had ever released. As the policy paper stated, it would be important for China to 'strengthen and enhance China-EU relations', which were 'an important component of China's foreign policy' (FMPRC 2003). The report further made clear that China 'is committed to a long-term, stable and full partnership with the EU'. The strategic partnership was in 2010 upgraded by both parties to also encompass foreign affairs, international security, climate change, and global economic governance (Kirchner, Christiansen & Dorussen 2016: 2).

The convergence of interests related to important topics in international relations such as international peace and security, prosperity, and sustainable development, which formed part of both China's two centenary goals and the EU's 2020 strategy, led them to launch the common China-EU 2020 Strategic Agenda in 2013, in which both recognized each other as 'important actors in a multipolar world' and their mutual 'responsibility for promoting peace, prosperity and sustainable development for the benefit of all' (FMPRC 2013: 3). With the Strategic Agenda, both China and the EU sought to further deepen their already existing Strategic Partnership of 2003.

The 2003 policy paper and the 2013 Strategic Agenda were followed by a new Chinese EU policy paper in 2014. This paper recognized the important developments that had taken place in China-EU relations since 2003 and placed the relationship at the centre of a new world order where a reconfiguration of power had triggered the rise of new centres of economic and political significance. As the policy paper emphasized, the EU had become an important strategic partner for China in its 'effort to pursue peaceful development and multi-polarity' (FMPRC 2014); two of China's most important strategic goals in international relations (Michalski & Pan 2017b: 2).

Although from the Chinese perspective the partnership has experienced several setbacks since 2003, such as the failure of the EU to lift the arms embargo, the refusal to grant China the Market Economy Status (MES), and the more recent challenges on trade and investments, it is seen by China as a significant component of contemporary international relations, and the partnership stands out as one of the most comprehensive partnerships between two major powers (Michalski & Pan 2017a: 611). In its early stages, the strategic partnership led some scholars to argue about the emergence of a China-EU 'axis' in world affairs (Shambaugh 2004: 248). More recently, it has raised concerns in the US that the growing partnership could potentially undermine the transatlantic alliance. This concern was reinforced when the US' traditional allies joined the China-initiated Asian Infrastructure Investment Bank (AIIB) against the desire of the US which perceives the initiative as a threat to the existing Bretton Woods institutions of global economic governance (Higgins & Sanger 2015). For China, however, its relationship with the EU is an important aspect of China's comprehensive foreign policy for the new century, which is defined in terms of four major dimensions: great powers as the key, neighbouring countries as the priority, developing countries as the basis, and multilateralism as the key venue (Wang & Song 2016: 3).

Against this background, the relationship with the EU is part of the first dimension of China's comprehensive foreign policy for the new century and is regarded as an integral part of its desire to build a long-term relationship with the major powers in the world based on mutual benefit and win-win cooperation. Thus, rather than being understood as a new 'axis' in world affairs or as a relationship aimed at weakening the transatlantic alliance, it would be more correct to place China's relationship with the EU within its overall framework of building stable relations with all the major powers in the world in order to foster 'stability and balanced development that contributes to global peace, tranquillity, and harmonious development', as emphasized by Chinese Foreign Minister Wang Yi (MFAPRC 2017).

The China-EU strategic partnership and the China-EU 2020 Strategic Agenda can be said to form the foundations of China-EU cooperation on international security. An important aspect of China-EU security cooperation is related to nuclear non-proliferation and their active roles in mediating between countries standing off in nuclear crises, as explained in detail in the EU-China joint declaration on non-proliferation and arms control of 2004. Since becoming a member of the Nuclear Non-proliferation Treaty in 1992, China has clearly signalled its desire to prevent the spread of nuclear weapons and has actively been working for denuclearization by joining all multilateral regimes of nuclear non-proliferation (Attina 2017: 189). In order to prevent the spread of nuclear weapons, China has closely cooperated with the EU and they both had leading roles in solving the Iranian nuclear crisis and in reaching the signature of the JCPOA in Vienna in July 2015.

More recently, China and the EU have opposed the US' unilateral withdrawal and re-imposition of economic sanctions against Iran. In the joint statement that followed the 20th China-EU Summit, both sides clearly underlined their commitment to the JCPOA by stating that the 'JCPOA is a key element of the global non-proliferation architecture' and a 'significant diplomatic achievement', and that they 'welcome the fact that the IAEA has again confirmed the continued adherence by Iran to its nuclear-related commitments' (MFAPRC 2018). As a consequence of the US unilateral re-imposition of sanctions on Iran, the EU and China have also shown a growing interest in structural changes of the global financial system to reduce the world's financial dependence on the US (Rosenberg & Saravalle 2018). In addition to the bilateral cooperation, as exemplified by the Iranian nuclear crisis, China and the EU also have significant cooperation through multilateral fora, such as for example the Nuclear Security Summit (NSS) and the International Atomic Energy Agency (IAEA). In China's White Paper on the EU of 2014, the Chinese government clarified that it had an interest to continuously strengthen bilateral and multilateral cooperation with the EU on non-proliferation, by stating that both sides should 'commit to jointly upholding the authority of the multilateral disarmament regime' and 'strengthen international nuclear security'. The policy paper also urged stronger cooperation 'to prevent weaponization and an arms race in outer space and safeguard peace and security' (MFAPRC 2014).

Although cooperation on nuclear non-proliferation has stood out as an important aspect of China-EU security cooperation, there are other issue areas where both actors have converging interests and cooperation. These include UN peacekeeping operations, transnational terrorism, antipiracy, and drug trafficking, among others. Thus, China-EU security cooperation can be said to have a great potential for getting strengthened and further deepened in order to cover many aspects of global security, both in terms of traditional and non-traditional security issues.

China and the US-EU relationship

With the end of the Cold War, the transatlantic alliance continued to be the primary instrument through which the US and Europe sought to deal with challenges to international security, as the interventions in the civil war following the break-up of Yugoslavia and the NATO expansion towards Eastern Europe illustrated. In China, the end of the Cold War and the victory of the West was both a relief as the Soviet threat diminished and a time of suspicion towards the intentions of the West. Western sanctions imposed on China, and the attempt to intervene in China's domestic affairs on grounds related to human rights and democracy in the early years of the post-Cold War era, increased the Chinese suspicion of a potential Western attempt to seek regime change. In particular, US unilateralism following the fall of the Soviet Union was of great concern, as the US was attempting to create a unipolar world and embarked on its mission of liberal hegemony (Mearsheimer 2018; Walt 2018). By the end of the 1990s and early 21st century increasing US unilateralism and assertiveness in international politics also led to growing concerns in Europe. For example, then French President Jacques Chirac argued in 1999 that France should counteract US 'hyperpower' through French-led multilateral initiatives (*New York Times* 1999), while former German Chancellor Gerhard Schröder argued in 2003 that 'security in today's world cannot be guaranteed by one country going it alone' and that it 'can be achieved only through international cooperation' (Schröder 2003).

By that time, the EU had already built a more constructive relationship with China than the US had, based on the depiction of the EU and China as 'major global powers' (Michalski & Pan 2017a: 618). For example, interventions in Chinese domestic affairs related to human rights, the crisis related to Taiwan, and the US bombing of the Chinese embassy in Belgrade under the Clinton administration created serious tensions between China and the US. Meanwhile, the EU decided to halt any arms sales to Taiwan, accepted participation in the China-led initiative of a bilateral human rights dialogue in 1995 and the Leader's Summit in 1998, which set in motion direct bilateral strategic communication (Zhou 2017: 4). The EU's motivation for pursuing a more constructive and active policy towards China was based on the desire to facilitate China's integration into the international community and to assist China in its modernization process (Michalski & Pan 2017b.)

The constructive relationship with the EU soon led China to regard the EU as a 'comprehensive strategic partner' (Chen 2012: 18). For example, in its 2003 China policy paper, the European Commission stressed that 'the EU and China have an ever-greater interest to work together as strategic partners to safeguard and promote sustainable development, peace, and stability' (European Commission 2003: 3). After forging the strategic partnership, several EU countries proposed lifting the EU arms embargo and granting China MES. This period of the relations between China and the EU was by some depicted as a time of a 'love affair' (Aggarwal & Newland 2015: 9), while other scholars defined the US-EU relationship as a period of a 'transatlantic rift' (Shambaugh 2005).

However, China's expectations for the EU relationship and the comprehensive strategic partnership were soon disregarded, as the EU bowed to the US pressure against lifting the arms embargo and granting China MES (Lanteigne, Thygeson & Sverdrup 2016: 17). The US made it clear that by lifting the arms embargo the EU would potentially impact the balance of power in the Asia-Pacific in favour of China vis-à-vis US allies in the region (Cuyckens 2012: 305). These developments were soon followed by official meetings between the German Chancellor Merkel and French President

Sarkozy with the exiled Dalai Lama, and later on by the exclusion of China from the EU's Galileo Satellite project. Finally, the EU labelled China as the single most important challenge to the EU's trade policy. At this time, it became clear for the Chinese leadership that the EU was unable to act independently from the US (ibid.: 305).

With the financial crisis in 2008 and the finalization of the Lisbon Treaty, China's views on the EU-US relationship again experienced several changes. From the Chinese perspective, the EU was perceived as being serious in its attempt to forge an independent course in its foreign policy and to establish strategic relations with China and other key players in the world. It was also perceived that the EU now had moved towards a more pragmatic approach in its foreign relations than earlier. Around the same time, the US announced its strategy of 'rebalancing to Asia', which later was changed to the 'pivot' strategy (Clinton 2011), and more recently, the 'Open Indo-Pacific Strategy' under Trump (Landler 2017). The US pivot strategy made it clear for the Chinese leadership that the US intended to contain the revitalization of China (Xiang 2012). The EU, on the other hand, did not express any willingness to take part in the US pivot strategy and rather sought to form an independent Asia strategy.

However, major differences in the EU and the US strategy towards China and the region became clear with the creation of the AIIB, as major EU countries decided to join the bank while the US perceived it as a potential threat to the existing US-dominated Bretton Woods institutions and urged EU member states not to join. These differences have increased with the more recent policies of the Trump administration. The increasing US tendency to seek unilateral solutions to global challenges, and its recent protectionist policies, coupled with its zero-sum approach to China, is perceived by China to be driven by a Cold War mentality based on power politics and aimed at containing the revitalization of China (Xinhua 2017a). The EU approach to China is, on the other hand, not characterized by any fundamental strategic disputes, and differs from the US by its focus on assisting China in its modernization process and its interest in integrating it more fully into the international order (Michalski & Pan 2017b). Thus, China perceives the EU as a more constructive and important partner in the triangular relationship in order to balance US unilateralism, oppose protectionism, and uphold multilateralism and win-win cooperation between the world's major powers (Global Times 2018). This view was made clear by China's Foreign Minster Wang Yi during a meeting with Federica Mogherini, where he stated that 'China and the EU are two forces for stabilisation. They need to step up strategic communication and cooperation to firmly support multilateralism and international rules' (Zheng 2018).

China and global governance

As noted earlier in this chapter, China firmly attaches itself to the prevailing order, but it does however perceive this order as partial to the interests of

Western powers (especially the US), and unrepresentative of the values and concerns of non-Western states. Therefore, we argue that China has taken the role of an 'order-shaper', seeking to reform the existing institutions of global governance and ultimately shaping their future. For this reason, it is of crucial importance to understand China's order-reforming activities and strategies. In this regard, it is important to also keep in mind, as we mentioned earlier, that world order rests on two fundamental components: (i) a balance of power and (ii) a consensus on the legitimacy of the existing arrangements (Kissinger 2014: 26). Therefore, whether China, together with the US and the EU, and other developed and developing countries manage to reform the existing arrangement will ultimately have an impact on the legitimacy of the evolving order, as we now find ourselves in an era of global power shift.

According to Chen, the order-reforming activities of China fall into two categories: 'reform from within' and 'reform from outside' (Chen 2016b). The first strategy of 'reform from within' concerns China's desire to reform the existing US-led international institutions through multilateral action with both developed and developing countries. Several important developments have proven that China's strategy of 'reform from within' is feasible, most notably the emergence of G20 as an important forum for global economic governance and the 2015 approval of the US Congress of the 2010 IMF reform in which China obtained the third largest voting rights in the IMF. However, the slow pace of any substantial reforms has also led China to focus on the strategy of 'reform from outside'. Chen identifies four sub-strategies under the general 'reform from outside' strategy. These are (i) creation of plurilateral regional orders, (ii) creation of plurilateral embedded orders, (iii) creation of plurilateral parallel orders, and (iv) creation of China-sponsored bilateral networks (Chen 2016a: 781).

The above-mentioned sub-strategies are not aimed at delegitimizing the existing international institutions, but rather at complementing them in areas in which they are weak or absent. A notable example of this is the creation of the Shanghai Cooperation Organization (SCO), which is a regional organization supportive of the first sub-strategy of creating 'plurilateral regional orders'. The main purpose of SCO is to promote cooperative security in the fight against separatism, terrorism, and religious extremism in Central Asia. One of the main characteristics of the SCO is that it is built on a strict inter-governmental principle, with mutual respect for each other's sovereignty and territorial integrity. A second example is the creation of the New Development Bank (NDB) and the AIIB, which Chen identifies as supportive of the third sub-strategy of 'plurilateral parallel orders'. Both the NDB and the AIIB have their headquarters in China. What makes these institutions part of the 'parallel orders' strategy is that they both have the potential to become alternative, or even rival, to those currently existing. For this very reason, the AIIB has been the target of US rhetoric, as previously discussed. Finally, China's Belt and Road Initiative is an example of the fourth sub-strategy, i.e. the creation of China-sponsored bilateral networks in its immediate neighbourhood and globally (Chen 2016b).

China's drive for a 'reform from outside' strategy has mainly been a result of the slow pace of reforms of the existing institutions to adapt to the new power realities in the world. As China and other developing countries become more influential, it is of crucial importance to accommodate their interests and rights within global governance in order to further strengthen the legitimacy of the existing institutions (Michalski & Pan 2017b: 2). For China, the most important aspects of the existing institutions that need to be reformed are their basic norms that tend to reflect, and reinforce, the interests and preferences of the developed West over the developing world. Some crucial examples are the prioritization of values like democracy and human rights over sovereignty and development. According to Pan (2012), conceptual gaps between China and the West constitute a foundational challenge in forging strong cooperation and partnership on major issues, such as international security.

An important conceptual gap between China, on the one hand, and the US and EU on the other is the concept of sovereignty. While respect for sovereignty is a guiding principle of Chinese foreign policy and regarded as a right of every nation-state, it is regarded from the EU and US as requiring accountability (ibid.: 21–23). On this basis, there are serious disagreements on topics such as economic sanctions and military interventions. While China adheres to the principle of non-intervention in other countries' domestic affairs, the EU and US do see coercive measures, such as sanctions, the use of force, and military intervention, as policy options if a state fails to govern in a certain manner (Meulen & Putten 2009: 6). This has led to serious frictions on issues such as those related to Taiwan, South and East China Seas, North Korea, the arms embargo, Libya, and Syria, among others. However, this does not mean that China is against interventions at all costs. China's endorsement of the 2005 World Summit document clearly shows that China embraces the idea of 'Responsibility To Protect' (R2P) and that China does not think states are immune from international reaction to crimes against humanity.

However, as this chapter has also made clear, China and the EU do share similar concerns related to increasing US unilateralism and protectionism. Furthermore, as the 20th China-EU Summit made clear, the EU is also committed to cooperate on the reform of the existing institutions of the international system, most prominently the WTO. Although there are several existing challenges between China and the EU, most prominently in trade and investment, European Commission President Juncker stated that he had 'always been a strong believer in the potential for EU-China partnership' and that in today's world 'where partnership is more important than ever before' the EU-China cooperation 'simply makes sense' (Font 2018).

In the joint statement that followed the 20th China-EU Summit, both sides reaffirmed their commitment to 'multilateralism and a rules-based international order with the United Nations at its core' (MFAPRC 2018).

Conclusion

The developments in international relations we are confronted with in the contemporary era are primarily caused by the changes in the underlying structure of the international political system. More specifically, the changes in the distribution of power have upset the balance of power and brought significant challenges to the legitimacy of the existing arrangements of world order. These arrangements, which were established by the end of WWII and came to encompass the entire world after the Cold War, are primarily reflecting the preferences and interests of their main founders, the developed countries of the West. Therefore, there should be no surprise that China perceives them as reflections of Western dominance.

It is furthermore important to note, as many examples of China's important involvement in global security governance this chapter have made clear, that China does not seek to undermine the existing arrangements of world order. China does not either seek to replace the US as a hegemonic power, as its call for a community of common destiny for humankind necessarily implies a peaceful and stable world order in which the major powers of the international system forge relationships based on mutual trust, mutual respect, and win-win cooperation, thus fostering a more multipolar, just, equitable, and legitimate global order.

China has a fundamental interest in safeguarding the existing arrangements of world order as its revitalization was made possible by its increasing integration with the world and as its further reform and opening-up process depends upon a stable and predictable rules-based order. At the same time, China also seeks to strengthen the legitimacy of the existing arrangements in order for them to better reflect the interests of the developing world in an era of global power shift. Consequently, China has emerged as an active 'order-shaper', seeking to reform the existing arrangements from within and from the outside. To this end, China seeks close cooperation with other major players in the world, but increasing US unilateralism and protectionism leaves the EU as the most important partner for China to achieve this end. Although China and the EU have shown willingness to cooperate on major issues, such as those related to global security governance, it would at the same time still be naïve to claim that the China-EU comprehensive strategic partnership represents any kind of 'axis' in terms of emerging global governance (Wæver 2017). Nevertheless, we argue that statements from the EU on the willingness to cooperate with China in reforming the existing arrangements of the international system, upholding multilateralism and the architecture of global governance, have the potential to establish a relationship that can become a potent force to prevent the fragmentation of the international system and weaken global governance at the time of the US withdrawal from its global leadership role.

References

Allison, G. (2017) *Destined for War: Can America and China Escape the Thucydides's Trap?* Boston, New York: Houghton Mifflin Harcourt.

Aggarwal, K.V. & A.S. Newland (2015) 'Introduction', in K.V. Aggarwal & A.S. Newland (eds.), *Responding to China's Rise: US and EU Strategies*, New York: Springer, 3–23.

Attina, F. (2017) 'Traditional Security Issues', in J. Wang & W. Song (eds.), *China, the European Union, and the International Politics of Global Governance*, Houndmills, Basingstoke, Hampshire: Palgrave Macmillan, 175–193.

Chen, Z. (2012) 'Europe as a Global Player: A View from China', *Perspectives* 20(2), 7–30.

——— (2013) 'The Efficacy of Post-Lisbon Treaty EU's External Actions and China-EU Strategic Partnership', in M. Telò & F. Ponjaert (eds.), *The EU's Foreign Policy: What Kind of Power and Diplomatic Action?* Surrey: Ashgate, 175–188.

——— (2016a) 'China, the European Union and the Fragile World Order', *Journal of Common Market Studies* 54(2), 775–792.

——— (2016b) 'China's Domestic Debate on Global Governance', *The Diplomat*, 23 November. Available at: https://thediplomat.com/2016/11/chinas-domestic-debate-on-global-governance/.

Clinton, H.R. (2011) 'America's Pacific Century', *Foreign Policy*, 11 October. Available at: https://foreign policy.com/2011/10/11/americas-pacific-century/.

Commission of the European Communities (2003) 'Commission Policy Paper for the Transmission to the Council and the European Parliament', *A Maturing Partnership – Shared Interests and Challenges in EU-China Relations*, 9 October, Brussels. Available at: https://eur-lex.europa.eu/LexUriServ/LexUriServ.do?uri=COM:2003:0533:FIN:EN:PDF

Cuyckens, H. (2012) 'The EU and China: Emerging Global Powers Capable of Balancing US Hegemony and Shaping a New World Order?' in J. Wouters, T. de Wilde, P. Defraigne & J.-C. Defraigne (eds.), *China, the European Union and Global Governance*, Cheltenham: Edward Elgar, 279–311.

Font, C. (2018) 'China, EU Can Exemplify Global Governance', *Global Times*, 19 July. Available at: www.globaltimes.cn/content/1111481.shtml.

Global Times (2018) 'China, EU Oppose Unilateralism Protectionism', 25 June. Available at: www.globaltimes.cn/content/1108352.shtml.

Higgins, A. & E.D. Sanger (2015) '3 European Powers Say They Will Join China-Led Bank', *New York Times*, 17 March. Available at: www.nytimes.com/2015/03/18/business/france-germany-and-italy-join-asian-infrastructure-investment-bank.html.

Jin, C. (2016) 'Challenges and Opportunities in the Sino-US Relations' [中美关系中的挑和机会战.中国人民大学国关系学院], Beijing: People's University Institute of International Relations, International Situation, 80–96.

Jin, C. & Huang (2015) 'Sino-US New Model of Big Country Relations: The Road of Mutual Benefit' (中美新型大国关系：合作供之路赢), *International Horizons*, Current Affairs Report 10, 36–37.

Kirchner et al. (2016) 'EU-China Security Cooperation in Context', in J.E. Kirchner et al. (eds.), *Security Relations Between China and the European Union: From Convergence to Cooperation?*, **Cambridge: Cambridge University Press**, 1–19.

Kissinger, H. (2014) *World Order: Reflections on the Character of Nations and the Course of History*, New York: Penguin Books.

Landler, M. (2017) 'Trump Heads to Asia With an Ambitious Agenda but Little to Offer', *The New York Times*, 2 November. Available at: www.nytimes.com/2017/11/02/us/politics/trump-china-japan.html.

Lanteigne, M. (2009) *Chinese Foreign Policy: An Introduction*, London: Routledge, 95–107.

Lanteigne, M., B. Thygeson & U. Sverdrup (2016) '"For Every Action ...": The American Pivot to Asia and Fragmented European Responses', Norwegian Institute of International Affairs and International Order and Strategy at Brookings, January.

Lieberthal, K. & J. Wang (2012) 'Addressing US-China Strategic Distrust', The John L. Thorton China Center at Brookings, Washington, DC.

Mardell, J. (2017) 'The Community of Common Destiny in Xi Jinping's New Era', *The Diplomat*, October. Available at: https://thediplomat.com/2017/10/the-community-of-common-destiny-in-xi-jinpings-new-era/.

Mearsheimer, J. (2004) '"Clash of the Titans", A Debate with Zbigniew Brzezinski on the Rise of China', *Foreign Policy* 146, 46–49.

——— (2018) *The Great Delusion: Liberal Dreams and International Realities*, New Haven and London: Yale University Press.

Meulen, M. & F.P. Putten (2009) *Great Power and International Conflict Management: European and Chinese Involvement in the Darfur and Iran Crisis*, Den Haag: Netherlands Institute of International Relations Clingedael.

Michalski, A. & Z. Pan (2017a) 'Role Dynamics in a Structural Relationship: The EU-China Strategic Partnership', *Journal of Common Market Studies* 55(3), 611–627.

——— (2017b) *Unlikely Partners? China, the European Union and the Forging of a Strategic Partnership*, Singapore: Palgrave Macmillan.

Ming, Z. (2018) 'China-EU Relations in the New Era', *EUObserver*, 29 January. Available at: https://euobserver.com/stakeholders/140728.

Ministry of Foreign Affairs of the People's Republic of China (2003) China's EU Policy Paper, Beijing, 13 October. Available at: www.fmprc.gov.cn/mfa_eng/wjb_663304/zzjg_663340/xos664404/dqzzyw t_664812/t27708.shtml.

——— (2013) China-EU 2020 Strategic Agenda for Cooperation Released at the 16th China-EU Summit, Beijing, 23 November. Available at: www.fmprc.gov.cn/mfa_eng/wjdt_665385/2649_665393/t1101804.shtml.

——— (2014) China's Policy Paper on the EU: Deepen the China-EU Comprehensive Strategic Partnership for Mutual Benefit and Win-win Cooperation, Beijing, 2 April. Available at: www.fmprc.gov.cn/mfa_eng/wjdt665385/wjzc s/t11 43406 .shtml.

——— (2017) Speech by Foreign Minister Wang Yi at the Opening of Symposium on International Developments and China's Diplomacy, Beijing, 10 December. Available at: www.fmprc.gov.cn/mfa_eng/wjdt_665385/zyjh_6 6539 1/t1518130.shtml.

——— (2018) Joint Statement of the 20th China-EU Summit, Beijing, 16 July. Available at: www.fmprc.gov.cn/mfa_eng/zxxx_662805/t157751 6.shtml.

Myers, S.L. (2018) 'With Ships and Missiles, China is Ready to Challenge U.S. Navy in Pacific', *The New York Times*, 29 August. Available at: www.nytimes.com/2018/08/29/world/asia/china-navy-aircraft-carrier-pacific.html.

Pan, Z. (2012) 'Sovereignty in China-EU Relations: The Conceptual Gap and Its Implications', in Z. Pan (ed.), *Conceptual Gaps in China-EU Relations: Global Governance, Human Rights, and Strategic Partnership*, London: Palgrave Macmillan, 19–34.

Rosenberg, E. & E. Saravalle (2018) 'China and the EU are Growing Sick of US Financial Power', *Foreign Policy*, 16 November. Available at: https://foreignpolicy.com/2018/11/16/us-eu-china-trump-sanctions/.

Schröder, G. (2003) 'Germany Will Share the Burden in Iraq', *The New York Times*, 19 September. Available at: www.nytimes.com/2003/09/19/opinion/germany-will-shar e-the-burden-in-iraq.html.

Shambaugh, D. (2004) 'China and Europe: The Emerging Axis', *Current History* 103(674), 243–248.

——— (2005) 'The New Strategic Triangle: US and European Reactions to China's Rise', *The Washington Quarterly* 28(3), 7–25.

The New York Times (1999) 'To Paris, US Looks Like a "Hyperpower"', 5 February. Available at: www.nytimes.com/1999/02/05/news/to-paris-us-looks-like-a-hyper power.html.

The State Council Information Office of the People's Republic of China (2013) The Diversified Employment of China's Armed Forces, Beijing, April. Available at: http://english.gov.cn/archive/white_paper/2014/08/23/content_281474982986506.htm.

——— (2015) China's Military Strategy, Beijing, May. Available at: http://eng.mod.gov.cn/Press/2015-05/26/content_4586805.htm.

——— (2017) China's Policies on Asia-Pacific Security Cooperation, Beijing, January. Available at: www.fmprc.gov.cn/mfa_eng/zxxx_662805/t1429771.shtml.

The White House (2017) National Security Strategy of the US of America. Washington, DC, December. Available at: www.whitehouse.gov/articles/new-national-security-strategy-new-era/.

Walt, M.S. (2018) *The Hell of Good Intentions: America's Foreign Policy Elite and the Decline of U.S. Primacy*, New York: Farrar, Straus and Giroux.

Wang, H. & N.J. Rosenau (2009) 'China and Global Governance', *Asian Perspectives* 33(3), 5–39.

Wang, J. & W. Song (2016) 'Introduction: New Players and New Order of Global Governance', in W. Jianwei & S. Weiqing (eds.), *China, the European Union, and the International Politics of Global Governance*, Houndmills, Basingstoke, Hampshire: Palgrave Macmillan, 1–13.

Wu, X. (2010a) 'China's International Orientation in the Fast-Changing International Situation', Beijing, *China International Studies*, January/February, 38–55.

——— (2010b) 'Understanding the Geopolitical Implications of the Global Financial Crisis. Centre for Strategic and International Studies', Washington, *The Washington Quarterly*, October, 155–163.

——— (2012b) 'The Trend of the US China Policy in the Next Four Years and China's Response', Beijing, *China International Studies*, November/December, 48–53.

Wæver, O. (2017) 'International Leadership after the Demise of the Last Superpower: System Structure and Stewardship', *Chinese Political Science Review* 2(4), 452–477.

Xiang, L. (2012) 'China and the "Pivot"' *Survival* 54(5), 113–112.
Xinhua (2016) 'Xi Calls for Reforms of Global Governance', 28 September. Available at: www. xinhuanet.com/english/2016–09/28/c_135720719.htm.
——— (2017a) 'Commentary: Xi Demonstrates China's Role as Responsible Country in New Year Address', 1 January. Available at: www.xinhuanet.com/english/2018-01/01/c_13686530 7.htm.
——— (2017b) 'China Urges the US to Abandon Cold War Mentality', 19 December. Available at: www.xinhuanet.com/english/2017-12/19/c_136838057.htm.
Zhao, S. (2012) 'Shaping the Regional Context of China's Rise: How the Obama Administration Brought Back Hedge in its Engagement with China', *Journal of Contemporary China* 21(7), 369–389.
Zheng, S. (2018) 'EU and Chinese Foreign Ministers Reaffirm Commitment to Multilateralism and Free Trade', *South China Morning Post*. Available at: www.scmp.com/news/china/diplomacy-defence/article/2158178/eu-and-chinese-foreign-ministers-reaffirm-commitment.
Zhou, H. (2017) 'An Overview of the China-EU Strategic Partnership (2003–2013)', in H. Zhou (ed.), *China-EU Relations: Reassessing the China-EU Comprehensive Strategic Partnership*, Beijing: Social Sciences Academic Press, 3–31.

4 Caught between a withdrawing hegemon and an emerging leader – what role for the European Union in the evolving US-China-EU 'triangle'?

Francesco Saverio Montesano

Introduction

The notion that the contemporary global order is somewhat 'in flux' has been popular in the academic and policymaking world for well over a decade (see e.g. Hurrell 2006; Smith 2012). Following the rather brief post-1989 unipolar phase, global politics have been witnessing significant shifts, with new actors emerging on the international stage and novel policy challenges (and ways to respond to them) gaining ground on key players' agendas. In particular, so-called 'global perspectives' have been on the rise, emphasizing interdependence and the need for coordinated responses on issues pertaining to global public goods. Global public goods are non-excludable and non-rival in consumption, and their benefits reach across borders, generations, and population groups and include climate stability, the multilateral trading system, and peace and security. In this light, interdependence is no longer a merely descriptive functional feature of the global system, but its management has come to represent a requirement that all actors aspiring to play a leading role within that system will have to meet.

The importance of effective 'interdependence management' in global governance is at its highest in the realm of (foreign and) security policy. Traditionally linked to military policy and therefore ascribed to the 'high politics' domain, in the post-Cold War period security has grown to encompass a much broader spectrum, reflecting an international system that has aptly been described in terms of 'complex interdependence' (Keohane & Nye 2001). In order to respond to the emergence of new, globalized threats, more and more issues, from trade to climate change to migration, have been 'securitized', that is, have undergone a process whereby state actors transform subjects into matters of 'security' (Buzan et al. 1998: 25). These issues present experts and policymakers with an unprecedentedly vast agenda combining traditional and non-traditional security items (Caballero-Anthony 2016).

The demands presented by this new strategic context are especially pressing for three actors who, given their overall economic, political, and security primacy, have occasionally been referred to as the sides of a 'global triangle': the United States (US), China, and the European Union (EU). In formal terms, the notion of a US-China-EU 'triangle' acting as a sort of global steering committee is rather misleading, given the lack of institutionalization of the actors' actual trilateral relations. A US-China-EU summit is hardly foreseeable in the near future, and Washington, Beijing, and Brussels overwhelmingly prefer to deal with each other bilaterally. Nevertheless, the combined relative weight of the three on a global scale makes this notion analytically useful, in that it underscores the importance of the three actors' approach to global governance and of their outlook on its dynamism (Montesano 2017).

This chapter examines the evolving strategic[1] stances of the three components of this global triangle, seeking to shed light on the respective conceptions of and approaches to their role as key players in global governance. Using analytical criteria partially drawn from Destradi's typology of 'empire', 'hegemon', and 'leader' (Destradi 2010), a comparative review is provided of each actor's foreign and security policy discourse, institutional reforms and policies, with particular emphasis on the respective security relations with the other two sides of the triangle. This review will reveal a very fluid situation. While the US appears to be veering away from proactive global security engagement, China has been stepping up its outreach and 'rule-making' ambitions in an increasingly assertive fashion. Meanwhile, although its actorness in the field of foreign and security policy remains contested, the EU has undoubtedly been making discursive and institutional progress to enhance its role.

Section 1 defines the key analytical concepts used to assess each actor's strategic posture. Section 2 conducts a comparative discourse analysis of key US, Chinese, and EU strategic documents, seeking to highlight the evolution in each actor's *self-representation* and *ends* vis-à-vis their role in foreign and security policy. Methodologically, this analysis will deliberately almost exclusively refer to primary sources (i.e. official documents). This is to maximize the focus on the actual discourse, thus minimizing the risk of 'scholarly bias' stemming from the incorporation of other secondary outlooks and also bolstering the original comparative contribution of this study. The third section compounds the previous section's discursive examination with a 'probe into practice', investigating whether changes in discourse are reflected in the more concrete *means* – both institutional and policy-related – deployed by each actor to put in practice their evolving stance towards global governance. Finally, the conclusion summarizes the findings and discusses their implications for the future role of all three actors in the context of a changing global order, with specific emphasis on the EU.

Conceptual framework

To analyse the three actors' changing understanding of their role as global foreign and security policy players, a conceptual framework needs to incorporate both self-centred (i.e. focusing on the actor's self-perception) and interdependent (i.e. related to the actor's approach to the international system) concepts.

To this end, Destradi's typology of regional powers' foreign policy strategies – expressed through different 'modes of primacy' – is especially insightful. Destradi's framework is three-pronged, hinging on the notions of empire, hegemony, and leadership, each differing in terms of the deploying actor's ends (goals), means, self-representation, and (external) legitimation (Destradi 2010: 926–927 – see also summarizing Table 4.1). The three strategic approaches are located on a continuum (Destradi 2010: 928), which is why the framework is well-suited not only to qualify US, Chinese, and European strategies in a 'static' fashion but also to delve into their diachronically varying nature.

The first strategy is *empire*. Defined as a 'system of domination based on the use or threat of military intervention', imperial primacy hinges on the unilateral use of (mostly) military means in order to pursue strictly self-interested ends. In terms of self-representation, imperial actors do not shy away from explicitly aggressive and threatening stances, clearly aimed at enforcing subordination and often resorting to 'exemptionalist' discourse, claiming the right to enforce rules upon others while refusing to abide by them (Rapkin 2005: 393). Normatively speaking, an empire is by definition not legitimate, since compliance is based on the 'physical' inability of subordinate states to resist the enforcement of imperial power. Given the nature of the current system, a full-blown imperial strategy is clearly unadvisable (and arguably unviable) for any actor seeking to play a key role: especially with regard to self-representation, this approach is openly hostile to any form of interdependence, thus clashing with the very core of contemporary global relations.

The second strategy is *hegemony*. It encompasses a broad spectrum of forms of power exercised through more 'subtle' ways than imperial ones. It fluctuates between coercive and benevolent rule, and the means used can be both material and ideational (normative). Overall, the ultimate aim of a hegemon is to establish an uncontested hierarchical order, whereby legitimacy plays a key role to minimize enforcement costs. Reflecting the higher diversity within this mode of primacy, Destradi identifies three sub-types of hegemony. *Hard hegemony* is defined as the establishment of an order for the realization of the hegemon's goals via coercion, but without the need to resort to military intervention. A hard hegemon pursues its self-interested ends using a combination of means including sanctions (mostly economic), threats (especially 'threats of exclusion'), and political pressure. Unlike empires, hard hegemons try to project a cooperative image of themselves, hence displaying high levels of divergence between self-representation and actual behaviour. Normatively speaking, subordinates' compliance in a hard-hegemonic order is overwhelmingly based on rational calculations about the costs of non-compliance, thus creating what has aptly been termed a 'pseudo'-form of legitimacy (i.e. not based on a genuine convergence of values and goals). *Intermediate hegemony* also aims at the establishment of an order for the realization of the hegemon's self-interested ends, but unlike hard hegemony it pursues these goals mostly via the provision of (material) benefits and inducements – also termed 'reward power' (Knorr 1975: 7). Like hard hegemons, intermediate hegemons also represent themselves as cooperative, thereby displaying moderate divergence between 'self-representation' and real behaviour. In terms of legitimation, there is still no real normative convergence between the hegemon and its subordinates, but the latter's compliance is at least partially 'genuine' since it is based on rational cost-benefit calculations, whereas in hard hegemony, it only hinges on the willingness to avoid costs. Finally, *soft hegemony* can also be defined as the establishment of an order for the realization of the hegemon's self-interested ends. However, these are pursued by means of normative persuasion and socialization, in line with the hegemon's self-representation as a fully cooperative actor. In a successful soft hegemonic order, subordinates comply due to the redefinition of their norms and values along hegemon-compatible lines, thus eventually bestowing complete legitimacy upon the hegemon itself. It is worth noting that, since socialization is a lengthy process that transcends the normal duration of a policy cycle, this type of hegemony usually follows a more coercive phase. Accordingly, the hegemon tends to first use a more decisive approach to force a change of policy on its subordinates, which is later supposedly internalized by the targets and leads to a deeper change in norms and values (Ikenberry & Kupchan 1990).

The third strategy is *leadership*. Unlike empires and hegemons, leaders do not seek to establish an order to pursue their self-interested ends. Rather, they act as trailblazers aiming at achieving *goals* that are shared by the community they are part of. Like soft hegemons, in order to pursue these goals they mainly rely on normative persuasion and socialization. However, since a leadership-based system is *not* hierarchical and compliance is therefore entirely based on willingness, the socialization process needs to be more advanced than in soft hegemony: subordinates are replaced by followers, and even the process of legitimation becomes less 'vertical' and more 'circular', given that followers and leader legitimize each other as they both play a role in the achievement of their common goals.

Before moving on to using these notions to analyse (both discursively and from a more institutional/policy angle) the strategic stances of the US, China, and the EU vis-à-vis the global order, two further theoretical caveats are needed. First, as mentioned before, it is important to stress that the strategies or 'modes of primacy' described above are 'ideal-types'. A successful strategy will usually integrate elements of several categories, especially at the level of means and self-representation. Second, and of particular relevance to the EU, the notion of *actorness* refers to the 'capacity to behave actively and deliberately in relation to other actors in the international system' (Sjöstedt 1977), and it is a clear prerequisite for any player aspiring to

Table 4.1 Modes of primacy

	Empire	*Hegemony*			*Leadership*
		Hard	*Intermediate*	*Soft*	
Definition	System of domination based on the use or threat of military intervention	Coercive order for the realization of the hegemon's goals.	Reward-based order for the realization of the hegemon's goals	Socialized order for the realization of the hegemon's goals	Pursuit of common goa via a leader-initiated socialization process
Ends	Self-interested	Self-interested	Self-interested	Self-interested	Common, shared
Means	Military	Sanctions, threats, political pressure	Material inducements (reward power)	Normative persuasion, socialization	Normative persuasion, socialization
Self-representation	Aggressive, coercive	Cooperative	Cooperative	Cooperative	Cooperative
Legitimation/ normative convergence	None	Pseudo-legit.	Partial	Legitimation	Legitimation
Compliance	Resistance/ subordination	Resistance/ only based on rational calculations of the costs of non-compliance	Based on rational cost-benefit calculations	Based on socialization	Willing followership

Source: Adapted from Destradi (2010: 926–927).

an imperial, hegemonic or leading role. This is especially important when discussing the EU, as (real or perceived) actorness flaws have played a major role in informing the debate around the need for EU strategic changes (Jupille & Caporaso 1998; Bretherton & Vogler 2006).

Strategic discourse and the global role of the US, China, and the EU

To highlight the evolution in each actor's self-representations and ends with regard to their foreign and security policy postures, this section will carry out a comparative discourse analysis of key US, Chinese, and EU strategic documents. The subsequent section then focuses on the means, that is, the three actors' behaviours.

The US: from strategic hegemony towards 'selfish' withdrawal

Since the end of the Cold War, and drawing on already solid post-WWII foundations, the US built its virtually uncontested strategic primacy by relying on regionally differentiated hegemonic approaches that combined economic support and strategic/military alliances. While this unipolar status quo appeared indestructible, already over a decade ago some farsighted voices warned that things might change if (1) the call for global multipolar/multilateral governance became stronger; (2) US allies started to see a disjunction between the sources of their (US-guaranteed) security and those of an economically prosperous future; and (3) US global commitment witnessed a retraction (Ikenberry 2004). As it happens, all three conditions have started to be fulfilled during the past decade, something which – especially for the first two – is not surprising given the soaring interdependence described earlier.

Has the US picked up on these changes, and adjusted its strategic self-representation and ends accordingly? An overview of the most recent key US strategic documents (National Security Strategies, NSS) highlights interesting trends.

Despite the political differences between the incumbents, the 2002 and 2006 NSS, issued during the Bush administration, and the 2010 NSS – the first of the Obama presidency – illustrate similarly high levels of awareness regarding the need for the US to be an 'engaged' hegemon, stressing the importance of choosing 'leadership over isolationism' and of proactively supporting multilateralism and diplomacy in an interdependent global order (USA 2002, 2006, 2010). The objectives behind such engagement were obviously different, with Bush's foreign policy seeking to eventually make the US 'so much more powerful than any other state that strategic rivalries and security competition among the great powers will disappear, leaving everyone, not just the US, better off' (cited in Rielly 2008: 73). However, both Bush and Obama believed that primacy could only be achieved in a proactive way. When examining the two most recent NSS (2015 and 2017), and even though in terms of the modes of primacy the US discourse remains broadly hegemonic, it is possible to identify a much greater – and unprecedented – shift between Obama's strategy and Trump's.

The 2015 NSS is presented as 'a vision for strengthening and sustaining American leadership and confidently welcome the peaceful rise of other countries as partners to share the burdens for maintaining a more peaceful and prosperous world' and includes the US' pledge to 'uphold and refresh the international rules and norms that set the parameters for [...] collaboration and competition' (USA 2015: 29). This proactively cooperative tone is in line with the explicitly stated awareness that 'in an interconnected world, there are no global problems that can be solved without the United States, and few that can be solved by the United States alone' (ibid.: 3). Moreover, the document acknowledges the ongoing power shift dynamics but does not see them under a threatening or even confrontational light. Rather, the 2015 NSS emphasizes win-win cooperation and competition as the key to solving the transnational and largely shared challenges of our time, such as climate change and global health issues (Wright 2015).

Accordingly, the document places US *ends* squarely within the 'hegemonic' mode, yet without explicitly linking all sections to their pursuit.

For instance, values and democracy promotion are framed as intrinsically good for each society, without any mention of their 'use' for the US agenda. This strong universalistic discourse emphasizes a quite 'enlightened', integrating other actors' interests, understanding of (national) interests (Burchill 2005). It projects a form of *self-representation* that is remarkably close to the 'leadership' mode. This image is reinforced throughout the NSS via the strongly positive emphasis on multilateralism, in both the security and the economic domains. The US is presented as a leading force *within* the 'post-World War II legal architecture', which is 'essential to the ordering of a just and peaceful world' (USA 2015: 23). In this light, and in combination with the keen awareness of the evolving nature of the global order mentioned above, the document stresses the need to keep engaging in multiple fora in a flexible fashion, so as to 'uphold and refresh the international rules and norms that set the parameters for [...] collaboration and competition' (ibid.: 29). Moreover, while the NSS acknowledges the importance of US strategic strength, it does not advocate a military build-up, but rather pushes for targeted specialization as the preferred option to combat complex transnational security challenges. Accordingly, it favours openness to peaceful cooperation even with actors described as 'competitors' (China and Russia), rejecting coercion and instead promoting 'strategic patience' as the best way to deal with a number of threats (ibid.: ii; 24–25). This emphasis on 'soft', non-coercive means offers further evidence of the Obama administration's significant distance from both empire and hard hegemony in its 2015 self-representation.

In apparent continuity with the 2015 document, the 2017 NSS – the first issued by the Trump administration – also explicitly acknowledges the changes in the global strategic context. However, while its predecessor stressed far-reaching cooperation in a rules-based international order as the ideal response, the tone struck by the 2017 Strategy – and further reinforced in the 2018 National Defence Strategy – is very different. First, the 2017 document presents a very strong emphasis on the US' own national interests, hence immediately distancing its *self-representation* from the 'leadership' type. It stresses how US primacy guarantees global benefits to all allies and partners but clearly subordinates this to the effective protection of the 'four key national interests' (US homeland and way of life; US prosperity; US military superiority; US influence) (USA 2017). The overwhelmingly self-centred, 'America First'-based *ends* go hand in hand with a much more hands-off stance on multilateralism, reflecting not only the US' diminished interest in proactive integration but also a certain ignorance of the cooperation-dependent nature of the current system and challenges. While the 2017 NSS does see it as crucial that the US retains multilateral leadership (ibid.: 17), this is mostly so as to prevent strategic rivals (especially China and Russia) from monopolizing key institutions and fora to pursue their 'disruptive goals'. Additionally, it advocates selective engagement, explicitly prioritizing those multilateral settings (notably IMF and WTO) that 'serve US interests', while exhibiting strong reticence vis-à-vis 'new' (i.e. not

US-initiated) arrangements (ibid.: 40–41). The combination of this remarkably withdrawn stance in global governance and the much more confrontational discourse towards other major powers results in an overall strategic approach that seems to be out-of-touch with the reality of interdependence.

Trump administration's strategy illustrates a clear friction between a superficial acknowledgement that 'something has changed' in global security and the ends and means that the US focuses on to pursue its own interests. While it appears to grasp that the new global security environment makes every domain of US preeminence 'contested', its foreseen response is a strongly isolationist one. The strategy deliberately omits the soaring interdependence levels and expounds a 'beautiful vision' of world affairs being conducted by 'strong, sovereign and independent nations' (USA 2017: ii). In stark contrast with the 2015 NSS, it ignores key transnational challenges such as climate change and pandemics, focusing instead on the need to bolster US military superiority in order to stave off the alleged existential threats posed by America's rivals, who have become much more dangerous in their pursuit of a world 'antithetical to US interests' thanks to their being 'unencumbered' by values (ibid.: 25–28). Trump's overall approach to international relations appears strongly transactional, emphasizing 'zero-sum', unilateral views that stand in stark contrast with the multilateral cooperation advocated by most other major players, including China and the EU (Montesano 2017: 2), as further discussed below.

Altogether, the US current foreign and security policy strategy is characterized by a fundamental clash. On the one hand, a superficially, yet strongly hegemonic (and – at times, due to the underlying exemptionalism – even imperialist) and competitive discourse. On the other hand, a self-representation highlighting a much more detached approach to global governance, which points towards an overall withdrawal not only from trailblazing leadership-based modes of primacy, but away from *all* modes of primacy. This clash, as we will also elaborate in Section 3, reinforces the likelihood of greater US isolationism and withdrawal from concrete hegemonic/leading initiatives in the near future. Overall, especially considering how the 2017 NSS shies away from any mention of the US proactive involvement in the reform of the international system, a further weakening of the US' rule-making role can be expected, which will in turn deepen what has aptly been termed a global 'power vacuum'.

China: towards assertive global engagement

Over the past two decades, China has been undergoing a true strategic doctrinal shift, moving away from the 'low-lying' stances of the Deng era towards gradually much more proactive global engagement. The new leadership of the Chinese Communist Party (CCP), with Xi Jinping at the helm, has developed a very ambitious roadmap designed to turn China into a moderately prosperous society by 2021, a developed country by 2035 and a first-rate national power with a world-class military by 2050 (Zhao 2017). Accordingly, China portrays its mid-century self as a global leader in every area of human consequence: economics and trade, science and technology, military and defence, culture and governance (Kuhn 2017).

China's drive to transition into a new global role begs the question of which mode(s) of primacy best describe its recent and current behaviour. An overview of Beijing's two key strategic documents of the past decade provides a good picture of its evolving stance.

The first document is the 2010 White Paper on China's National Defence, published during Hu Jintao's presidency (PRC 2010). The paper illustrates China's awareness of the opportunities and challenges of a highly interdependent global system, characterized by 'irreversible' progress 'toward economic globalization and a multipolar world' and by 'irresistible' trends 'toward peace, development and cooperation', but also by intensifying 'international strategic competition' and 'increasingly integrated, complex and volatile' security threats. From a Chinese perspective, this complex context is however seen with enhanced confidence, given how China has 'important strategic opportunities for its development, and the overall security environment for it remains favourable'. With specific regard to security policy, the document heralds China's 'new concept' based on 'mutual trust, mutual benefit, equality and cooperation' and aimed at fostering 'together with other countries, an international security environment of peace, stability, equality, mutual trust, cooperation and win-win'. Moreover, it advocates a defence policy that is 'defensive in nature' and in line with China's striving for the kind of 'peaceful development' that will eventually make a significant contribution to world peace. In this light, it acknowledges its rising military expenditure but stresses how its modernization is happening 'at a reasonable and appropriate level', and with an emphasis on confidence-building 'based on the principles of holding consultations on an equal footing, mutual respect for core interests and recognition of major security concerns, not targeting at any third country, and not threatening or harming other countries' security and stability'.

From this analysis, it is remarkable to note how the 2010 Paper is completely devoid of primacy-related discourse, be it imperial, hegemonic, or even leadership-oriented. It explicitly states that 'China will never seek hegemony, nor will it adopt the approach of military expansion now or in the future, no matter how its economy develops', as it pursues 'military relations that are non-aligned, non-confrontational and not directed against any third party, and promotes the establishment of just and effective collective security mechanisms'. In stark contrast with the US discourse, heavily centred on the importance of its alliance system and characterized, especially in 2017, by a rather confrontational approach, China's *self-representation* in 2010 is thus one of a fully cooperative player, committed to playing a constructive strategic role in the pursuit of *ends* that are seen as crucial by the whole international community. In this respect, although there is no explicit reference to it, said ends are in line with those of a player seeking 'leadership'. Additionally, the paper does emphasize the link between China's growing contributions to international security and its role as a 'responsible *major* power'. The positive correlation between the two seems to hint at China's awareness that its strategic standing on the global stage is likely to increase and, thus, at Beijing's willingness to step up its ranking in a more hierarchical way by more openly pursuing one of the modes of primacy.

This becomes evident when comparing the 2010 White Paper with the 2015 Military Strategy (PRC 2015). The 2015 document restates China's understanding of interdependence and emphatic opposition to 'hegemonism and power politics in all forms'. However, the strategy published under Xi Jinping exhibits significant changes in terms of China's *self-representation* as a global actor. While still a 'large developing country', China is aware that its 'comprehensive national strength, core competitiveness and risk-resistance capacity are notably increasing, and China enjoys growing international standing and influence', and such confidence is bolstered by the fact that the 'world economic and strategic centre of gravity is shifting ever more rapidly to the Asia-Pacific region'. Beijing realizes that its greatly enhanced clout can be translated into enhanced global presence, via the provision of global public (security) goods and by its ability to project (peaceful) power in much greater scale and scope. Thus, it is not surprising that the 2015 Strategy highlights the role of a 'strong military', stressing the importance of building and developing the armed forces in order to guarantee the 'great rejuvenation of the Chinese nation' under the 'absolute leadership' of the CCP. Overall, the 2015 discourse is much more China-centric than the 2010 one and illustrates Beijing's resolve to step up its global role in an unprecedentedly assertive fashion.

For the first time, the 2015 Strategy explicitly mentions how China's *ends* can be pursued including forceful means, maintaining that 'a holistic approach will be taken to balance war preparation and war prevention, rights protection and stability maintenance, deterrence and warfighting, and operations in wartime and employment of military forces in peacetime'. Stress will be placed on 'farsighted planning and management to create a favourable posture, comprehensively manage crises, and resolutely *deter and win wars*' (PRC 2015, emphasis added). Hence, while the goals remain strictly non-hegemonic, the *means* to tackle what are well-understood as new, composite (i.e. traditional and non-traditional) threats have been witnessing a marked upgrade to include 'harder' ones. Additionally, it is worth noting the diminished emphasis on non-interference as a guiding tenet of China's foreign policy: the 2015 document never mentions it explicitly, nor does it bring up the Five Principles of Peaceful Coexistence,[2] which used to be ubiquitous in all Chinese White Papers, thereby signalling the greater relaxation of China's previously untouchable normative tenets in view of taking on its new responsibilities.

To sum up, the 2015 document clearly links China's stronger military profile with its stronger presence on the global stage: not a hegemon nor (explicitly) a leader, but certainly a key actor who will strive 'to shoulder more international responsibilities and obligations, provide more public security goods, and contribute more to world peace and common development'. As will be elaborated later on, the document – also in light of its emphasis on the importance of a strong(er) central leadership – lays the foundations for the even more assertive turns taken by some of China's top brass in the last couple of years.

The EU as a strategic actor: a non-hegemonic 'influencer'?

In its external projection, the EU's strongest assets lie unquestionably in its trade clout. While official EU discourse rejects the notion of a 'trade-based' hegemon, evidence shows that the EU's trade liberalization agenda often trumps normative goals (Orbie 2008), and that its counter-hegemonic rhetoric is in fact a discursive cloak: normative goals are very difficult to achieve, and the EU uses its 'conflicted' nature to legitimize its aggressive market-enhancing trade policies (Bailey & Bossuyt 2013).

However, against said hegemonic elements, the EU's clout in foreign and security policy has traditionally been much weaker, owing to institutional and material constraints, and has been one of the key reasons behind the doubts cast over its nature as a fully fledged global actor, let alone a hegemon or a leader. As will be elaborated below, the past 15 years have witnessed significant institutional and policy steps to improve the Union's strategic actorness, and much has changed since Larsen's 2002 assessment of the EU as a (military) actor 'with regional focus but global ambitions' (Larsen 2002: 296). In order to answer the question of whether these new tools can help the EU measure up to the US and China and carve a stronger global role for itself as the balance within the 'triangle' changes, it is important to first analyse Brussels' key strategic documents of the new millennium, to see whether and how the EU's self-representation and ends have changed.

The first document is the 2003 European Security Strategy (ESS) (EU 2003). In line with the documents previously analysed, the ESS illustrates awareness of the complex interdependent nature of current global security, stressing how 'no single country is able to tackle today's complex problems on its own' and underlining how 'internal and external aspects of security are indissolubly linked' (ibid.: 2). However, the document is also underpinned by remarkable confidence in what was (perceived as) a more stable and predictable world: 'Europe has never been so prosperous, so secure nor so free. The violence of the first half of the 20th Century has given way to a period of peace and stability unprecedented in European history', and '[l]arge-scale aggression against any Member State is now improbable' (ibid.: 3). In this context, the ESS argues that the non-traditional security threats facing Europe (notably terrorism and organized crime) cannot be tackled by purely military means, and instead require a multifaceted approach for which the EU allegedly is 'particularly well equipped'. However, the document is far from being concrete vis-à-vis what the EU can concretely achieve (its *ends*), and such ambiguity is further fuelled by its assessment of the EU's policy objectives, which states that the EU has made progress, but still needs to become more active, capable, and coherent (ibid.: 11–13), hence openly acknowledging rather severe actorness flaws.

The most characterizing feature of the 2003 ESS is, however, its very strong normative premise based on promoting an international order hinging on 'effective multilateralism'. Framed by the advocacy for a rules-based order and the key role of multilateral institutions and regional organizations, the ESS' discourse is a very strongly values-based one:

> The quality of international society depends on the quality of the governments that are its foundation. The best protection for our security is a world of well-governed democratic states. *Spreading good governance, supporting social and political reform, ... establishing the rule of law and protecting human rights are the best means of strengthening the international order.*
>
> (EU 2003: 10, emphasis added)

This clearly Eurocentric normative approach underscores the EU's *self-representation* as a key normative player, whose soft power – especially in its neighbourhood – will be crucial to bolster security and stability. However, it is worth noting here that there is not a single mention of 'leadership' nor 'hegemony' throughout the document, which further reinforces the rather unclear depiction of the EU's actual and/or envisaged global strategic positioning.

The ESS' rather patent lack of realism, presenting the EU simultaneously as a normative leader and a (significantly) flawed actor, is greatly reduced in its successor, the 2016 Global Strategy (GS) (EU 2016). The GS begins by offering a much less rosy image of the EU's internal and external strategic context, mentioning how its 'wider region' has become more unstable and insecure, and even going so far as to mention an ongoing 'existential crisis'. Nevertheless, the GS is also a much better grounded document, suggesting a clear agenda which takes stock of previous mistakes in order to concretely improve the EU's global role, with a view of making it 'stronger' and, eventually, strategically autonomous. As far as *self-representation* is concerned, the GS clearly draws a lot of confidence from the ongoing implementation of the new tools made available by the 2009 Lisbon Treaty and, while maintaining a certain emphasis on the role of normative instruments, it also argues that 'the idea that Europe is an exclusively "civilian power" does not do justice to an evolving reality', where 'soft and hard power go hand in hand'. Throughout the GS, building on the awareness of the role of multilateralism and rules-based interdependence in a world where international politics can no longer be seen as a zero-sum game (in line with China, and in stark contrast with the Trump administration's 2017 NSS), the EU presents itself as a responsible global stakeholder seeking (the *ends*) to advance a rules-based order. This, however, is to be achieved according to what the GS terms 'principled pragmatism': balancing values and interests as the key to foster strategic effectiveness.

The far-reaching (discursive) impact of principled pragmatism is evident in the GS' call to reform global governance along 'effective' lines, arguing that 'resisting change risks triggering the erosion of such institutions and the emergence of alternative groupings to the detriment of all EU Member States' (EU 2016: 39) – a pragmatic view, once again, more in line with the Chinese rather than with the American discourse. Effectiveness-oriented pragmatism is also mentioned in the sections devoted to the EU's concrete approach to security issues: externally, the GS advocates an integrated approach which blends civilian and military resources to enhance the EU's profile; internally, the GS introduces the so-called 'joined-up' approach aimed at improving vertical (i.e. between member states and EU institutions) and inter-institutional coherence and effectiveness of the EU's external policies.

Despite its drive to bolster the EU's global profile, like the ESS, the GS never mentions the EU as an actor that might take on the strategic role of a hegemon or even a leader. Instead, it focuses on 'co-responsibility' as the 'guiding principle in advancing a rules-based global order' (EU 2016: 18). This highlights the ingrained conviction that the EU's way to global relevance is via cooperation and rules-based but normatively (gradually more) flexible multilateralism. Despite the GS' undeniable acknowledgement of the progress made by the EU in terms of strategic *means*, it also illustrates an overall modest self-representation, suggesting that Brussels' preferred mode of primacy (better: influence) might be at most that of a co-leader.

Means to ends? Strategic policy and institutional developments of the US, China, and the EU

This section, by way of a probe into their practice, focuses on whether the aforementioned changes in discourse (*self-representation* and *ends*) are reflected in the more concrete *means* – both institutional and policy-related – deployed by the three actors to put in practice their respective evolving stance towards global governance. Using illustrative examples to examine the three actors' behaviour, it assesses the degree of coherence between strategic discourse and practice and makes some informed predictions concerning the future role each of the actors might play in global politics.

The US: opening up a power vacuum?

Recent trends in US strategic discourse mark a rather generalized withdrawal from all modes of primacy, seemingly heralding the overall weakening of

Washington's rule-making role. Moving from discourse to practice, President Trump's 'America First'-based self-reliance implies indeed a number of strategic stances and policies that appear to corroborate the aforementioned discursive angle.

Since the inception of the new administration, US scepticism towards multilateralism and interdependence has witnessed a remarkable rise in most strategic domains. Among the most blatant examples of this stance is undoubtedly President Trump's Iran policy. In stark contrast with the other original signatories of the 2015 Joint Comprehensive Plan of Action (JCPOA) – also known as the 'Iran Nuclear Deal', the result of painstaking negotiations that led to Teheran tightly restricting its nuclear ambitions for a decade or more in return for ending the sanctions that had crippled its economy, Trump constantly ramped up its hostile rhetoric against Iran and the 'horrible' JCPOA (Landler 2018). Rhetoric was eventually backed up by action on 8 May 2018, when the US announced its withdrawal from the deal, along with the reinstatement of the previous sanctions and the 'consideration' of new ones. Trump's decision drew strong criticism from the vast majority of the international community, including the EU and China, who saw the US move as a direct threat to the international non-proliferation architecture, and, being directly against the still-valid UN Security Council resolution endorsing the nuclear deal, as a hazard to international security in general (Landler 2018).

As mentioned in other chapters of this volume, Trump's isolationism has also been patent in the field of international trade. Having barely been sworn in, in January 2017 Trump signed an executive order to withdraw the US from the Trans-Pacific Partnership (TPP) Agreement. More recently, Trump has brought his defence of US 'national interests' to the next level, levying harsh tariffs on both long-standing allies (EU, Mexico, Canada) and global competitors (notably China), thereby igniting a trade war allegedly aimed at preventing foreign powers from using the US as a 'piggy bank' (Shear & Porter 2018). Even without venturing into scenarios about how this might lead to the demise of the WTO-based multilateral trading system (Donnan 2018), these ongoing trade hostilities have already succeeded in torpedoing the final communiqué of the June 2018 G7, hence providing further evidence of the US' lack of commitment towards ensuring the stability of the multilateral establishment, with repercussions for the domain of foreign and security policy more widely.

Trump's vocal anti-multilateralism has also been recently underscored by the withdrawal from the UN Educational, Scientific and Cultural Organization (UNESCO) and from the 'hypocritical and self-serving' United Nations Human Rights Council (*Reuters* 2018b). Additionally, the discursive snub to transnational, non-traditional security issues has already found concrete confirmation, especially in the field of climate change with the June 2017 announcement of the US retreat from the 2015 Paris Agreement.

Overall, these key examples of recent US strategic policies confirm the shift towards a strongly transactional, zero-sum approach to international relations of the Trump administration, overwhelmingly focused on defending very narrowly defined national interests and seemingly uninterested in the pursuit and/or maintenance of any form of hegemony, leadership, or even mere participation in global strategic governance. If all modes of primacy can only be attained via the deployment of resources aimed at incentivizing some form of order-based consensus, at present the US appears to be very unwilling to invest said resources. With regard to its structural power, the US was the main architect of virtually all the international regimes and institutions that – to this day – constitute the backbone of international economic and security relations. However, now that this order is being 'shaken' by new and increasingly loud reformist voices, Washington is opting for self-centred withdrawal instead of constructive flexibility. This is likely to create and magnify what has aptly been termed a 'power vacuum' in the global order, thereby opening up greater room for other, more flexible international actors to take on a more 'managerial' role in global affairs (Montesano 2017: 2–3).

China: a fledgling leader?

Against the background of a withdrawing US, China is very much on the prowl for a brighter spot on the global stage. When looking at China's concrete strategic decisions since the 2015 Military Strategy, it is clear how its discursive assertiveness has been consistently backed up by action.

First, during the March 2018 National People's Congress, Foreign Minister Wang Yi was promoted to State Councillor. According to observers, this move reflects the leadership's desire to ensure that China's growing global political and economic interests are reflected in an increased diplomatic presence (Ng 2018). Moreover, it should be noted that, shortly before his promotion, Minister Wang confirmed the ongoing centralization of China's diplomacy around President Xi: 'Chairman Xi Jinping, as the chief architect of China's major-country diplomacy, has been personally involved in planning and conducting "brilliant" head-of-state diplomacy, [which] enhanced China's profile and influence' (Gao 2018). In addition to higher-profile diplomacy, Xi's tenure has been so far characterized by increasingly frequent 'aggressive' statements, the most recent going so far as to underline China's resolve to fight even 'bloody battles' to 'take its place in the world' (Griffiths 2018). Although 'physical' (i.e. with casualties) confrontations have not taken place yet, episodes such as the Doklam standoff with India in mid-2017 and the unprecedentedly large-scale military drill in the contested waters of the South China Sea in April 2018 (*Reuters* 2018a) certainly add credibility to such statements.

In this light, it is worth noting some of the steps that have been taken to enhance China's military profile, seen by Xi as crucial to buttress Beijing's 'major-country' role. In 2009, China's defence expenditure was RMB 495.11 billion, and in 2016 this figure had almost doubled to RMB 954.35 billion. In 2018, the government announced a further 8.1 per cent increase to 1.11 trillion (*Xinhua* 2018). While this data unquestionably attests to Beijing's significant investment into its hard power, it is also important to stress that, in fact, defence expenditure, while on the rise in absolute (and lately also in relative terms), has significantly decreased as a percentage of overall government spending compared to 10–15 years ago (from over 11 per cent to less than 7 per cent) (ChinaPower 2018). This appears to corroborate China's insistence that its military rise is – against the 'China-threat' voices – 'reasonable and appropriate' (PRC 2015).

Additionally, also in line with the discursive rejection of any attempt at 'spoiling' the global order, as well as with the discursive 'relaxation' of previously untouchable non-interference tenets, China's contribution to multilateral peacekeeping initiatives has been soaring. In December 2010, the People's Liberation Army (PLA) had 1,955 officers and servicepeople deployed in nine UN mission areas – already more peacekeeping personnel than any other permanent member of the UN Security Council. As of February 2018, the total number of Chinese peacekeepers is 2,518 in ten missions (compared to 1,077 Italians, 820 French, and only 57 US) (UN 2018).

China's efforts to enhance its image as a responsible power, aware of the changing global security environment, are also very evident in the field of the securitized matters of climate change and sustainable development, where China is rapidly becoming a trailblazer at both the domestic and the global levels. Governance-wise, Beijing's support was vital for the successful adoption of the Paris Agreement, but its commitment to tackle this issue extends far beyond it. In 2016, China invested USD 87.8 billion in renewable energy – the highest amount in the world (the EU invested USD 70.9 billion, and the US USD 58.6 billion) – and spent a record USD 32 billion on renewable projects abroad. In 2017, it was set to launch the world's largest emissions trading system (ETS) which, if successful, will create major worldwide incentives (Montesano 2017: 3). China's ETS has been encountering some issues in the transition from the seven regional 'pilot' schemes to full-scale national implementation, particularly with regard to data accuracy. Nevertheless, the phasing-in continues, and already a total of 250 million tonnes of carbon dioxide had changed hands by the end of October 2018, versus 200 million at the end of 2017 (*Reuters* 2018c).

Overall, these trends seem to confirm China's willingness to bolster its profile as a comprehensive and more capable security actor, able to better deal with the composite nature of new threats and, thus, to provide more public security goods. Hence, while on paper China keeps rejecting any allegation of pursuing hegemony, its *self-representation*, *ends*, and *means* are increasingly aligning according to criteria that match the profile of an international actor seeking some forms of primacy. Beijing's preferred mode, based on discursive and concrete evidence, would probably fit between soft hegemony and leadership. However, both modes require an order hinging on a degree of normative socialization, and China has always been highly reticent vis-à-vis normative-based alliances. This begs the question of which 'set of values' Beijing will rely on to buttress its soft power, which so far has been very much initiative-based (cf. for instance the emphasis on 'win-win connectivity' underpinning the Belt and Road Initiative). Additionally, despite its strong discursive support for multilateralism, overall China retains a preference for bilateral dealings, even in its new global initiatives. This has led several actors (including in the EU) to question Beijing's real motives, concerned that its cooperative stances might in fact be a shrewd façade concealing a much more realist 'divide and rule' strategy (Narramore 2008).

Therefore, when it comes to envisaging China's global strategic role in the medium to long term, discourse, practice, and norms paint quite a complex picture. On the one hand, China's support for multilateral solutions to global strategic challenges is supported by steadily growing material and political resources, hence making Beijing a good candidate to be a reformist yet not subversive steering power. On the other hand, China's discursive rejection of both hegemony and outright leadership (although this seems to be slowly changing), together with the generalized scepticism – both in China and abroad – with regard to its normative ability to build a consensus-based order, certainly constitute significant hindrances to any form of future hierarchical primacy.

The EU: a growing strategic arsenal for co-leadership?

While the two global heavyweights are moving in very different strategic directions, the EU has been trying to reform its foreign and security policy along more pragmatic lines, seeking to step up its effectiveness by means of a more 'flexible' understanding of its core multilateral tenets. Discursively, this is evident in the transition from the 2003 Security Strategy to the 2016 GS. In practice, the EU's strategic actorness has made significant strides over the past 15 years.

At the beginning of the millennium, lacking EU strategic capabilities were a major concern both within and outside the EU, with even the more optimistic observers arguing that in any security partnership (especially the transatlantic one) the EU could at most contribute the 'softer' (i.e. non-military) elements, while its allies would have to take care of the hard power dimension (Schweiss 2003). Since then, the EU has invested a lot of political and material resources to try and overcome the label of a strictly 'civilian' power (Duchêne 1972; Hill 1990).

In operational terms, 2003 saw the launch of the first EU mission abroad (EUPM in Bosnia), and since then as many as 35 military operations and civilian missions have been initiated and/or completed, hence attesting to the strong drive in Brussels to build up concrete strategic capabilities (Di Mauro et al. 2016).

These operational developments have gone hand in hand with important institutional progress, which enabled raising the EU's strategic profile. In this respect, the turning point was the 2009 Lisbon Treaty, which laid the legal foundations for a thorough overhaul of the EU's foreign and security policy. The Treaty established the European External Action Service (EEAS) and, in order to improve consistency and coordination with other EU institutions, created a High Representative of the Union for Foreign Affairs and Security Policy with a second 'hat' of Vice President of the European Commission. Additionally, it significantly expanded the so-called Petersberg Tasks (military and security priorities) introduced by the Amsterdam Treaty[3] (EU 2009). With the aforementioned changes now in place, the focus has been gradually shifting towards improving the EU's defence efficiency track record. To use the words of High Representative Federica Mogherini, '[w]hile the EU as a whole invests half of what the USA does in defence, the output of this investment is only comparable to 15 per cent of the US output' (EEAS 2017a). To tackle this issue, which has become even more pressing in light of the growing uncertainty brought about by the erratic and confrontational behaviour of the Trump administration as well as by the gruelling Brexit negotiations, 2017 saw the establishment of the first-ever EU command centre and of the European Defence Fund, seeking to boost and streamline Europe's defence capabilities, which at this stage has a budget of EUR 5.5 billion (EEAS 2017b).

Moreover, following a formal decision at the end of 2017, in 2018 the Council officially kicked off the implementation of Permanent Structured Cooperation (PESCO) on security and defence. Coordinated by the EEAS and the European Defence Agency (EDA), PESCO is a Treaty-based framework and process to deepen defence cooperation among EU member states who are capable and willing to do so. A total of 25 member states have decided to participate and have identified the first 17 collaborative PESCO projects, including the establishment of a European Medical Command and an EU Training Mission Competence Centre. The aim is to jointly develop defence capabilities and make them available for EU military operations, thus enhancing the EU's capacity as an international security partner and maximizing the effectiveness of defence spending. It will also 'help reinforce the EU's *strategic autonomy* to act alone when necessary and with partners whenever possible' (EEAS 2018, emphasis added).

In addition to these developments in the field of 'hard' security, the EU has become one of the most experienced global players when it comes to addressing non-traditional security issues: challenges arising mainly out of non-military sources, such as health hazards, resource depletion, migration, and climate change (Montesano 2017: 4). Especially on environmental issues, the EU is widely regarded as a leader, having launched the world's first major carbon market (the ETS in 2005) and consistently providing substantial funding to develop sustainable technologies.

Overall, it is therefore possible to argue that, although it remains the least internally consistent actor of the 'triangle', the EU's profile as a global strategic player is definitely on the rise. Complementing the analysis of the previous section, the growth of EU strategic capabilities corroborates the discursive preference for a path to global relevance hinging on proactive co-operation and underlines Brussels' drive to strengthen its strategic profile in order to be considered as an 'equal' by both Washington and Beijing beyond the economic dimension. Nevertheless, the capability build-up needs to be assessed in the context of the strictly non-hegemonic approach, emphasizing rules-based multilateralism and overall weaker than before in advocating values-based primacy. Hence, building a primacy-oriented hierarchical consensus is not an EU priority. Strategic developments in Brussels are aimed at gaining actorness rather than actual primacy. Nevertheless, given the EU's expertise in 'interdependence management', it is not far-fetched to envisage some forms of European co-leadership with other key actors in a number of – especially non-traditional – strategic fields.

Conclusion

This chapter has shown how the three sides of the so-called global triangle have, over the past 15 years, developed very different, constantly evolving approaches vis-à-vis their strategic outlook on the global order, in both discourse and practice.

In the US, the Trump administration has been veering towards a strongly inward-looking approach, prioritizing the pursuit of narrow, self-centred national interests and being very sceptical towards the very multilateral order the US shaped and upheld for over 60 years. Strategically, Washington's withdrawal from constructively contributing to global governance is creating a power vacuum in many domains. The US is actively dismantling the (more or less hard) hegemonic role it had played for decades and is seemingly uninterested in reforming its primacy towards 'softer' modes, hence inevitably depleting its rule-making capital.

In China, the growing discursive strategic assertiveness characteristic of Xi's leadership is being backed up by concrete institutional and policy initiatives, which some see as evidence of a Chinese ploy to take on a disruptive, even subversive global role. However, when combining discourse and practice, we find evidence of Beijing's strong emphasis on an indeed more proactive yet responsible engagement *within* the multilateral system. Moreover, China's uneasiness with regard to presenting itself as a normative actor, and therefore to building a hierarchical consensus-based order, adds further weight to the hypothesis that it is not seeking hegemonic or even leadership-based primacy – at least for the time being.

In the EU, a stronger foreign and security policy institutional framework has provided fertile ground for Brussels to step up its strategic profile, in both discourse and practice. However, these developments fall within a strictly non-hegemonic environment, wherein the key goal is not primacy, but rather fully fledged external actorness. Additionally, the EU's distance from any form of hegemonic posturing has increased in the past few years, with the 2016 GS formalizing a more pragmatic outlook, and therefore reducing the emphasis on enforcing a values-based order. These developments also attest to the high awareness at the EU level of the importance of strategic flexibility in such an interdependent global context.

Overall, we are witnessing a very fluid situation in the global order, particularly in the realm of security, as the securitization of numerous new domains is generating an unprecedentedly vast strategic agenda combining traditional and non-traditional elements. Addressing this situation would normally require all actors holding or aspiring to primacy roles to reframe their strategy along interdependent lines.

Our analysis of three key global players reinforces the notion that the global security order is in a transitional phase, characterized by the lack of any actors fully committed to pursuing and/or maintaining primacy, in any mode. This relatively 'rudderless' context does certainly generate a degree of instability, but it also opens up greater chances for 'new' actors to take on a more prominent role. Provided that they find ways to coherently and consistently translate their discursive synergies vis-à-vis global strategic interdependence into concrete actions, the EU and China might well be able to capitalize on this window of opportunity.

In this light, growing pragmatic adaptability is likely to help the EU strengthen its position both within the 'triangle' and on the broader global stage. With regard to the former, while transatlantic ties are and will remain crucial, the EU has not been oblivious to Washington's increasingly withdrawn and self-centred approach to global governance. As aptly put by German Chancellor Angela Merkel after the May 2017 G-7 Summit, Europe is aware that it 'must take its fate into its own hands', thereby signalling a willingness to look past its traditional ally and seek other partners to pursue its global agenda. In this regard, China's new global engagement could provide a significant opportunity. Despite their divergences (in both the political and the economic domains[4]), the EU and China have shown openness to a flexible approach to global governance. Bearing in mind that they also share a certain reluctance towards actively seeking strategic primacy, Brussels and Beijing are potentially well-placed to provide some form of co-leadership in a number of domains – starting from non-traditional ones, which are less politically sensitive and where US influence is weakest – and to help build and strengthen a reformed order (Chen 2016).

In light of the power vacuum created by the US, joining forces in a more systematic way could help the EU and China lead the way towards the establishment of a global strategic agenda characterized by greater inclusivity and understanding of current interdependence trends – hence also more open to reform – than the US-led one. A systematization of EU-China strategic relations would require an even stronger formalization of their bilateral endeavours, so as to develop more consequential links between dialogues and concrete initiatives. Especially in the field of security, while Brussels and Beijing have cooperated with some success in areas such as antipiracy, nuclear security, and science and technology, such cooperation remains at present rather sporadic.

While hurdles to deeper bilateral cooperation obviously originate from both sides, from an EU standpoint the main challenges are those hindering its progress towards full strategic actorness, and therefore towards any mode of primacy, including co-leadership. The tallest order is doubtlessly internal coherence, which has lately come under great strain due to intertwining internal and external issues, such as migration and the rise of sovereigntist populism across member states. The EU's strategic prowess relies on its ability to present itself as a 'straightforward' player on the global stage. This, in turn, heavily depends on the existence among the member states of a minimum of consensus with regard to what the EU's overarching strategic role should be. At present, despite the EU-level progress mentioned above, this consensus appears to be dangerously low. If European leaders wish to capitalize on the current window of opportunity offered by the evolving global strategic dynamics, revitalizing said consensus is a top priority.

Notes

1 For the purposes of this chapter, unless otherwise stated, 'strategic' is used as an umbrella term referring to issues pertaining to foreign and security policy.
2 Mutual respect for each other's territorial integrity and sovereignty; mutual non-aggression; mutual non-interference in each other's internal affairs; equality and cooperation for mutual benefit; peaceful co-existence.
3 These tasks were set out in the Petersberg Declaration adopted at the Ministerial Council of the Western European Union (WEU) in June 1992. In 1997, the Treaty of Amsterdam formally incorporated them in the Treaty of the European Union. Following the 2009 Lisbon Treaty 'expansion', they now include humanitarian and rescue tasks; conflict prevention and peacekeeping tasks; tasks of combat forces in crisis management, including peacemaking; joint disarmament operations; military advice and assistance tasks; post-conflict stabilization tasks.
4 A detailed analysis of the current hindrances in EU-China relations is beyond the scope of this chapter. For a cursory overview, see, e.g., Yu (2018).

References

Bailey, D. & F. Bossuyt (2013) 'The European Union as a Conveniently-conflicted Counter-Hegemon through Trade', *Journal of Contemporary European Research* IX(4), 560–577.

Bretherton, C. & J. Vogler (2006) *The European Union as a Global Actor*. 2nd ed., London: Routledge.

Burchill, S. (2005) *The National Interest in International Relations Theory*, Basingstoke: Palgrave Macmillan.

Buzan, B., Waever, O. & J. de Wilde (1998) *Security: A New Framework for Analysis*, Boulder: Lynne Rienner Publishers.

Caballero-Anthony, M. (2016) *An Introduction to Non-Traditional Security Studies-A Transnational Approach*, Thousand Oaks: SAGE Publications.

Chen, Z. (2016) 'China, the European Union and the Fragile World Order', *Journal of Common Market Studies* LIV(4), 775–792.

ChinaPower (2018) *What does China Really Spend on its Military?.* [Online] Available at: https://chinapower.csis.org/military-spending/ [Accessed 2 June 2018].

Destradi, S. (2010) 'Regional Powers and Their Strategies: Empire, Hegemony, and Leadership', *Review of International Studies* XXXVI(4), 903–930.

Di Mauro, D., Krotz, U. & K. Wright (2016) *EU's Global Engagement: A Database of CSDP Military Operations and Civilian Missions Worldwide. Codebook*, Florence: EUI.

Donnan, S. (2018) 'US Fires First Shot in Trade War with Allies', *Financial Times*, 31 May.

Duchêne, F. (1972) 'Europe in World Peace', in R. Maybe (ed.), *Europe Tomorrow*, London: Fontana/Collins, 32–49.

EEAS (2017a) *Defending Europe: European Defence Fund – Factsheet*, Brussels: EU.

——— (2017b) *Growing EU Military Power at Service of Peace, UN Charter and Multilateralism*, Brussels: EU.

——— (2018) *Permanent Structured Cooperation (PESCO) – Factsheet.* [Online] Available at: https://eeas.europa.eu/headquarters/headquarters-Homepage/34226/permanent-structured-cooperation-pesco-factsheet_en [Accessed 20 May 2018].

EU (2003) *A Secure Europe in a Better World*, Brussels: European Union.

——— (2009) *The Lisbon Treaty and its Implications for CFSP/CSDP*, Brussels: DG EXPO.

——— (2016) *Shared Vision, Common Action: A Stronger Europe- A Global Strategy for the European Union's Foreign and Security Policy.* [Online] Available at: http://europa.eu/globalstrategy/en/global-strategy-foreign-and-security-policy-european-union [Accessed 2 August 2017].

Gao, C. (2018) 'Despite Its Global Expansion, China Stresses No Intention to Displace US', *The Diplomat*, 8 March.

Griffiths, J. (2018) 'China Ready to Fight 'bloody battle' against Enemies, Xi Says in Speech', *CNN*, 20 March.

Hill, C. (1990) 'European Foreign Policy: Power Bloc, Civilian Model – or Flop?' in R. Rummel (ed.), *The Evolution of an International Actor: Western Europe's New Assertiveness*, Boulder: Westview Press, 31–55.

Hurrell, A. (2006) 'Hegemony, Liberalism and Global Order: What Space for Would-Be Great Powers?' *International Affairs* LXXXII(1), 1–19.

Ikenberry, J.G. (2004) 'American Hegemony and East Asian Order', *Australian Journal of International Affairs* LVIII(3), 353–367.

Ikenberry, J.G. & C.A. Kupchan (1990) 'Socialization and Hegemonic Power', *International Organization* XLIV(3), 283–315.

Jupille, J. & J.A. Caporaso (1998) 'States, Agency, and Rules: The European Union in Global Environmental Politics', in C. Rhodes (ed.), *The European Union in the World Community*, Boulder: Lynne Rienner Publishers, 213–229.

Keohane, R.O. & J.S. Nye (2001) *Power and Interdependence: World Politics in Transition.* 3rd ed., New York: Longman.

Knorr, K. (1975) *The Power of Nations: The Political Economy of International Relations*, New York: Basic Books.

Kuhn, R.L. (2017) 'New Era on the Road to 2050', *China Daily*, 28 October.

Landler, M. (2018) 'Trump Abandons Iran Nuclear Deal He Long Scorned', *The New York Times*, 8 May.

Larsen, H. (2002) 'The EU: A Global Military Actor?' *Cooperation and Conflict* XXXVII(3), 283–302.

Montesano, F.S. (2017) 'Global Politics and the Evolving EU-US-China Triangle: An Opportunity for EU Leadership?' *CEPOB – College of Europe Policy Brief*, November.

Narramore, T. (2008) 'China and Europe: Engagement, Multipolarity and Strategy', *The Pacific Review* XXI(1), 87–108.

Ng, T. (2018) 'China Promotes Foreign Minister Wang Yi to State Councillor, General Wei Fenghe Named Defence Minister', *South China Morning Post*, 19 March.

Orbie, J. (2008) 'The European Union's Role in World Trade: Harnessing Globalisation?' in J. Orbie (ed.), *Europe's Global Role*, Farnham: Ashgate, 35–66.

PRC (2010) *China's National Defense in 2010*, Beijing: Information Office of the State Council.

——— (2015) *China's Military Strategy*, Beijing: Information Office of the State Council.

Rapkin, D.P. (2005) 'Empire and its Discontents', *New Political Economy* X(3), 389–411.

Reuters (2018a) *China's Xi Presides over Large-scale Naval Display in South China Sea.* [Online] Available at: www.reuters.com/article/us-china-military-xi/chinas-xi-presides-over-large-scale-naval-display-in-south-china-sea-idUSKBN1HJ27M [Accessed 17 June 2018].

——— (2018b) *U.S. Quits U.N. Human Rights Body, Citing Bias vs. Israel, Alarming Critics.* [Online] Available at: www.reuters.com/article/us-un-rights-usa/u-s-quits-u-n-human-rights-body-citing-bias-vs-israel-alarming-critics-idUSKBN1JF24X [Accessed 21 June 2018].

——— (2018c) *China Says Work Far from Complete on National CO2 Scheme.* [Online] Available at: www.reuters.com/article/us-climate-change-china/china-says-work-far-from-complete-on-national-co2-scheme-idUSKCN1NV04N [Accessed 14 October 2019].

Rielly, J. (2008). 'The Bush Administration's Foreign Policy Legacy', *Politique Américaine* III(12), 73–86.

Schweiss, C.M. (2003) 'Sharing Hegemony- The Future of Transatlantic Security', *Cooperation and Conflict* XXXVIII(3), 211–234.

Shear, M.D. & C. Porter (2018) 'Trump Refuses to Sign G-7 Statement and Calls Trudeau 'Weak'', *The New York Times*, 9 June.

Sjöstedt, G. (1977) *The External Role of the European Community*, Stockholm: Saxon House.

Smith, M.A. (2012) *Power in the Changing Global Order – The US, Russia and China*, Cambridge: Polity Press.

UN, P. (2018) *Troop and Police Contributors.* [Online] Available at: https://peacekeeping.un.org/en/troop-and-police-contributors [Accessed 15 March 2018].

USA (2002) *The National Security Strategy of the United States of America*, Washington: The White House.

——— (2006) *The National Security Strategy of the United States of America*, Washington: The White House.
——— (2010) *National Security Strategy*, Washington: The White House.
——— (2015) *National Security Strategy*, Washington: The White House.
——— (2017) *National Security Strategy of the United States of America*, Washington: The White House.
Wright, T. (2015) *Interpreting the National Security Strategy*, s.l.: Brookings.
Xinhua (2018) *China to Increase 2018 Defense Budget by 8.1 Percent*. [Online] Available at: www.xinhuanet.com/english/2018-03/05/c_137016482.htm [Accessed 15 May 2018].
Yu, J. (2018) 'The Belt and Road Initiative: Domestic Interests, Bureaucratic Politics and the EU-China Relations', *Asia-Europe Journal* XVI(3), 223–236.
Zhao, L. (2017) 'PLA to be World-Class Force by 2050', *China Daily*, 27 October.

5 The United States in a global triangle? Re-configuring US-EU and US-China foreign policy and security relations

Alan K. Henrikson

Introduction: America between Atlantic and Pacific, and global, orientations

The relationships of the United States of America (US) with Europe, including members of the European Union (EU), and with the countries of Asia, including the People's Republic of China (PRC), have a high degree of specificity. Historically, the pattern of US transatlantic and especially transpacific relationships has been bilateral rather than multilateral – or even plurilateral. Situated on an island-like North American continent, the US, in contrast with the great powers of Europe or the large countries of Asia, is not embedded in a matrix of international complication. There is thus a flexibility in its strategy and diplomacy – even a natural tendency towards unilateralism in its behaviour.

Moreover, with its widely separated Atlantic and Pacific coastlines, the American nation 'faces' in two directions, both eastward and westward. There remains a tension between these two outward orientations. The divergence in national outlook is temporal as well as geographical. What is sometimes called Atlanticism looks towards the past – to the nation's rich European heritage. The country's Pacific identity, increasingly rooted in demography as well as in geography, points to the future – towards a destiny mixed, both in community and in competition, with countries of Asia. The idea of an American 'pivot' towards the Asia-Pacific, although a 21st-century concept, derives from earlier times. Even at the turn of the 20th century, there was a vision of the country entering a 'Pacific Age' (McDougall 1993). A fundamental difference between then and now is that the Atlantic and Pacific policy concerns of the US cannot easily be kept distinct. The globe is 'smaller'. The European interests of the US and its interests in major countries of Asia are more and more interconnected. This is true, of course, in the trade field. It is equally evident in the field of foreign policy and security relations.

In considering the question of whether the US along with the EU and the PRC constitute a Global Triangle, an analyst must keep in mind the insular, yet central, position of the US in the midst of a World Ocean, a geopolitical context sometimes serene and sometimes roiling (Henrikson 1980:

73–100). The only formal three-party relationship of importance that the US government has entered into is the North American Free Trade Agreement (NAFTA) with Canada and Mexico, recently renegotiated as the US-Mexico-Canada Agreement (USMCA). It has largely kept a free hand, insisting even in its most solemn security commitment, notably the North Atlantic Treaty of 1949, that, as made explicit in Article 11, its independent 'constitutional processes' are unaffected (North Atlantic Treaty Organization 2016). Are existing American commitments, including the mutual-defence pledge of NATO, stable? Will a new formation of allied partners, including the Pacific, somehow emerge? What shape might it take? It must be acknowledged at the outset that the likelihood of an explicit Global Triangle being formed among the US, EU-Europe, and PRC-China especially in the domain of foreign and security policy – in which vital national interests may be perceived to be at stake – is not very high. Three-way coordination among the three entities is much easier to imagine in the area of international economic relations or possibly also in the environmental realm, where American, European, and Chinese populations have similar natural-resource and health concerns and face a challenge of climate change that is planetary in scope.

Threesomes of any kind are awkward arrangements. A comprehensive three-way, globe-spanning combination of the US, Europe, and China, with their very different historical starting points, geographical stances, and political systems, would at present be impossible to establish. A knowledgeable European commentator, Simon Duke, wonders, when considering the idea of such a triangle: 'Twosome can work, but can a *ménage à trois*?' (Duke 2016: 130–133). Might it not be feasible, nevertheless, that in light of genuine problems threatening international stability in various locations of the world, for the leaderships of the US, EU, and PRC to find specific bases for cooperation in the foreign policy and security field? What otherwise might remain a sharply competitive, and even conflictual, set of relationships could thereby be transformed into a functional, if probably only implicit Triangle of a kind.

Much would depend, it is here hypothesized, on the practical *configuration* of the relationship – that is, not just on the vision of a 'Triangle', which is an abstract geometrical conception, but also on the operational design, the actual procedural mechanisms, for the interaction of the three parties. Analogizing from the organizational-and-computational field, one might liken this to 'configuration management (CM)', the process by which the performance of a complex system, with its many component parts and subsystems, is monitored and maintained (Jonassen Hass 2003). In operational terms, this may require the imaginative conceptualization and careful construction of new diplomatic modalities – a *re*-configuring for communication, short-term crisis control, and even possible long-term collaboration. A brief review of the logic, history, and workings of other security-related foreign policy triangular formations that have existed, and the relationship of the US to them, may suggest how such a global triplice might be formed and function, i.e., actually 'work'.

Triangles, equilibrium, and order: US international roles, past and present

International 'triangles' are often ephemeral. Rather than simply disappearing, however, they can be transitional, giving way to other, smaller or larger combinations. Logically, and historically, three players usually are not enough, numerically, to form the basis of a lasting international order. There is always the possibility that two of the players will unite against the third. If there are four players, two pairs of players may separate, creating in effect a 'bipolar' situation, one side of which probably will be stronger, and may seek to dominate the other. If there is a fifth player, for whose support the two sides may need to compete, a *stable* balance is more likely to emerge (Gulick 1955: 4, 8–9, 65–67, 302–303; Kaplan 1967: 34–35).

In a three-way power formation, there usually is a leader, which can be either the strongest power or the one that is, even if somewhat weaker and less directly engaged, the 'balancer' of the other two. A balancer can be either an enforcer, if strong, or a mediator, even if not. History is replete with examples. The US itself, although never in an institutionalized way, has been a player in international triangles in both senses – enforcer and mediator. President Woodrow Wilson sought to end the 1914–1918 war between the Triple Alliance and the Triple Entente – first by diplomatic intervention, through his emissary Edward M. House, and then, when that effort failed, through military intervention. At the Paris Peace Conference in 1919, Wilson saw the US as a neutral arbiter, trying to reconcile the demands of the Allies with the longer-term interests of the defeated Central powers while negotiating the creation of the first general international organization, the League of Nations (Cooper 2001; MacMillan 2002).

President Franklin D. Roosevelt, arguing that 'neutrals are parties at interest in a modern war' (Dallek 1995: 216), also attempted to exert a moderating influence, with the democracies and dictatorships in Europe and also in upholding the Open Door Policy in the Far East. When the US went to war following the Japanese attack on Pearl Harbor on 7 December 1941, it quickly became the leader of a coalition, the 'United Nations' – essentially an enforcement role.

From WWII, three 'Super-Powers' (Fox 1944) – the US, Britain and the Commonwealth, and the Soviet Union – emerged. These soon resolved into the Big Two: America and Russia – the 'Rivals', as the historian Adam Ulam characterized them (Ulam 1971). They competed for resources, space, and influence in what was fundamentally a bipolar world system. At the same time, countries of Western Europe and the PRC were striving to assert collective identities, with the aim of becoming independent poles. In the case of Europe, this aspiration was encouraged by US President John F. Kennedy in Philadelphia on 4 July 1963, where he stated, '[w]e do not regard a strong and united Europe as a rival but as a partner' (Kennedy 1963). In the case of China, the US government during the presidency of Richard Nixon, who travelled to the PRC in 1972, in effect recognized 'one China' – the PRC with Taiwan – as such a pole with a carefully worded Shanghai Communiqué (Kissinger 1979: 1079, 1492). Through the 'triangular diplomacy' that President Nixon and his national security adviser, Henry Kissinger, conducted, the US used the modality of its new relationship with China as leverage in dealing with Russia – both in arms control negotiations and in addressing regional issues, including the conflict in Vietnam. President Nixon understood America's global challenge in economic as well as geopolitical terms. He envisioned a five-power global equilibrium. In terms of 'economic potentialities', there are, he stated, 'five great power centers in the world today' – 'five great economic super powers: the US, Western Europe, the Soviet Union, Mainland China, and, of course, Japan' (Nixon 1971). The later administration of President Jimmy Carter, who was advised by Zbigniew Brzezinski, built upon this five-power foundation with a liberally oriented 'trilateralist' strategy. This involved policy coordination, mainly in the economic field, among the US plus Canada, the major countries of Western Europe, and Japan – all 'industrialized democracies'. The primary mechanism for this coordination was the Group of Seven (G7), focusing on problems of the developing world rather than on East-West issues.

There is, at present, no evidence of anything like a security-oriented Triangle among the US, the EU, and the PRC – either a *strategic* triangle like the American-Chinese-Soviet geopolitical relationship of the 1980s or even a less power-driven *diplomatic* triangle, as it might be called. The former, the late-Cold War-era 'strategic' triangle, functioned somewhat as a zero-sum game, with the gains of one party being balanced, more or less equivalently, by others' losses. Material strength was the primary determinant. The addition of the masses-and-forces of any two of them – Washington and Beijing – would work, commensurately, to the disadvantage of the third – Moscow. Theoretically, there did not need even to be actual interaction among them, other than the strategic interaction itself. By contrast, a 'diplomatic' triangle would be responsive to current events, and it would involve communication and, conceivably, could even result in cooperation. Such an American-European-Chinese triangular relationship, by involving negotiation, would be contingent, interactive, and positive-sum (Ross et al. 2010: 1–2).

The likelihood of such an evolution depends heavily on the US, not only on its power but also on its policies – and American domestic support for those policies. The spectacle of internal 'polarization' (Schultz 2018) in the US at present and the sometimes unilateral assertions of power by the American government have caused European and Chinese governments to push back, occasionally even to do so together as well as along with others. This certainly was evident when the new US presidential administration under Donald J. Trump in June 2017 withdrew from the 2015 Paris Agreement on climate change. It was evident as well in the strong denunciation, expressed by overwhelming votes at the United Nations in both the Security Council and the General Assembly, of the decision of the Trump administration to recognize Jerusalem as the capital of Israel. The position of EU member states favouring a two-state solution, with Jerusalem serving as a capital for both Israelis and Palestinians, was made explicit by Federica Mogherini, the EU High Representative for the Common Foreign and Security Policy (Cowell 2017). Less frontally, but no less firmly, the Chinese foreign ministry expressed its concern and long-standing support for a Palestinian state 'along the 1967 borders with East Jerusalem as its capital' (Gao 2017). This is an illustration, at the diplomatic level, of 'contingent' cooperation by two of the three members of a putative US-EU-PRC foreign policy and security triangle.

Beyond such specific policy differences, there is a broader, more conceptual difference separating the US from the EU, especially the major powers among its members, and the PRC as well. As the scholar David Shambaugh has observed, 'Europe and China have common interests in multipolarism and multilateralism' (Shambaugh 2005: 21). Other large entities including Russia and India also tend to favour a pluralistic world order, allowing each major power to play a leading part. Multipolarism, of course, is not the same as multilateralism, a diplomatic concept denoting many parties (or, more exactly, 'sides'). Multilateralism is not only quantitative but also qualitative. It implies normative consensus and collective decision-making (Ruggie 1993: 3–4). Such international cooperation the US has, at times, strongly resisted, most recently in the name of national 'sovereignty' (The White House 2017: 1, 4, 7, 40, 55).

A partial test of whether a Triangle – a truly systemic, interactive, three-way configuration – does or could exist, it may be postulated, is the following: Does the interest, policy, and action of each of the three parties actually *constrain* the other two parties, preventing them from doing what they otherwise would do independently? Does their relationship, further, *compel* them to do what an initiating party – in the present case, the US government – prefers and itself chooses to do? For such a three-way causal linkage to exist, it needs not to be the case that all of the interacting movements are of the same kind and equal in strength, as in an abstract 'equilateral' triangle. The pattern of interaction in the peace-and-security field, where military strength matters most, might be quite different from that in the economic-financial field or environmental-resource field. The overall politico-geometric configuration may have different shapes at different levels, from the subregional to the global.

In order to test the above hypothesis, of an increasing actual political sensitivity and even diplomatic mutuality of the US, the EU, and the PRC, in a kind of 'managerial' trinity, let us examine their interaction (or lack thereof) in addressing three major regional situations of international concern. The first is the challenge posed by the Islamic Republic of Iran's nuclear programme, along with its missile testing and support for violent activity in neighbouring countries. The second is the problem of territorial jurisdiction and freedom of sea and air communication in the South China

Sea. The third is the danger that has been posed by the testing of nuclear weapons by the Democratic People's Republic of Korea (DPRK) and its frequent rocket launches. With regard to each of these problematical situations, the US, the EU, and the PRC all have taken policy positions, with the US being the strongest upholder of the pre-existing international order but finding itself unable to resolve the problems without the cooperation of others.

Transatlantic cooperation: the US-EU side of a triangle

The principal instrument of US transatlantic policy in the security field has been the North Atlantic Alliance – in its institutional embodiment, NATO. American relations with countries of Europe in the context of the Marshall Plan, which helped to make possible the Common Market and later the EU, did not initially involve cooperation in the field of foreign and security policy. There was some foreign policy coordination, nonetheless, in the context of the European Recovery Programme (ERP) and the Organization for European Economic Cooperation (OEEC). This began to change further in the late 1980s when, as the Cold War ended, the prospect opened of rejoining Eastern and Western Europe. As part of a policy initiative, the 'New Atlanticism', President George H.W. Bush in an address in Boston in May 1989 declared:

> We are ready to develop with the European Community and its member states new mechanisms of consultation and cooperation on political and global issues, from strengthening the forces of democracy in the Third World to managing regional tensions to putting an end to the division of Europe.

As his Secretary of State, James Baker, explained, there would be increased 'substantive overlap' between the work of NATO and that of the primarily European institutions. He recommended, in an unprecedented move, a formal relationship – even a treaty was considered – between the US and the European Community. The result, after a willing response from the European Community, was the Declaration on EC-US Relations – the Transatlantic Declaration (TAD) – of 23 November 1990 (Henrikson 1993). Since that time, political cooperation has greatly increased between the US government with the European institutions.

The Middle East, where American and European interests overlap, has been a particular focus of attention for the US and the EU and its member states. The 1979 Iranian Revolution challenged the existing regional order. The occupation of the US embassy in Tehran by protesters – the hostage crisis – was an affront to the US presidency of Jimmy Carter and to American people, as well as a violation of the Vienna Convention on Diplomatic Relations. Even after the crisis itself was resolved, with the release of the hostages and some Iranian financial assets, the bitter memory of the embassy capture and a failed rescue attempt precluded the possibility of direct bilateral communication between the US government and authorities of the revolutionary Islamic regime thereinafter. European countries with historical ties and their own substantial economic connections with Iran, notably Great Britain, France, and Germany – the E3 – stepped in to fill the diplomatic breach concerning the Iranian nuclear programme. For a time Europe seemed the 'good cop' to the American 'bad cop', but the tactics were not well coordinated. Eventually, the US and Iran made direct contact in secret talks between their representatives in Oman (Landler 2016: 233–259). The EU, through the office of its High Representative, became the *primus inter pares* of a negotiating group including the US and other permanent members of the United Nations Security Council – the P5+1 or, as German diplomats prefer, the E3/EU+3. The result, attributable in significant part to the convening power of the EU and the skill of its representatives who served in the role of go-between among the six powers while US negotiators dealt with their Iranian counterparts in hammering out an agreement, was the Joint Comprehensive Plan of Action (JCPOA) concluded on 14 July 2015 (Kerry 2018: 484–523).

Denounced by Donald Trump as a candidate and also after being elected President as the 'worst deal ever', the JCPOA, in which the EU as well as its member states have a major political and economic stake, has required a strong European public defence. High Representative Federica Mogherini rushed to Washington shortly after President Trump's inauguration to seek reassurance that the Iran nuclear agreement would continue to have official US support. The new administration already had put Iran 'on notice' over its test-firing of a ballistic missile. It had also denounced as 'terrorist' Iran's support for the government of Bashar al-Assad in Syria and its aid to Hezbollah and other groups engaged in conflict throughout the region. Despite HR Mogherini's efforts and the insistence of other participants, including the International Atomic Energy Agency (IAEA), that the Iranian government was carrying out its obligations under the JCPOA, President Trump decided to 'decertify' the Iranian nuclear agreement. This left it up to Congress to decide whether to reimpose sanctions against Iran that had been lifted along with the July 2015 agreement. Congress did not act to do so. The 'real stress test' of the EU's ability to constrain the US, causing it to adhere to the JCPOA, was yet to come (Blockmans & Viaud 2017). Matters came to a head when on 8 May 2018, President Trump definitively announced that the US would withdraw from the JCPOA (Landler 2018). 'We will be instituting the highest level of economic sanctions', he declared, with the warning: 'Any nation that helps Iran in its quest for nuclear weapons could also be strongly sanctioned by the US' (Trump 2018). For European and other countries with economic ties to Iran, this was an unmistakable threat of secondary sanctions if they did not comply with this coercive form of American leadership.

In another region of the world – the South China Sea and its surrounding areas – there are also conflicts in which the US and the EU and its member states have similar, even shared interests in resolving. Some are value-related. In the South China Sea itself, major jurisdictional, geostrategic, and economic issues – maritime sovereignty, freedom of navigation and overflight, fishing rights, and exploitation of seabed resources – are at stake. The PRC, asserting historical rights, has aggressively drawn a broad 'nine dash line' around its projected sphere of control and has built artificial structures within it, including docking facilities and runways, thus fortifying its expansive claims. Moreover, it has flatly rejected the 2016 verdict of the Permanent Court of Arbitration in The Hague in favour of the position of the Philippines, which, despite its superior legal position, soon appeared to accommodate itself to the reality of China's greater size and power and its proffer of economic benefits.

In these circumstances, it is principally the US, with its large naval presence in the Asia-Pacific area and its security relationships with the countries of the region, that is endeavouring to uphold international law and to maintain peace and security there. During the earlier administration of President Barack Obama there was a noted policy shift – a 'pivot', or rebalancing – of attention and some military personnel to the Pacific, both to support US bilateral alliances and to assure Americans and others of uninhibited access to the markets of Asia (Clinton 2011). At the occasion of the 2017 Shangri-La Dialogue in Singapore, Secretary of Defense James Mattis, a former Marine Corps general who had led the Central Command (CENTCOM) and previously the NATO Transformation Command, stated on behalf of the Trump administration that the US had 'a deep and abiding commitment to reinforcing the rules-based international order'. Recognizing that economic and political 'friction' was to be expected, Mattis warned that 'we cannot accept Chinese actions that impinge on the interests of the international community'. The US would 'continue to fly, sail and operate wherever international law allows', he declared, and it would 'demonstrate resolve through operational presence in the South China Sea and beyond' (Mattis 2017).

European policies regarding the region have varied considerably with countries' national interests – in the area itself and also at home. The long history of European – Italian, Spanish, Portuguese, Dutch, British, French, and, later, also German and Belgian – connection with the Chinese and other peoples of Asia and the Pacific is rich and profound, and it has left a differentiated legacy.

France and Britain are at the forefront. At the 2017 Shangri-La Dialogue the French Minister of Armed Forces, Sylvie Goulard, pointed out that France has '1,600,000 nationals in the region, vast territories and an exclusive economic zone stretching over 9 million square kilometers between the Indian Ocean and the Pacific Ocean' (Goulard 2017). The French government 'intends to exercise its responsibility by participating in a constructive and attentive manner to the evolutions of the regional security architecture' (ibid.). For France this included participation in a demonstration of naval deterrence. The flagship FS *Mistral* along with the frigate *Courbet* were deployed during the 'Jeanne d'Arc 2017' operational mission in the area. The *Mistral* carried two helicopters with a British naval detachment, as Goulard noted, 'showing our joint operational know-how and the solidarity of the Europeans' (ibid.). The commitment of France and Britain, with its continuing Commonwealth ties and interest in Hong Kong, to bilateral cooperation in the maritime realm, including the sea routes of the Indian Ocean and the Asia-Pacific, was confirmed by the UK-France Summit in January 2018 (United Kingdom-France Summit Communique 2018). For Britain, with the possibility of a 'hard Brexit' from the EU looming, its old relations with the 'Anglosphere' may gain in importance. Like France, it has continued to send warships through the region in coordinated freedom of navigation operations (FONOPS). France's government under President Emmanuel Macron has heightened the involvement of its naval and air forces in the region. Yet he stressed that France, which would be the last country of the EU to have territories in the Pacific if Britain leaves, does not want to antagonize China (*The Straits Times* 2018).

At the organizational level of the EU, where consensus is required among a much wider range of countries, the solidarity shown has been shallower. The EU's statement on the South China Sea problem that followed the Arbitration Court's decision reflected the differing interests that individual members had with regard to Chinese companies investing in their domestic economies (Emmott 2016). 'Europe Can't Save the South China Sea', an observer frankly commented (Scimia 2017). High Representative Mogherini acknowledged in the EU declaration that member states of the EU, as contracting parties of the UN Convention on the Law of the Sea (UNCLOS), were 'committed to maintaining a legal order of the seas' and 'the peaceful settlement of disputes'. However: '[t]he EU does not take a position on sovereignty aspects relating to claims'. The statement drew attention to the dispute settlement mechanisms of UNCLOS and the EU's own status as a High Contracting Party to the 1976 Treaty of Amity and Cooperation in South East Asia, and it did affirm: 'The EU stands ready to facilitate activities which help to build confidence between the parties concerned' (Council of the EU 2016). By contrast, a US official statement made following the Arbitral Award emphasized the fact that 'the Tribunal unanimously found that the Philippines was acting within its rights' in initiating the arbitration, and noted that 'the Tribunal's decision is final and legally binding' (Kirby 2016). The US-EU 'side' facing the challenge posed by China in the South China Sea was clearly less than solid.

The most serious threat to international peace and security in the Pacific sphere was in Northeast Asia, on the Korean peninsula. Since the conflict in Korea that ended with an uneasy truce in July 1953, the Republic of Korea and the DPRK have been at daggers drawn along a Demilitarized Zone intersecting the 38th Parallel. In 2003, the DPRK withdrew from the

Nuclear Non-Proliferation Treaty (NPT), which prompted the beginning of Six-Party Talks in Beijing including the two Koreas, Japan, the US, and the Russian Federation as well as China. Discontinued in 2009 following a North Korean satellite launch, the Six-Party Talks have not been resumed. The new North Korean leader, Kim Jong-un ('Rocket Man', as President Trump then belittlingly called him), relied on nuclear weapon and missile testing – on deterrence – to assure his regime's survival. Yet, in a remarkable joint declaration made with South Korean President Moon Jae-in at Panmunjom on 27 April 2018, Kim Jong-un 'confirmed the common goal of realizing, through complete denuclearization, a nuclear-free Korean Peninsula' (Taylor 2018). More remarkable still, when a South Korean emissary to the White House reported that Kim Jong-un said that if the American president would join him in a summit meeting the two could produce a historic breakthrough, President Trump 'accepted on the spot' (Baker & Choe 2018). Their meeting took place in Singapore on 12 June 2018. The result was a joint statement envisioning 'a lasting and stable peace regime on the Korean Peninsula' (*The New York Times* 2018) with, however, little indication as to how that might be brought about.

Although their policies regarding North Korea, formulated in UN Security Council Resolutions dating from 2006, are basically the same, the US and the EU have very different positions in relation to the Korean situation. The US is a formal ally – a treaty partner – of South Korea. It has more than 37,000 personnel stationed there, and it is committed to defend the country. American support of the Republic of Korea, and of US forces on the peninsula and in the wider area, has been augmented by installation of the Terminal High-Altitude Area Defence (THAAD) system to intercept and destroy any incoming missiles. The Trump administration's decision in October 2018 to withdraw from the 1987 Intermediate-range Nuclear Forces (INF) Treaty in response to Russian violations of it will permit the US to develop a land-based intermediate-range ballistic missile system for Northeast Asia (Boot 2018). A military balance is being maintained, arguably at a higher level of tension, not only with North Korea but with neighbouring China as well.

Some European countries were involved in the Korean War. The United Nations Command (UNC), led by the US, was composed of 16 countries including Great Britain, the Netherlands, Belgium, and Luxembourg. France sent a volunteer force, the *Bataillon français de l'ONU*. When in 1953 the armistice was signed, and a Neutral Nations Supervisory Commission (NNSC) established, the UNC side chose Sweden and Switzerland to be two of the four members (the other two, for the DPRK and Chinese side, were Czechoslovakia and Poland). Although the NNSC as a group has ceased to function, the Swedish and Swiss governments maintain small presences at Panmunjom and also have diplomatic missions in the North Korean capital. Sweden's embassy in Pyongyang serves as the 'protecting power' under the Vienna Convention on Diplomatic Relations for interests of the

US. Countries of the EU, along with Switzerland, thus do have a stake in the maintenance of peace in Korea – largely an economic and diplomatic stake (European External Action Service 2018). The US has an existential commitment.

The US has retained the lead in dealing with the challenge posed by North Korea and its nuclear and missile programmes. In January 2018, under the co-chairmanship of Secretary Rex Tillerson and Canadian foreign minister Chrystia Freeland, ministers of some 20 countries, including European and other 'Sending States' involved in the Korean War, met in Vancouver to discuss support for South Korea and ways to end the crisis on the peninsula. The Chinese government, sounded out by the Canadian government, declined to participate, given the 'UN Command' historical association of the meeting, but it was kept apprised (Smith 2018).

The EU, although it had indicated through High Representative Federica Mogherini that it would be ready to serve as mediator with the aim of freezing North Korea's nuclear weapons and missile programmes, has remained on the sidelines. Several EU member states having embassies in Pyongyang, including the Czech Republic and Poland, and old connections with the communist government there, explored the possibility of European mediation in joint meetings with North Korean officials in September 2017. Their efforts were complicated, however, by the sanctions being imposed by the EU, which went beyond even those mandated by the UN Security Council. 'The North Koreans are starting to see the EU as a US puppet, but we stress that we are an honest broker', commented one European diplomat. 'They want to talk to the US', acknowledged another (Emmott 2017). Should American leadership fail in dealing with the North Korean problem, it has been argued very speculatively, Europe could play a role as a moderator, 'not *despite* but *because of* its distance from the conflict' (Hilpert & Meier 2018: 83).

Transpacific cooperation: the US-PRC side of a triangle

The US and the PRC have long been Cold War adversaries and, to this day, have profound differences of policy and interest with regard to regional and other foreign policy issues – even as their economic relations have expanded and deepened. The latent hostility between them – less ideological than situational, an incumbent power and a rising power – is such that there is serious discussion, even among some knowledgeable American analysts, of a possible US-PRC military showdown. Political scientist Graham Allison, analogizing from ancient history, has written *Destined for War: Can America and China Escape the Thucydides Trap?* (Allison 2017). Peter W. Singer and August Cole, in their well-informed techno-thriller, *Ghost Fleet: A Novel of the Next World War*, demonstrate how a military conflict between the US and the PRC, with Russia also becoming involved, might actually happen (Singer & Cole 2015). Theirs is but a cautionary story, yet a serious one.

It was fear of Russia, not of China, that was the motive factor behind the US 'triangular diplomacy' of the early 1980s. Henry Kissinger explains the origins of that three-way strategic relationship less in diplomatic than in geopolitical terms: the government in Beijing took the initiative (e.g., its inviting the US ping-pong team to visit China) because of its sense of military vulnerability vis-à-vis Moscow. Academic experts who were focused narrowly on China did not see 'the possibility that the Chinese might have an incentive to move toward us *without* American concessions because of *their* need for an American counterweight to the Soviet Union', Kissinger recalls (Kissinger 1979: 165). He and President Nixon were actually surprised by how 'easy' it was therefore to make arrangements for their trips to China. The basic cause – the compellent – was the pre-existing three-way power relationship – 'triangular' *avant la lettre*. The American-Chinese common front against possible Soviet aggression, though implicit, was made clear in a joint statement opposing 'hegemony' in the Shanghai Communiqué of 28 February 1972 (ibid.: 1490–1492). When in 1978 the pragmatic Deng Xiaoping became paramount leader in Beijing, realistic jokes were made, nervously in Moscow, about China's being 'the 16th member' of NATO (a position actually filled by Spain in 1982).

That 'triangular' power configuration of the 1970s no longer exists. The overall rise of the PRC in recent decades, including the significant increase in its military and naval capabilities, has placed the US-China strategic relationship – and the China-Russia relationship as well (Arbatov & Dvorkin 2013) – on an entirely different footing. The strategic 'partnership' envisioned between Washington and Beijing began as a dialogue between political leaders only, with little involvement of 'the bureaucracy' on either side. 'We only began to feel its weight and its resistance', according to Kissinger aide Richard Solomon, 'when we established liaison offices in 1973' (Association for Diplomatic Studies and Training n.d.). In January 1979, the establishment of formal diplomatic relations – and embassies – during the Carter administration facilitated some actual US-Chinese military cooperation, including America arms sales and the operation of a joint listening post in Xinjiang. Additional mechanisms eventually were created to regularize the Washington-Beijing relationship, notably the administrative 'Dialogues': Deputy Secretary of State Robert Zoellick's Senior Dialogue and Secretary of the Treasury Henry Paulson's Strategic Economic Dialogue during the George W. Bush administration. Under the Obama administration, these were combined as the US-China Strategic and Economic Dialogue (SandED), with a 'Strategic Track' and an 'Economic Track'. These bodies performed a 'managerial' function of a diplomatic kind.

The US-PRC managerial relationship has undergone a modification, though not a profound change, as a result of the personal meeting between President Donald Trump and President Xi Jinping at Mar-a-Lago in April 2017. A multi-track 'comprehensive dialogue mechanism' was agreed upon by them. Within that framework, there would be a separate

US-China Diplomatic and Security Dialogue (DandSD) which could focus more sharply and in greater depth on critical issues in that domain, notably the North Korean problem, than was felt to be possible under the broader SandED. The first meeting of the Diplomatic and Security Dialogue took place in Washington in June of that year, under the co-chairmanship of the two countries' top diplomatic and military officials. Other dialogues – the Comprehensive Economic Dialogue, Law Enforcement and Cyber Strategic Dialogue, and Social and People-to-People Dialogue – were scheduled to meet later. The creation of the DandSD, while a formal and procedural innovation, did not itself indicate a discontinuity in American policy. However, President Trump's continuing criticism of China's 'unfair' trade practices, and the attitude of hostility that this connotes, along with the retaliatory economic measures he has ordered (Office of the United States Trade Representative 2018), call into question the possibility of closer US-PRC political cooperation. So, too, does even the uncertain rapprochement between Washington and Pyongyang, which has visibly increased anxiety in Beijing (Wong 2018).

It does not appear that there is an intention on either the American side or the Chinese side to form anything like a 'G-2' – a cooperative combination to provide global public goods. The 'G-2' idea, put forward initially by C. Fred Bergsten of the Petersen Institute for International Economics (Bergsten 2008) and conceptually broadened by former National Security Adviser Zbigniew Brzezinski to include cooperation in the security field, as well as the economic field, was premised on the basic equality in size of the two societies as well as on their 'complex interdependence'. Invoking previous Chinese President Hu Jintao's concept of 'a harmonious world', Brzezinski, well known as an original proponent of 'trilateral' cooperation among the industrial democracies of North America, Western Europe, and Japan, came to envision 'a comprehensive partnership, paralleling our relations with Europe and Japan' (Brzezinski 1983: 53–55; Brzezinski 2009). Thus, a Washington-Beijing 'G-2' would not be a political duopoly but rather part of a larger system of global management, including other major players – notably the EU and Japan – in possibly varying configurations to deal with international problems.

The problem of a nuclear-capable Iran under Islamic control has been of significant concern to both Washington and Beijing, even if from quite different geographical and ideological perspectives. In the days of the Carter administration, Iran was thought of strategically as a 'regional influential' (Brzezinski 1983: 53–54). The Trump administration, closely aligned with Israel and also with Saudi Arabia, has identified the Islamic government of Iran as a major adversary. China's Iranian interests, which are mainly economic and focused on oil, predate the 2015 JCPOA which, as it made possible the lifting of sanctions, enhanced the prospects of Chinese-Iranian economic cooperation. As a participant in the P5+1 talks, China is a stakeholder in the agreement and a vital one (Singh 2015). 'China is needed as a direct participant in the dialogue with Iran', as Zbigniew Brzezinski pointed out, 'for China will also be affected if the effort to negotiate ends in failure' (Brzezinski 2009). China, though a relatively passive player, has strongly supported the EU and the E3s in their insistence that the JCPOA should be upheld. The Chinese position, joined to that of the EU, thus has been an important constraint on US policy, as is the pro-Iranian position of the Russian Federation.

One must add Japan as constraining factor as well. Although not a member of the P5+1 negotiating group, Japan, which has frequently served on the UN Security Council as a non-permanent elected member, has long had an economically significant relationship with Iran – and is disinclined to confront it. Japanese diplomacy could be an emollient, perhaps even more – for example by offering practical cooperation with Iran in the field of nuclear safety (*The Japan Times* 2016) should an opportunity for that again arise. In the short run, however, the action of the US administration in unilaterally disavowing the JCPOA has proved these constraints to be ineffective.

In the South China Sea, it is China that is the driving, and the disruptive, force. The US, with its hub-and-spoke alliance system and its naval and air coverage of the Pacific, remains the principal defender of the region's international security order. While opposing China's jurisdictional claims and its threatening military installations and operations (Beech 2018), the US government, as a matter of policy, favours a non-adversarial approach to conflict resolution. As an example, it supports the Association of Southeast Asian Nations (ASEAN) countries' work in negotiating a Code of Conduct with the PRC (Lee 2017; Mogato & Shepherd 2017). Where they have 'overlapping interests', as Secretary of Defense Mattis emphasized at the 2017 Shangri-La conference in Singapore, they 'seek to cooperate with China as much as possible'. Even where they 'disagree', they will 'seek to manage competition responsibly because we recognise how important US-China relations are for the stability of the Asia-Pacific' (Mattis 2017). In October 2018, Secretary Mattis met with his Chinese counterpart, Defence Minister Wei Fenghe, on the sidelines of an ASEAN security conference in Singapore. 'We're two large powers, or two Pacific powers, two economic powers. There's going to be times we step on each other's toes, so we're going to have to find a way to productively manage our relationship', he said. 'And the military relationship is to be a stabilizing force in the relations between the two countries' (Burns 2018).

In Northeast Asia, the US security relationships with Japan and with South Korea are the structural underpinnings of the region's stability, as well as of the American defensive positions there. They are also an implicit counterbalance to China, which perceives an offensive capability, if not necessarily intent, in the US presence. The THAAD missile system with its X-band radar, Chinese military analysts contend, threatens China's 'strategic deterrence' capability and could even become an interoperable part of a 'multilateral' Ballistic Missile Defense (BMD) linked to that of other US

Asian allies (Yao 2017). General Joseph F. Dunford, Jr., chairman of the US Joint Chiefs of Staff, sought to clarify the purpose of American strategy during a visit to Beijing in August 2017 when he met with President Xi Jinping and senior Chinese military leaders: 'We have a long-term alliance commitment with South Korea' (Perlez & Choe 2017). As for North Korea, he explained that, while the US favoured a peaceful outcome to the standoff with Pyongyang, 'we are also being prudent in preparing military options' (ibid.). Prudence required prevision as well as preparation. 'So we think it is better to talk about those military options in advance' (ibid.). Dunford was manifestly eager to improve communication between the American and Chinese militaries, partly to reduce the risk of miscalculation. The two sides signed an agreement while he was in Beijing calling for periodic talks between top generals. At the level of defence ministers, too, contact would be maintained, despite tensions over tariffs and other matters (*South China Morning Post* 2018). This could only be a partial basis, however, for an American-Chinese transpacific partnership.

EU-China: forging a *three*-sided global triangle?

The missing piece in a conceivable US-EU-PRC foreign policy and security triangle is the EU-PRC 'lateral', mainly because the EU as such does not have a military presence in the Asia-Pacific region. It lacks a capacity for coercion and thus, to a degree, for consideration in that sphere. The policies of the EU regarding China, in contrast with those of the US and of NATO, have not stressed security, but rather have emphasized economic relations and, less consistently, human rights. The 'strategic partnership' that the EU and PRC formed in 2003 does not encompass military cooperation, although the two have conducted joint exercises in the Indian Ocean in response to Somali piracy there (Men 2014: 3, 6). The US government, given its Asia-Pacific security responsibilities, has been concerned about the destabilizing effect of European sales of arms to China. There were sharp differences between the EU and the US in the 2003–2005 period over the possible lifting the EU embargo on arms exports, dating from the 1989 Tiananmen Square massacre. Europe did at that time accede to American wishes, which indicated a predominance of the US-EU side of the triangle over the EU-China side (Archick, Grimmitt & Kan 2006). The arms sales issue has largely been resolved, although specific concerns relating to dual-use technology and components of weapons remain (Vennesson 2007; Stumbaum 2009; McMillan 2014). A new complication may be the effect of 'Brexit' on the EU arms embargo, as British arms producers would no longer be bound by it (Harding 2016). The embargo thereby could unravel and, somewhat perversely, add hard military content to the EU-PRC 'strategic relationship'.

A 'management configuration' necessary to bring about a more structured, and operationalized, way of maintaining stability in the north-eastern and other parts of Asia-Pacific sphere clearly has not been devised. The US, partly as a counterweight to China (not for the surely futile purpose of 'containing' it but to assure its own and its friends' and allies' freedom of naval manoeuvre and shipping), is giving priority in its latest National Security Strategy to 'Indo-Pacific' quadrilateral cooperation (The White House 2017: 45–47). The geometric figure of a 'Quad', composed of the US, Japan, Australia, and India, was advanced first by the Japanese government of Prime Minister Shinzo Abe during 2006–2007. It has regained currency (Panda 2017). Conceivably, with greater European involvement in assuring the maritime security of the Asia-Pacific region (Andre 2017), the Quad could develop into an effective 'Quint', with almost global extent. For China, such a formation might appear ominous. It could also, however, lead to relations of pragmatic cooperation in foreign policy and security affairs in the Indo-Pacific.

Conclusion

The political geometry of international relations in the world's foreign policy and security domain is changing, owing not only to shifts in the underlying geopolitical balance but also to events, which can be shaped (or misshaped) by diplomatic initiative. The notion of a Global Triangle of the US, the EU, and the PRC as a *political* construct, whose members are able to work together in close diplomatic cooperation, does seem at present unrealistic. The idea is not, however, wholly fantastic. There have been and still are lesser pieces of such a potential configuration, including actual instruments for its operational management, in place. These include the Six-Party Talks framework; the 'club' of European embassies in Pyongyang; the Shangri-La Dialogue; the Canadian-led 'Vancouver Group'; the dialogue relationships of the US, EU, and PRC with the ASEAN group of countries; the P5+1 (E3/EU+3) formation that produced the JCPOA with the Islamic Republic of Iran; the high-level US-PRC military exchanges; and, centrally, American, European (now including the EU itself), and Chinese cooperation within the United Nations system.

There is a further, circumstantial factor that may engender greater system cooperation in foreign policy among the members of a new Big Three: the common challenges they face in the global environment. This includes 'the global security environment, an environment that has no geographic boundaries', General Denis Mercier emphasized when serving as Supreme Allied Commander of NATO's Transformation Command. Today's crises 'become more and more interrelated and the same actors may interact differently according to the situation, which makes situational understanding more difficult', he noted. 'In this complex global security environment, no nation or organization can manage a crisis on its own'. This new circumstance, Mercier suggested, 'may lead us to consider scenarios that would engage a wider range of partners out of the Euro-Atlantic area, explore innovative decision-making architectures to face future transnational challenges and help define the required needs to empower all parties who could play a role in global security' (Mercier 2017). That partnership certainly would include the PRC as well as other nations in the broader Indo-Asia-Pacific sphere. The image of a 'Global Triangle' of the US, the EU, and mainland China may help to re-configure foreign policy and security cooperation among themselves and also with others.

References

Allison, G. (2017) *Destined for War: Can America and China Escape the Thucydides Trap*, Boston: Houghton Mifflin Harcourt.

Andre, D. (2017) *The Asia Pacific and Europe's Maritime Security Strategy*, Center for International Maritime Strategy, 29 March.

Arbatov, A. & V. Dvorkin (2013) 'The Great Strategic Triangle', *The Carnegie Papers*, April, Carnegie Moscow Center, Carnegie Endowment for International Peace.

Archick, K., R. Grimmitt & S. Kan (2006) *European Union's Arms Embargo on China: Implications and Options for U.S. Policy*, Washington: Congressional Research Service, 26 January.

Association for Diplomatic Studies and Training. (n.d.) 'Richard Solomon, Ping-Pong Diplomat to China'. Available at: adst.org/oral-history/fascinating-figures/richard-solomon-negotiating-peace-by-other-means.

Baker, P. & S.-H. Choe (2018) 'With Snap "Yes," Trump Rolls Dice on North Korea', *The New York Times*, 11 March.

Beech, H. (2018) 'As Beijing Flexes Muscles, Waves of Risk Churn South China Sea', *The New York Times*, 4 September.

Bergsten, C. (2008) 'A Partnership of Equals', *Foreign Affairs*, July/August.

Blockmans, S. & A. Viaud (2017) 'EU Diplomacy and the Iran Nuclear Deal: Staying Power?' *Policy Insights*, no. 2017–28, Centre for European Policy Studies, 14 July.

Boot, M. (2018) 'On the INFD Treaty, Trump Finally Gets Something Right', *The Washington Post*, 24 October.

Brzezinski, Z. (1983) *Power and Principle: Memoirs of the National Security Adviser, 1977–1981*, New York: Farrar Straus Giroux.

——— (2009) 'The Group of Two that Could Change the World', *Financial Times*, 13 January.

Burns, R. (2018) 'Mattis Meets his Chinese Counterpart, But No New Agreements', *The Washington Post*, 18 October.

Clinton, H. (2011) 'America's Pacific Century', *Foreign Policy*, 11 October.

Cooper, J. (2001) *Breaking the Heart of the World: Woodrow Wilson and the Fight for the League of Nations*, Cambridge: Cambridge University Press.

Council of the EU (2016) 'Declaration by the High Representative on Behalf of the EU on the Award Rendered in the Arbitration between the Republic of the Philippines and the People's Republic of China', General Secretariat, Press Release 442/16, July 15.

Cowell, A. (2017) 'E.U. Leaders Reject Netanyahu on Jerusalem Recognition', *The New York Times*, 11 December.

Dallek, R. (1995) *Franklin D. Roosevelt and American Foreign Policy, 1932–1945*, New York: Oxford University Press.

Duke, S. (2016) 'EU-China Security Relations: Twosomes Can Work, But Can a *ménage à trois*?', *EU-China Relations: New Directions, New Priorities*, Discussion Paper, Friends of Europe/Les amis de l'europe, Summer, 130–133.

Emmott, R. (2016) 'EU's Statement on South China Sea Reflects Divisions', *Reuters*, 15 July.

——— (2017) 'EU's Diplomatic Back Channel in Pyongyang Goes Cold', *Reuters*, 3 October.

European External Action Service (2018) 'Federica Mogherini Expresses Full Support for Denuclearization and Peace on the Korean Peninsula', Press Release, Seoul, 6 August.

Fox, W. (1944) *The Super-Powers: The United States, Britain, and the Soviet Union – Their Responsibility for Peace*, New York: Harcourt, Brace.

Gao, C. (2017) 'What's China's Stance on Trump's Jerusalem Decision?', *The Diplomat*, 7 December.

Goulard, S. (2017) 'Upholding the Rules-Based Regional Order: Sylvie Goulard', Minister for Armed Forces, France, IISS Shangri-La Dialogue 2017 Second Plenary Session, 3 June. Available at: www.iiss.org/en/shangri-la-dialogue/archive/shangri-la-dialogue-2017-a321/plenary-2-faad/goulard-7854.

Gulick, E. (1955) *Europe's Classical Balance of Power: A Case History of the Theory and Practice of One of the Great Concepts of European Statecraft*, New York: W.W. Norton.

Harding, R. (2016) 'Japan Fears Brexit Blow to EU Arms Embargo on China', *Financial Times*, 4 July.

Henrikson, A. (1980) 'America's Changing Place in the World: From "Periphery" to "Centre"?', in J. Gottmann (ed.), *Centre and Periphery: Spatial Variation in Politics*, Beverley Hills: SAGE Publications, 73–100.

——— (1993) 'The New Atlanticism: Western Partnership for Global Leadership', *Revue d'intégration europeénnne/Journal of European Integration* 16(2–3), 165–191.

Hilpert, H. & O. Meier (2018) 'Disentangling Rather than Cutting the Gordian Knot: The North Korea Conflict and the Role of Europe', in H. Hilpert & O. Meier (eds.), *Facets of the North Korea Problem: Actors, Problems and Europe's Interests*, SWP Research Paper 12, Berlin: Stiftung Wissenschaft und Politik, December, 73–83.

Jonassen Hass, A. (2003) *Configuration Management Principles Practice*, Boston: Addison-Wesley.

Kaplan, M. (1967) *System and Process in International Politics*, New York: John Wiley and Sons.

Kennedy, J. (1963) 'Address at Independence Hall, Philadelphia', July 4, 1963, The American Presidency Project. Available at: www.presidency.ucsb.edu/us/?pid=8756.

Kerry, J. (2018) *Every Day Is Extra*, New York: Simon and Schuster.

Kirby, J. (2016) 'Statement by John Kirby on Decision in the Philippine-China Arbitration', 12 July, U.S. Embassy and Consulate in Korea, https://kr.usembassy.gov/p_gov_071216.

Kissinger, H. (1979) *White House Years*, Boston: Little, Brown and Company.

Landler, M. (2016) *Alter Egos: Hillary Clinton, Barack Obama, and the Twilight Struggle Over American Power*, New York: Random House.

——— (2018) 'Trump Abandons Iran Pact He Long Scorned', *The New York Times*, 9 May.

Lee, Y. (2017) 'A South China Sea Code of Conduct: Is Real Progress Possible?', *The Diplomat*, 18 November.

MacMillan, M. (2002) *Paris 1919: Six Months that Changed the World*, New York: Random House.

McDougall, W. (1993) *Let the Sea Make a Noise: A History of the North Pacific from Magellan to MacArthur*, New York: BasicBooks.

McMillan, S. (2014) 'Europe's Arms Trade with China', *The Strategist*, 11 February.

Mattis, J. (2017) 'The United States and Asia-Pacific Security: General (Retd) James Mattis', Secretary of Defense, IISS Shangri-La Dialogue 2017 First Plenary Session, 3 June. Available at: www.iiss.org/en/events/shangri-la-dialogue-2017-a321/plenary-1-6b79/mattis-8315.

Men, J. (2014) 'EU-China Security Relations', *Policy Report*, August, S. Rajaratanam School of International Studies (RSIS), Nanyang Technological University, Singapore.

Mercier, D. (2017) General Denis Mercier, Supreme Allied Commander Transformation, NATO, Shangri-La Dialogue 2017 Special Session Two, 3 June. Available at: www.iiss.org/en/events/shangri-la-dialogue/archive/shangri-la-dialogue-2017-4f77/special-sessions-7894/session-2-c938.

Mogato, M. & C. Shepherd (2017) 'Australia, Japan, U.S. Call for South China Sea Code to be Legally Binding', *Reuters*, 7 August.

Nixon, R. (1971) 'Remarks to Midwestern News Media Executives Attending a Briefing on Domestic Policy in Kansas City, Missouri', July 6, 1971, The American Presidency Project. Available at: www.presidency.ucsb.edu/ws/?pid=3069.

North Atlantic Treaty Organization (2016) *The North Atlantic Treaty*, Washington, 4 April 1949. Available at: www.nato.int/cps/ic/natohq/official_texts_17120.htm.

Office of the United States Trade Representative (2018) 'President Trump Announces Strong Actions to Address China's Unfair Trade', Press Release, March.

Panda, A. (2017) 'US, Japan, India, and Australia Hold Working-Level Meeting on Quadrilateral Regional Cooperation: The 'Quad' is Back', *The Diplomat*, 13 November.

Perlez, J. & S.-H. Choe (2017) 'Bannon and Dunford Remarks Muddle U.S. Strategy for North Korea', *The New York Times*, 16 August.

Ross, R., Ø. Tunsjø & T. Zhang (2010) 'Introduction', in R.S. Ross, Ø. Tunsjø & T. Zhang (eds.), *US-China-EU Relations: Managing the New World Order*, London: Routledge, 1–2.

Ruggie, J. (1993) *Multilateralism Matters: The Theory and Praxis of an International Form*, New York: Columbia University Press.

Schultz, K. (2018) 'Perils of Polarization for U.S. Foreign Policy', *The Washington Quarterly* 40(4), 7–28.

Scimia, E. (2016) 'Europe Can't Save the South China Sea', *The National Interest*, 24 July.

Shambaugh, D. (2005) 'The New Strategic Triangle: U.S. and European Reactions to China's Rise', *The Washington Quarterly* 28(3), 7–25.

Singer, R. & A. Cole (2015) *Ghost Fleet: A Novel of the Next World War*, Boston: Houghton Mifflin Harcourt.

Singh, M. (2015) 'The Sino-Iranian Tango: Why the Nuclear Deal is Good for China', Snapshot, *Foreign Affairs*, 21 July.

Smith, M.-D. (2018) 'Canada Appears Offside with the U.S. after Inviting China to Sidelines of Vancouver North Korea Meeting', *National Post*, 12 January.

South China Morning Post (2018) 'China's Defence Minister to Visit US, James Mattis Says', Agence France-Presse, 28 October.

Stumbaum, M.-B. (2009) *Risky Business? The EU, China and Dual-use Technology*, Occasional Paper, European Union Institute for Security Studies, October.

Taylor, A. (2018) 'The Full Text of North and South Korea's Agreement, Annotated', *The Washington Post*, 27 April.

The Japan Times (2016) 'Japan to Offer $2.2 Million to Iran for Nuclear Safety Cooperation', Kyodo, 8 December.

The New York Times (2018) 'The Trump-Kim Statement: Read the Full Text'. 12 June.

The Straits Times (2018) 'France Challenges Beijing in South China Sea', Agence France-Presse, 12 June.

The White House (2017) National Security Strategy of the United States of America, Washington, December.

Trump, D. (2018) 'Remarks by President Trump on the Joint Comprehensive Plan of Action', 8 May. Available at: www.whitehouse.gov/briefings-statements/remarks-president-trump-joint-comprehensive-plan-action.

Ulam, A. (1971) *The Rivals: America and Russia Since World War II*, New York: Viking Press.

United Kingdom-France Summit Communique 2018, Royal Military Academy Sandhurst, 18 January.

Vennesson, P. (2007) 'Lifting the EU Arms Embargo on China: Symbols and Strategy', *EurAmerica* 37(3), September, 417–444.

Wong, C. (2018) 'China Could be Excluded from Peace Talks after Donald Trump-Kim Jong-un Summit, Analysts Say', *South China Morning Post*, 1 May.

Yao, Y. (2017) Major General (Retd) Yao Yunzhu, People's Liberation Army, 'Nuclear Dangers in the Asia-Pacific', Special Session One, IISS Shangri-La Dialogue, 3 June. Available at: www.iiss.org/en/events/shangri-la-dialogue/archive/shangri-la-dialogue-2017-4f77/special-sessions-7894/session-1-475b.

Part III

Economics and trade

6 EU-China-US trilateral relations

Status quo, problems and perspectives

Ding Chun

Introduction

Relations between China, the EU and the US are important elements of the world economic structure. The US is the most advanced economy in the world, the EU is the largest and most successful economic union in the world and China is the largest developing country in the world, and the triangular relationship among the three economies has a decisive influence on the global economy. According to World Bank statistics, China, the US and the EU accounted for 60.98 per cent of global gross domestic product (GDP) in 2015 and 61.11 per cent in 2016. The relationship is important not just because of their share of global GDP and trade and investment flows but also because of their role in the making of the global economic order. While trade and investment flows are important, attention is also focused on how global rules will be set, with China, the EU and the US playing a key role. The global economic order is increasingly under challenge and China, as a major economic and political actor, plays a significant role in how it will be remade. Since the late 1970s China has emerged as a major economy and transformed its economic relations with the EU and US and also the global economic order. Thus, the policies adopted by China are not only bilateral in importance but are a determining factor in the global order. Increasing apparent frictions in bilateral relationships are a result of China's growing importance in quantitative terms, but also of the qualitative changes in the global economic order that are occurring. These changes are demonstrated by developments in trade and investment flows and also in governance institutions such as the World Trade Organization (WTO).

Since China began its policy of opening and reform, its role in global trade and investment flows has grown in importance, as has its role in global institutions. While China's policy has been to accommodate itself to the existing global order through domestic reform and joining institutions such as the WTO, nevertheless, it has faced challenges in doing so. China's rise has posed challenges for itself, its major economic partners and the global

The author cordially thanks Diwen Jiang, Jiawei Yang, Yiwei Ma and Xiaowen Wang from School of Economics, Fudan University, and Duncan Freeman from College of Europe for their contributions.

order which they have created. How China manages the triangle with the EU and US will be central to how the global order is constituted. Although China does not view the two in the same way, it considers both as vital in its bilateral relationships and also to the global order. While the economic relationships between China and the other two members of the triangle are key for China, the entire triangle will be important in determining the future global order and China's position in it. China has asserted its willingness to support globalization and the existing global order, most notably in the speech by President Xi Jinping at Davos in 2017 since China has been a major beneficiary of the global economic that has emerged in the last four decades. According to China's Ministry of Commerce (2017c), the total volume of China, US and EU trade reached a record high in 2016. The total exports of China, the US and the EU accounted for 46 per cent of the world's total exports in 2016, while China accounted for 17 per cent, the EU and the US accounted for 16 per cent and 14 per cent, respectively. The total imports of China, the US and Europe account for 45 per cent of global imports. The US accounts for 18 per cent of the total global imports, and the EU and China account for 15 per cent and 12 per cent, respectively. However, following the crisis which began in the US and Europe in 2008, the global economic recovery has been sluggish and uncertain. According to the Chinese government, during this period China's economy has entered a 'new normal' in which it seeks slower but higher quality growth, and its GDP growth rate has dropped from 10.6 per cent in 2010 to 6.7 per cent in 2016. After President Trump came to power, he adopted an 'America First' strategy that has involved frequent use of import tariffs which have had an impact on the development of the world economy, while at the same time providing a large domestic deficit spending stimulus. The EU faces many internal and external problems, such as the continuing European debt crisis, the refugee crisis, terrorism, populism, Brexit and the crisis in Ukraine, bringing great uncertainty to the EU's future economic development. Against this background, the future development of Sino-EU and Sino-US relations in the current economic situation concerns not only the fundamental interests of all three but also the prosperity and stability of the global economy.

This chapter is organized as follows. It first analyses the current situation of Sino-EU and Sino-US trade and investment and then analyses the problems of Sino-EU and Sino-US trade and investment. Finally, this chapter analyses the prospects of China, EU and US economic relations in the global context.

Sino-EU and Sino-US trade and investment

Based on the international division of labour, the economies of China, the US and the EU are highly complementary. In terms of their trade in goods, China has a long-term surplus in trade in goods with the US and with the EU, while China has a growing deficit in trade in services with the US and the EU. The differences in Sino-EU and Sino-US trade are mainly manifested in the structure of trade in goods. In the field of investment, since China has accelerated its 'go global' strategy, China became a net investor in the US and the EU from the point of view of direct investment flows. However, in terms of the direct investment stock, China's stock of direct investment in the US and in the EU still lags behind the US and the EU's direct investment stock in China and is only a small fraction of the investment stocks that the EU and US have in each other's economies.

China has long-term trade surplus with both the US and the EU. Since China joined the WTO, trade between China and the US and between China and the EU has developed rapidly. China was the largest trading partner of the US in 2016, with 21.1 per cent of US imports coming from China and 7.8 per cent of US exports going to China. China is the EU's second-largest trading partner with 20.3 per cent of the EU's imports coming from China and 9.5 per cent of the EU's exports going to China.

The total volume of trade in goods between China and the US increased from USD 181.6 billion in 2003 to USD 410.9 billion in 2008; compared to 2003, the total volume of US exports to China in 2008 increased by 149 per cent to USD 71.3 billion. Compared to 2003, the total volume of China's exports increased by 122 per cent to USD 339.6 billion in 2008. After the financial crisis, the US economy recovered and Sino-US trade continued to grow steadily. From 2008 to 2016, the average annual growth rate of exports of US goods to China was 6.2 per cent. The average annual growth rate of US imports of goods from China was 3.9 per cent. In 2016, the total trade volume between China and the US reached USD 5,782 billion. Since the establishment of the Comprehensive Strategic Partnership between China and the EU in 2003, the trade in goods between China and the EU has developed rapidly. From 2003 to 2008, the average growth rate of the total trade volume between China and the EU reached 35.8 per cent. The EU's exports to China increased from EUR 41.47 billion to EUR 78.3 billion, while the EU's imports from China increased from EUR 106.5 billion to EUR 249.1 billion. Due to the impact of the financial crisis and the debt crisis in Europe, the EU's imports of Chinese goods decreased after 2009, while the exports of goods to China increased steadily. With the economic recovery of the EU in recent years, the EU has maintained a relatively steady increase in the import and export of goods with China. In 2016, the total volume of trade between China and the EU reached EUR 514.7 billion (Eurostat).

As can be seen from Sino-EU and Sino-US trade statistics (Figure 6.1), trade in goods between China and the EU, China and the US has shown an upward trend. However, China's exports of goods to the EU and the US both decreased in 2016.

There is considerable research on the reason why the trade deficits exist. In terms of industrial structure, the EU and the US and China are at different stages of development. According to the theory of comparative advantage, the developed modern service industries and technology-intensive industries in the EU and the US were bound to shift their low value-added and labour-intensive industries to the places that have abundant labour,

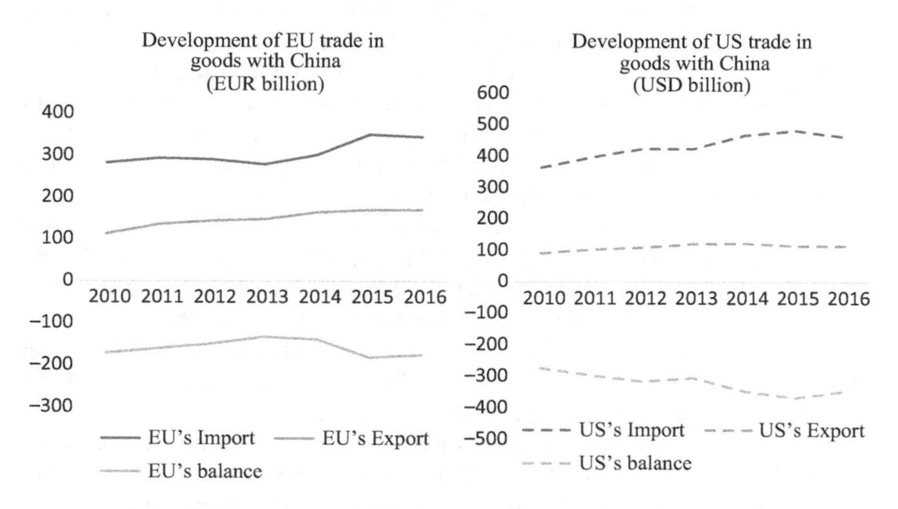

Figure 6.1 Trade in goods of Sino-EU and Sino-US.

such as China. They then imported a large amount of low value-added manufacturing products from China, resulting in a trade deficit (Fu & Zhu 2008; Zhang 2009; Bao 2010; Yeats 2010; Duan & Jiang 2012). From the trade protection point of view, the EU and the US policy of limiting high-tech exports to China is also an important factor in causing the deficit. For example, Ju et al. (2012) think that the trade imbalance between China and the US is largely due the fact that 'the US exports too little to China'. While the US has relatively few exports to China in its comparative advantage industries, Premier Li Keqiang said in March 2017 that if the EU removed restrictions on its high-tech exports to China, the trade imbalance would have been significantly improved (*Guanchazhe* 2017). In addition, the exchange rate (García Herrero & Koivu 2007) and statistical factors are also important reasons for the huge deficits.

As can be seen from Table 6.1, the share of machinery and transportation equipment (including electronic equipment, communications equipment and vehicles) in the imports and exports of the EU, the US and China in 2016 is high. This implies that the trade between China and the EU and between China and the US shows strong characteristics of intra-industry trade. The EU and the US have similar structures of imports from China. However, from the perspective of the export structure of the EU and the US to China, there are some differences. The share of machinery and transportation equipment (including electronic equipment, communications equipment and vehicles, etc.) in EU exports to China has reached more than 50 per cent. To some extent, this shows China's reliance on the EU's technology. Chemicals and related products ranked second in the EU's exports to China, but raw materials and other products ranked second in US exports

Table 6.1 The structure of trade in goods

	Share of EU's Imports from China (per cent)	*Share of US Imports from China (per cent)*	*Share of EU's Exports to China (per cent)*	*Share of US Exports to China (per cent)*
Food and live animals	1	1	4	5
Beverages and tobacco	0	0	1	0
Crude materials, inedible, except fuels	1	0	6	23
Mineral fuels, lubricants and related materials	0	0	2	2
Animal and vegetable oils, fats and waxes	0	0	0	0
Chemicals and related products, n.e.s.	5	3	13	12
Manufactured goods	13	11	8	5
Machinery and transport equipment	50	52	54	44
Miscellaneous manufactured articles	29	31	9	8
Commodities and transactions n.c.e.	0	1	1	1
Other	0	0	1	0

Source: Eurostat, USITC.

to China, accounting for 23.1 per cent, far higher than the EU's share of raw material exports to China, indicating that China relies more on the import of raw materials from the US than the EU.

Contrary to the trade in goods between China and the EU and US, the notable feature of trade in services between China and the EU and US is that the EU and the US both have long-term trade surpluses with China. At present, according to Eurostat, the US is the EU's largest service trade partner and China is the third largest service trade partner. According to figures released by China's Ministry of Commerce, the US is China's (the Mainland) largest service trade partner, and the EU is the third largest service trade partner. As can be seen from the service trade figures of the EU, the US and China (Figure 6.2), after the financial crisis and the debt crisis in Europe, the EU's service exports to China increased from EUR 19.5 billion in 2010 to EUR 36 billion in 2016. The EU's imports of services from China increased from EUR 17.2 billion in 2010 to EUR 25.7 billion in 2016. Trade in services between China and the US also increased rapidly in recent years. In 2016, the total volume of trade in services exported by the US to China reached USD 47.9 billion, an increase of 115 per cent over 2010. The total volume of US service imports from China reached USD 32.9 billion, with an increase of 213 per cent over 2010. According to China's Ministry of Commerce (2017b), the US is the country with the largest service trade surplus with China. In general, the US and the EU both have a long-term service

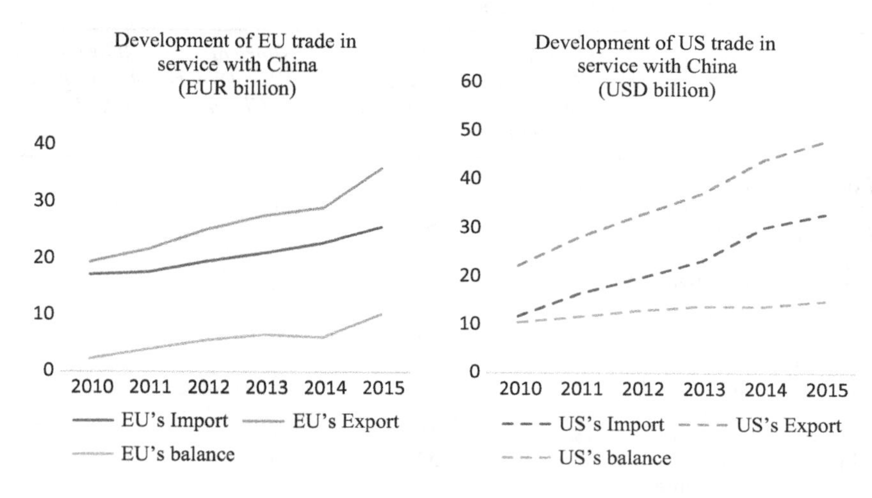

Figure 6.2 Trade in services.
Source: Eurostat, USITC.

trade surplus with China. However, the EU's surplus with China has been on the rise, while the US surplus with China has tended to be stable.

The reason why the EU and the US have a surplus with China in trade in services lies mainly in the weak development of China's service industry, its small added value and the insufficient competitiveness (Chen & Whalley 2014). However, the service deficit is also a phenomenon of the process of China's economic restructuring and upgrading. As China's supply-side structural reform deepens, the potential for service industry development will continue to be realized and its development momentum will gradually increase and China's competitive advantage in service trade will gradually emerge.

Both inward foreign direct investment (IFDI) and outward foreign direct investment (OFDI) can promote economic and employment growth in a country (Morck et al. 2008; Whalley & Xin 2006; Liu & Li 2013; Nicolas 2014; Liu & Mao 2016). It also plays an important role in improving a country's technology and adjusting its economic structure. From the perspective of China, the implementation of the 'One Belt One Road' and 'Made in China 2025' strategies, as well as the inherent demand of Chinese enterprises to upgrade and enhance their international competitiveness, make direct investment an important means to promote China's economic development.

Both the US and the EU have been the major destinations of foreign direct investment (FDI) in the world because of their legal systems, infrastructure and high labour quality. In 2016, China's direct investment in the EU reached EUR 35 billion, an increase of 77 per cent over 2015, while the EU's direct investment in China was EUR 7.6 billion, the fourth consecutive year of decline. After 2013, China became a net direct investor in the EU, and in 2016, China's net direct investment in the EU reached EUR 27.4 billion. Although the EU promulgated a regulation on screening of FDI in 2019, this will not cause a significant change in the situation that the EU remains a major destination for overseas investment. In 2016, China's direct investment in the US reached USD 46.2 billion, three times that of 2015, while US direct investment in China was USD 13.8 billion, relatively stable from the previous year. China became a net investor in the US in 2015 with a net investment of USD 32.4 billion in 2016.

The high technology of the EU and the US is an important driving force for the direct investment of Chinese enterprises. In addition, the attraction of the US financial markets and the EU's strategic assets are also important factors that affect Chinese enterprises' direct investment in the US and the EU. After China's reform and opening up began in the late 1970s, it promoted the development of its economy by attracting a large amount of FDI. Although China has become a net investor in terms of the flow of direct investment to the EU and to the US, the EU and the US are still net investor countries in China in terms of direct investment stocks.

From the Sino-EU and Sino-US investment stock figures, it can be seen that the EU's stock of direct investment in China is still much higher than that of China's direct investment in the EU. However, it is foreseeable that as China increases its direct investment in the EU and the US, the gap between the Sino-EU and Sino-US investment stocks will continue to shrink.

Chinese private-owned enterprises have played an important role in China's OFDI. Among the top five Chinese investors in the EU, three of them are private companies. And in the top five Chinese investors in the US, two are joint venture and one is private. Hence, it can be seen that Chinese private-owned enterprises have played an important role in China's outward investment.

Problems of Sino-EU and Sino-US trade and investment

China, the US and the EU are in different stages of development. There are big differences in economic structure and comparative advantages between them. Therefore, there are bound to be problems between China, on the one hand, and the EU and US, on the other hand, in trade and investment. From China's point of view, it mainly complains about the trade protectionism of the EU and the US, their technological protectionism, the failure to fulfil Article 15 of the 'Protocol to China's Accession to the WTO' and a series of 'Anyone but China' strategies. From the perspective of the EU and the US, the EU and the US are mainly dissatisfied with aspects of China such as its imperfect intellectual property protection system, restrictions on industrial policies and market access, and overcapacity in sectors such as steel production.

China's concerns

Due to differences in the export structure between China and the EU, China and the US, China's long-term trade surplus with both the EU and the US is due to the fact that Chinese products can enter the world market at lower prices. The EU and US believe that their enterprises can't compete with Chinese enterprises in the international market. In turn, the economic development of the EU and US has been affected, resulting in long-term trade friction between China and the EU and US. In recent years, in order to counter the impact of the financial crisis and debt crisis, the trade protection measures taken by the EU and the US have both greatly increased trade frictions between China and the EU and between China and the US.

Take the antidumping and countervailing investigations initiated by the EU and the US as an example. From the EU perspective, from 2012 to the third quarter of 2016, the EU launched antidumping and countervailing investigations against China as many as 29 times, accounting for 45 per cent of total EU investigations. Referring to China's steel industry, the EU Ambassador in China Hans Dietmar Schweisgut pointed out that China must seriously deal with its steel production capacity. The EU accused China of dumping steel and imposed high duties on imports of steel products. In September 2017, the EU conducted an antidumping and countervailing investigation on products such as fibreglass and tartaric acid from China. From the perspective of the US, according to data collected by the US International Trade Commission, a total of 118 antidumping and countervailing investigations were launched by the US between 2012 and 2016, of which 36 were against China, accounting for 35.5 per cent of the total. In August 2017, US President Trump directed US Trade Representative Robert Lighthizer to decide whether to initiate a '301' investigation of China's trade-related intellectual property policies and practices in accordance with the US Trade Act 1974. In September 2017, the US International Trade Commission released findings on the photovoltaic industry and concluded that imported crystalline silicon solar cells and their packaging products had caused serious damage to the domestic photovoltaic industry in the US, which is extremely unfavourable to photovoltaic manufacturing enterprises outside the US. In addition, a US report on 'Assuring the US Long-Term Leadership in the Semiconductor Industry' has expressed concern about the development of the Chinese semiconductor industry.

Investment can promote the growth of the local economy by creating jobs. Therefore, Sino-EU and Sino-US direct investment have become an important driving force for economic development. With the rapid development of China's economy, China became a net investor in the EU and the US. However, with the increase in investment, the investment friction between China and the EU, China and the US have also gradually increased.

The reason why the EU and the US have limited investment from China is mainly because the EU and the US are worried that the investment by Chinese enterprises will cause loss of core technology. For example, in 2016, Chinese company Midea acquired the KUKA robotics company in Germany, which triggered concerns over loss of technology to China. In February 2017, the economic ministers of Germany, France and Italy even proposed establishing a 'firewall' to counter Chinese enterprises' investment in advanced technology assets. The US Foreign Investment Commission (CFIUS) increased the number of cases reviewed involving mergers and acquisitions by Chinese companies of US businesses on the ground of national security. According to the China's Ministry of Commerce (2017a), the US President has rejected only three mergers and acquisitions cases since the CFIUS Board was established in 1975, and all three cases involved Chinese investors: The first was the acquisition of Mamco Manufacturing, a Seattle-based aircraft parts manufacturer by CATIC in 1989; the second case was in 2012 when a branch of Sany Heavy Industry acquired a wind farm group in Oregon; the third came in 2016, when Fujian Hongxin Investment Fund acquired the German-based chip-equipment maker Aixtron.

According to Article 15 of China's WTO accession agreement, the use of 'surrogate country' data by WTO member countries in their antidumping investigations on Chinese exports should have been terminated on 11 December 2016. This is an obligation that WTO member states must fulfil under international treaties and the treatment that China can enjoy as a member of WTO. However, the EU and the US did not fulfil their obligations as scheduled and continued to take protectionist measures against Chinese goods. China has argued that as the two leading developed economies in the world, the EU and the US should signal to the international community and the market respect for international rules.

In recent years, a series of bilateral or multilateral agreements have been signed among the US and the EU and other countries. These include the Trans-Pacific Partnership Agreement (TPP), which was a comprehensive free trade agreement (FTA), also known as the 'economic NATO', the purpose of which was to promote free trade in the Asia-Pacific region. It included the main elements of a typical FTA: trade in goods, rules of origin, trade remedies, sanitary and phytosanitary measures, technical barriers to trade, trade in services, intellectual property, government procurement and competition policy. However, on 23 January 2017, Trump announced that the US withdrawal from the agreement following his election as President of the US.

The Transatlantic Trade and Investment Partnership (TTIP) was a trade preferential agreement initiated by the EU and the US aimed at building a free trade zone between the EU and the US and stepping up bilateral trade with the EU and the US. According to the EU's estimate, once the TTIP came into force, it would have increased the output value of the EU and US economies by EUR 119 billion and EUR 95 billion each year, and also influence the formulation of international trade rules. The negotiations on TTIP were abandoned after the election of President Trump.

The Trade in Services Agreement (TiSA) is a trade agreement launched by the WTO's 'Real Good Friends of Services', a sub-group of a few WTO members, dedicated to promoting trade liberalization in services. At present, the member countries account for more than 70 per cent of the total world trade in services, with 23 members. One thing in common in this series of agreements is that China is not involved in any of them.

EU and US concerns

The EU and the US have always placed great emphasis on the protection of intellectual property. For example, in the US President's national trade policy agenda of 2017, intellectual property protection is considered as an important part of US trade policy. The US administration argues that China lacks an effective legal system to protect intellectual property rights. Although China amended its relevant laws and regulations that protect the interests of domestic and foreign investors based on the agreement on WTO trade and intellectual property after China's accession to the WTO, they still need further improvement. The relatively imperfect intellectual property protection system in China and the lack of law enforcement will continue to hinder trade and investment between China and the US and EU.

Regarding China's industrial policy, both the EU and the US believe that China will continue to pursue a wide range of industrial policies, which will limit the import of foreign goods and restrict the entry of foreign manufacturers and service providers into the Chinese market. The Chinese government has provided a large amount of financial, resource and regulatory support to industrial enterprises. The continuous strengthening of industrial policies has led to unfair competitive conditions. The main beneficiaries are Chinese state-owned enterprises and other enterprises in China that seek to upgrade their position in the economic value chain. In terms of market access, the EU hopes that China will open its government procurement market, eliminate access restrictions for key strategic industries and eliminate the restrictions on foreign ownership of Chinese companies. The EU and the US also hope that China will become more open in the service sector (including banking services, insurance, communications services and network-related services (including cloud services)). The EU and the US also hold that China should provide greater equality and reciprocity in terms of trade and investment.

The steel sector is an important foundation for EU and US industry. Iron and steel workers are still an important force in EU and US society. Both the EU and the US believe that global steel demand is weak and the global steel industry is suffering from the crisis of overcapacity and that overcapacity in China's steel industry is one of the major causes of overcapacity in the global steel industry. Hans Dietmar Schweisgut, EU ambassador to China, pointed out in 2016 that overcapacity in China's steel industry is one of the most important issues for the EU stating that China's efforts were 'not going quite far enough' (Martina 2016), while the US Secretary of Commerce Penny Pritzker said, 'China must take timely and concrete actions to reduce its excess production and capacity' in the steel industry, or else face trade protection measures imposed by other countries (Blenkinsop & Wong 2016).

In addition to the EU and US common concerns about China, there are differences between them. For example, the US government has said that trade deficits with China, the RMB exchange rate, agricultural products and some legal frameworks in China are also US concerns (US Trade Representative 2017).

Sino-EU, Sino-US economic cooperation prospects

From the perspective of the US, before Trump was elected as president, it hoped to maintain its leading position in the global economy and restructure global economic rebalancing. Since Donald Trump was elected as president, he has implemented the 'America first' strategy, giving top priority to US interests and attempting to revive the US manufacturing industry. Trump has criticized FTAs and threatened withdrawal from the North American FTA, which has been renegotiated. From China's perspective, it is playing an increasingly important role in world economic governance and has strengthened its relations with other countries through the establishment of FTAs, the implementation of the 'One Belt One Road' strategy and the establishment of institutions such as the Asian Infrastructure Investment Bank. Trump's election as President did not change China's stance of opening up and cooperation. President Xi Jinping said at the Davos Forum in early 2017 that China will never close its door and is committed to pushing forward globalization and global governance reform. At 19th CPC National Congress, President Xi Jinping made it clear that China will adopt policies to promote high-standard liberalization and facilitation of trade and investment and will implement the system of pre-establishment national treatment plus a negative list across the board, significantly easing market access, further open the service sector, and protect the legitimate rights and interests of foreign investors. All businesses registered in China will be treated equally. From the perspective of the EU, the high dependence of the EU on the US has determined that the EU will surely be affected by the strategic shift of the US. Trump's unfriendliness to the EU after his election as the President of the US (evidenced by Trump openly supporting Brexit and Eurosceptics; the US conducting Article 232 investigations of steel exports including from China and the EU) made German Chancellor Angela Merkel state that, '[w]e Europeans have our fate in our own hands' after the G7 summit in 2017. At the same time, the EU will continue to uphold openness and oppose protectionism and support global trade rules and will play an increasingly important role in global economic governance.

First of all, although the EU economy is recovering, it has been hit hard by both the financial and debt crises and by Brexit, and the cooling of relations between the EU and the US is also a factor of uncertainty. The cooperation between China and the EU has become an important driving force for the economic development of the EU. With regard to the US, the US market has always been a traditional export market valued by China, and the US is also China's largest trade surplus partner. This complicated relationship between China and the US makes Sino-US economic cooperation inevitable. In November 2017, Trump made a visit to China and signed a cooperation agreement worth up to more than USD 250 billion. This is the manifestation of the inevitable. Furthermore, China is the largest US creditor nation, but China will gradually buy the euro in order to diversify its investment.

China's 'Belt and Road Initiative' also welcomes participation by EU member states and the US. China will continue to pursue friendly cooperation between the US and the EU at the same time.

Due to their different stages of development and industrial structure, frictions between China and the EU, China and the US will be inevitable. First, on the issue of the trade deficit, China is a developing country and according to the theory of comparative advantage in trade, developing countries will exhibit a trade surplus in some fields when they trade with developed countries. In the context of globalization, there is always a trade surplus in the process of industrialization in a country (including developed countries such as the US and Japan that have experienced a goods trade surplus). The trade deficit between the US and China is mainly determined by the economic structure of the two countries, industry competition and the division of labour in international industry. Due to the similar economic development between the EU and the US, trade frictions will be inevitable between China and the EU as the volume of trade goes up.

Second, the issue of protectionism in the EU and the US will persist. Protectionism has always existed in the US, and Trump has intensified the policy. In order to restore economic growth after suffering the debt crisis in Europe, the EU has also been adopting trade protectionist measures to protect its own industry. The EU's trade and investment strategy 'Trade for All: Towards a more responsible trade and investment policy' of 2015 and its other policies surely clash with China in trade and investment. The EU also proposed that trade and investment policies should promote its values and use trade as a powerful tool to solve the problems of 'human rights', 'anti-corruption' and 'good governance'. These issues have long been the focus of controversy between China and the EU in trade and investment. It is foreseeable that there will be more disputes between China and the EU, China and the US on trade protection.

Finally, on the competition among Chinese, US and EU companies. As China's economy enters a 'new normal', China will make large-scale investments in fields such as scientific research and innovation. The adjustment of China's industrial structure and industrial upgrading will speed up. The relatively low position of Chinese enterprises in the global division of labour will be significantly improved, and thus be a competitor with the US, the EU and other developed countries in some fields. The complementarity of trade between China and the US and between China and the EU will decrease and friction which is caused by competition will also be inevitable.

The global economy is slowly recovering, but at the same time, the world is suffering from the negative impact of anti-globalization manifestations such as trade protectionism and populism. The global per capita income gap has widened, and environmental problems have also threatened the development of the global economy. There is no doubt that there are many uncertainties in the global economic development. China, the US and the EU are the three largest economies in the world, and there is no other country can replace them in a short period of time. The mode of production cooperation brought by globalization will continue without much impact from anti-globalization forces. Only through cooperation can achieve a win-win result. The cooperation among China, the US and the EU in global economic governance will continue. At the same time, the three economies must take on more responsibilities for global governance. Therefore, in the face of common global problems and the assumption of the common responsibility of global economic governance, the fundamental interests of China, the US and the EU for promoting global economic development and governance through cooperation have not changed. The trilateral relations between China, the US and the EU will be based on a kind of bilateral cooperation for a long time. Therefore, the trade and investment patterns among the three will not change much.

References

Bao, J. (2010) 'On Interdependence of Trade and Economic Growth between China and Europe and Policy Choice for New Protectionism', *Journal of International Trade* 5, 29–37.

Blenkinsop, P. & S.-L. Wong (2016) 'As Global Steel Crisis Grips, China says March Output was a Record', *Reuters*, 18 April. Available at: nwww.reuters.com/article/us-china-steel-overcapacity/as-global-steel-crisis-grips-china-says-march-output-was-a-record-idUSKCN0XF2LI.

Chen, H. & Whalley, J. (2014) 'China's Service Trade', *Journal of Economic Surveys* 28(4), 746–774.

Duan, Y. & X. Jiang (2012) 'The Impact of Sino-EU Trade on Bilateral Economy and Employment', *Journal of International Trade* 8, 29–39.

Fu, Q. & Z. Zhu (2008) 'Empirical Study on the Impact of US FDI on China- US Bilateral Trade Imbalances', *Journal of International Trade* 7, 77–81.

García Herrero, A. & T. Koivu (2007) 'Can the Chinese Trade Surplus Be Reduced through Exchange, Rate Policy?' Bank of Finland Transition Economies, BOFIT Discussion Paper No. 6/2007.

Guanchazhe (2017) 'Li Keqiang Discusses EU-China Trade Deficit: Releasing Hold of Technology Exports can Significantly Improve It' [李克强谈中欧贸易逆差：放开对华技术出口可改善], 15 March. Available at: www.guancha.cn/economy/2017_03_15_398889.shtml.

Ju, J., H. Ma, Z. Wei, Y. Qian & Q. Liu (2012) 'Anti-Comparative Advantage', *China Economic Quarterly* 11(3), 805–832.

Liu, H. & Li, S. (2013) 'Influence of FDI on China's Economic Growth and Employment——Based on the VAR Model', *Journal of International Trade* 4, 105–114.

Liu, H. & H. Mao (2016) 'Effects of Manufacturing OFDI on Domestic Value-added in Exports', *China Industrial Economics* 7, 91–108.

Martina, M. (2016) EU 'Ambassador to China Urges Beijing to Do More to Cut Steel Output', *Jakarta Globe*, 9 May. Available at: https://jakartaglobe.id/context/eu-ambassador-china-urges-beijing-cut-steel-output/.

Ministry of Commerce of the People's Republic of China (2017a) 'Research Report on China-US Economic and Trade Relations', 25 May.

——— (2017b) 'Ministry of Commerce: The US is the Country of Origin of China's Largest Trade Deficit in Services' [商务部：美国是中国服务贸易逆差最大来源国]. Available at: http://chinawto.mofcom.gov.cn/article/e/r/201707/20170702617113.shtml.
——— (2017c) 'EU-US-China Trade in Goods Accounts for Half of Global Trade' [欧盟、美国和中国货物贸易总额占全球贸易半壁江山]. Available at: www.mofcom.gov.cn/article/i/jyjl/m/201708/20170802636610.shtml.
Morck, R., B. Yeung & M. Zhao (2008) 'Perspectives on China's Outward Foreign Direct Investment', *Journal of International Business Studies* 39(3), 337–350.
Nicolas, F. (2014) 'China's Direct Investment in the European Union: Challenges and Policy Responses', *China Economic Journal* 7(1), 103–125.
US Trade Representative (2017) '2016 Report to Congress on China's WTO Compliance', January.
Whalley, J. & X. Xin (2006) 'China's FDI and Non-FDI Economies and the Sustainability of Future High Chinese Growth', *National Bureau of Economic Research, Inc.*
Yeats, A.J. (2010) 'China's Foreign Trade and Comparative Advantage: Prospects, Problems, and Policy Implications', World Bank.
Zhang, W. (2009) 'Causes of Sino-US Trade Imbalance and Relevant Analysis', *Finance & Trade Economics* 4, 71–76.

7 The European Union's trade strategy in the emerging tripolar structure with the United States and China

Sieglinde Gstöhl

Introduction: the emergence of a strategic triangle in trade

Much ink has been spilled in recent years about the rise of emerging economies and the related relative 'decline of the West' (see, for instance, Anderson et al. 2009; Kupchan 2012). This debate ponders in particular about whether and when China will achieve superpower status and the hegemony of the United States (US) will end, to what extent the European Union (EU) has become a genuine global actor, and about the prospects of great power competition in a multipolar world order.

Table 7.1 shows that the US and China are the EU's main trade partners. Although the EU is now importing more goods from China than from the US, the American market still is by far the largest market for European exports of goods, trade in services and foreign direct investment (FDI). Both the US and, to a lesser extent, the EU have run big trade deficits vis-à-vis China, and China has been criticized for building up massive foreign currency reserves due to market interventions. Yet, the US also has a trade deficit vis-à-vis the EU and other important trading partners.

Transatlantic trade is in fact more important than these conventional statistics show. Global value chains in many sectors have been rendering most exports the product of many intermediate imports. A new 'value-added' approach attempts to assess the impact of global value chains in international production by focusing on where value is actually created. 'In value-added

Table 7.1 Shares and ranking of leading EU trade and investment partners (2015)

EU shares of	*US (per cent)*	*China (per cent)*
Exports of goods to	20.7 (rank 1)	9.5 (rank 2)
Imports of goods from	14.4 (rank 2)	20.3 (rank 1)
Exports of services to	27.2 (rank 1)	4.5 (rank 3)
Imports of services from	31.0 (rank 1)	3.8 (rank 4)
FDI inward stocks	41.4 (rank 1)	0.6 (rank n/a)
FDI outward stocks	37.1 (rank 1)	2.4 (rank 5)

Source: Based on European Commission (2016b, 2017).

terms, the EU exports (and imports) relatively more to (from) the US and relatively less to (and from) China' (Hamilton 2016: 371). Moreover, services are more and more closely linked to merchandise trade. For the US and the EU the share of services in value-added exports is above 50 per cent (ibid.: 372). Hence, the transatlantic trade relationship still is by far the most important one for the EU. China's trade surpluses also reflect its current global role as a major assembler of goods, to which lower value is added.

The election of US President Trump in late 2016 has created uncertainty about the country's future trade policy. The EU-US negotiations on a Transatlantic Trade and Investment Partnership (TTIP) came to a halt. The President's first National Trade Policy Agenda pledged 'to expand trade in a way that is freer and fairer for all Americans' and to focus on bilateral rather than multilateral negotiations (United States 2017: 1). The Trump administration 'reject[s] the notion that the United States should, for putative geopolitical advantage, turn a blind eye to unfair trade practices' (ibid.). The President decided to withdraw the US from the Trans-Pacific Partnership (TPP) signed in February 2016, which involves 11 other Pacific Rim countries (without China), and to call for a renegotiation of the North American Free Trade Agreement (NAFTA) with Canada and Mexico, as well as of other free trade agreements (FTAs). Moreover, he triggered 'trade wars' with China, the EU and other trade partners by imposing (or threatening to impose) considerable tariffs on certain goods.

Having joined the World Trade Organization (WTO) only in 2001, China has hitherto lacked the will to assume any global leadership responsibility in trade. In response to Trump's policy, however, President Xi explicitly committed to developing global free trade and investment: 'China stands for concluding open, transparent and win-win regional free trade arrangements and opposes forming exclusive groups that are fragmented in nature' (Xi 2017). In addition to support for the WTO, China aims, according to the 13th Five-Year Plan (2016–2020), (1) to pursue FTAs and free trade trans-boundary projects, such as the 'One Belt, One Road' initiative; (2) to expand the volume of its trade in services; and (3) to turn itself into a 'trader of quality' (China 2016). With the ongoing negotiations on a Regional Comprehensive Economic Partnership (RCEP) – comprising the members of the Association of Southeast Asian Nations (ASEAN) and six countries with which ASEAN has FTAs (including China) – or the China-Japan-South Korea trilateral FTA talks, the Chinese government sought to hedge against the US influence in East Asia, and in particular the TPP (Song & Yuan 2012).

These recent developments in EU-US-China relations raise the question of whether the world is moving towards a new trade order and how the EU has been responding to such shifts. Therefore, this chapter examines to what extent changes in the international trade structure since the 1990s have contributed to adaptations of the EU's trade strategy. It draws on insights from major system-level International Relations (IR) theories – neorealism, neoliberal institutionalism and constructivism – and identifies changes in power constellations, institutions and ideas as potential explanatory factors, to the detriment of domestic issues.

First, this chapter shows that due to power-related, institutional and normative changes, the international trade structure is essentially becoming tripolar, yet without a shared EU-US-Chinese agenda. The global trade regime has since 1995 evolved in a mixed manner: whereas membership has grown and the dispute settlement system was strengthened, multilateral trade negotiations – the Doha Round – have been weakened. The WTO has since come under pressure for reform. Regarding ideas, trade in the 21st century has become not only more comprehensive and deeper but also more contested.

Second, this chapter argues that the EU's trade strategy has changed from 'managed globalization' putting the WTO first, to 'competitive liberalization' based on ambitious bilateral FTAs, and then gradually turned into a more assertive, geo-economic approach focusing on stricter reciprocity, enforcement and value promotion. Overall, ideas of trade liberalization continue to drive EU trade policy, and changes in the relative power positions, moderated by the institutional constraints of the WTO, provide considerable explanatory power both on the multilateral and bilateral levels.

The next section sets out the conceptual framework, followed by an analysis of the transformations of the international trade structure, before the different phases of the EU's changing trade strategy are discussed.

Conceptual framework

International order does not change easily since the organizing rules and institutions of world politics are embedded in wider structures, and opportunities for change arise mainly out of critical junctures such as wars and crises. Given this path dependence, rising states have to deal with legacies of deeply entrenched interests, ideas and institutional arrangements. Trade policy can be seen as a reaction to the constraints and opportunities flowing from the international political economy structures, which are likely to affect the preferences of societal actors, governments and EU institutions. These actors make their decisions based on the interests they have or ideas they hold.

Power, institutions and ideas roughly reflect the central tenets of mainstream IR theories. For neorealism, anarchy is the ordering principle of the international system; it constrains the behaviour of states and renders the relative distribution of power across states important. Neoliberal institutionalism attributes an important role to international institutions in shaping the international structure and mitigating the effects of anarchy. And constructivist IR theory is concerned with how ideas define international structure. As argued by Oriol et al. (2016: 16), 'any structure can be transformed into another one through normative, institutional and power-related changes'.

Drawing on a neorealist perspective, power is best captured by material resources (Waltz 1979: 192), and '[t]he structure of a system changes with changes in the distribution of capabilities across the system's units' (ibid.: 97). International power configurations may differ considerably between distinct policy domains. At the systemic level, economic power resources typically rely on relative shares of gross domestic product (GDP), trade or FDI.

Neoliberal institutionalism defines institutions as 'persistent and connected sets of rules (formal and informal) that prescribe behavioural roles, constrain activity, and shape expectations' (Keohane 1988: 383). International institutions 'can reflect, stabilise and perpetuate a given distribution of power and/or a given perception of legitimacy for actors and ideas' (Oriol et al. 2016: 6). They can thus also become a battlefield of shifts in power and ideas.

Ideas are beliefs held by individuals, describing intersubjective meanings which are to varying degrees shared by different actors, including about the legitimacy of the prevailing international order. Wendt (1999: 309) argues that 'the most important structures in which states are embedded are made of ideas'. According to Woods (1995: 161), 'a state perceives its international economic interests on the basis of a set of ideas or beliefs about how the world economy works and what opportunities exist within it'. Economic ideas such as neoliberalism, (neo)mercantilism or *dependencia* can influence trade policy, as can other, not necessarily commercial ideas, for instance about sustainable development or human rights.

Transformations of the international trade structure

The liberal international order established by the West claimed for many decades to have been based on open markets, rules-based relations, international institutions and progress towards liberal democracy (Ikenberry 2018: 11). This section traces how the international trade structure after the end of the Cold War has been shaped by power-related, institutional and normative factors.

Changes in the economic power constellation

For a long time after WWII, the US acted as a hegemon providing an open multilateral trading system as a collective good. The global power constellation changed significantly with the end of the bipolar structure and the dissolution of the Soviet Union. The immediate post-Cold War world was first characterized by a 'unipolar moment', with the US as the unchallenged superpower. The EU has undergone several rounds of enlargement in 1995, 2004, 2007 and 2013, acquiring more economic capabilities and – like the US – gaining the status of a 'global regulator' (Lavenex et al. 2017). At the beginning of the new millennium, the big states with large populations and often rapid economic growth – such as Brazil, Russia, India and especially China (BRIC) – appeared to be rising as first collective rival to the global economic dominance of the West. These emerging powers have increasingly contested the US' and the EU's ability to individually or jointly shape the international trade order, although the hope (or fear) that the BRIC countries would act as a new bloc has not been fulfilled.

Table 7.2 shows how the relative power positions of the EU, the US and China have changed in this period. In terms of population, China is much bigger than the EU-28 and the US together. The European and American shares in global merchandise trade have slightly declined, while China's share has been quadrupling from 1995 (3.6 per cent) to 2015 (14.8 per cent). The three powers hold now comparable shares in this field. The Chinese proportion of trade in services has been growing as well (largely due to tourism and transport) but is still roughly half as big as the EU or US shares. FDI is heavily dominated by the transatlantic economy with the EU as the largest host and provider of FDI despite considerable growth rates of Chinese investments abroad.

The EU, China and the US are clearly the three largest trade powers. For comparison, Japan's share in world trade in goods and services was in 2015 close to 5 per cent, its share in GDP 4.5 per cent, in FDI outward stock 7.8 per cent and in FDI inward stock only 1 per cent (European Commission 2017). A post-Brexit EU-27 will probably still hold the world's largest share of trade in services, but only the third biggest share of trade in goods and of GDP, behind China and the US.

International institutional changes

The core principles of the multilateral trade regime – already enshrined in the 1947 General Agreement on Tariffs and Trade (GATT) – are liberalization, non-discrimination, reciprocity and the peaceful settlement of trade disputes. These principles have known exceptions, for example the special

Table 7.2 Relative power positions of the EU, the US and China (1995–2015)

Global shares (in per cent) of	*EU-28*			*US*			*China*		
	1995	*2005*	*2015*	*1995*	*2005*	*2015*	*1995*	*2005*	*2015*
Population	8.5	7.6	6.9	4.7	4.5	4.4	21.2	20.0	18.6
GDP (PPP)	24.6	21.8	16.9	20.1	19.6	15.7	5.9	9.9	17.1
Trade in goods	18.8	17.5	14.9	17.4	16.6	14.3	3.6	8.9	14.8
Trade in services	24.0	24.1	22.7	18.6	17.4	16.7	2.4	4.4	8.8
FDI inward stocks	37.3	36.9	37.8	28.2	45.7	33.3	2.8	4.4	7.3
FDI outward stocks	43.1	43.9	48.0	34.2	53.1	37.7	0.4	0.8	6.3

Sources: Population based on World Bank, *World Development Indicators*; GDP and trade data (excluding intra-EU trade) for 2005 and 2015 based on European Commission (2016a, 2017); GDP and trade data (excluding intra-EU trade) for 1995 obtained from DG Trade. To allow for comparison, the EU-28 data are provided for all years.

and differential treatment of developing countries or the conditions under which FTAs are considered WTO compatible. Important changes have occurred in the organization's membership and coalition patterns.

WTO membership has increased from 128 GATT signatories at the end of 1994 to 164 members by the end of 2018, and 22 countries are still in the process of accession. In the WTO, and in the United Nations more generally, there are no agreed definitions of developed and developing countries, except for the least developed countries (LDCs). The vast majority of WTO members, including China, are developing countries by self-definition and therefore expect to benefit from special and differential treatment. The EU and all of its member states are members of the WTO, and with the entry into force of the Lisbon Treaty, all WTO-related aspects of trade policy became explicitly an exclusive competence of the Union.

The WTO is a member-driven, consensus-based organization and coalitions play an important role in the trade negotiations. For a long time, one of the most important informal groupings was the so-called Quad, consisting of the major Western trade powers (the US, the EU, Japan and Canada). Under its leadership, and in particular that of the US-EU tandem, many trade rounds were concluded (Mortensen 2009). In 2003 the G20, a new coalition of developing countries, was pressing for ambitious agricultural reforms in developed countries. With Brazil in the lead, it included for instance Argentina, Chile, China, India, Indonesia, Mexico, Nigeria, Pakistan, the Philippines and South Africa. Garcia-Duran et al. (2016) therefore call the 2003 WTO Ministerial Conference in Cancún a watershed moment of structural change. Moreover, an inner circle comprising the 'new Quad' – the EU, the US, Brazil and India – gained prominence in the Doha Round. Recently acceded members, that is, countries that joined the WTO after 1995 like China (in 2001) or Russia (in 2012), were reluctant to enter new commitments in the Doha Round negotiations because of the liberalization they had undertaken as part of their accession agreements. The expectations that the emerging powers would support the international liberal order and behave as 'responsible stakeholders' have, so far, not been fulfilled (Ahnlid & Elgström 2014). The established Western powers expected the rising powers to share the burden of running, including reforming, the global institutions from which they were benefitting as well. However, in the WTO India turned out to be a rather revisionist power, while Brazil became more supportive, and China reluctantly turned from free riding to a more active participation.

The WTO had introduced new rules for dispute settlement, including more detailed procedures and time frames, an appellate review of panel reports and the abolition of the veto of individual members. As a result, it has become more attractive for members to bring trade disputes to Geneva. The US and the EU have long been the heaviest users of the WTO dispute settlement system. In the period 1995–2016, around 40 per cent of all complaints involved either the US or the EU, and about 25 per cent of all disputes were directly between the two (Leitner & Lester 2017: 173). However, the number of complaints brought by them has declined in recent years, as other WTO members – such as China, India and Brazil – have become more active.

Overall, the world trade regime has since 1995 become quasi-universal in membership and more effective in trade disputes but arguably less so in multilateral trade negotiations (Poletti & De Bièvre 2016). The practice of consensus-based decision-making and of 'single undertaking' negotiations, which in the past facilitated complex package deals, have become highly cumbersome. This has led to calls for reforming the global trading system, for example making greater use of plurilateral agreements in the WTO (Hoekman & Mavroidis 2015).

Ideas-related changes

Goldstein (1989: 32) argues that 'policy change depends not only on new political coalitions but also on the ideas they carry and the institutional structures they meet'. The demand for change must be met by a supply of ideas on how to restructure politics or international institutions. The beliefs of policy-makers of which areas of trade should be liberalized or protected and how have undergone changes too. The post-WWII trade regime was essentially a liberal international economic order or what Ruggie (1982: 393) called 'embedded liberalism': multilateralism predicated upon domestic interventionism. Despite enormous differences among countries over the precise policies this implied, the fact 'that multilateralism and the quest for domestic stability were coupled and even conditioned by one another reflected the shared legitimacy of a set of social objectives to which the industrial world had moved' (ibid.: 398).

At the end of the Cold War, the ideas of market economy, trade liberalization and liberal democracy seemed to celebrate a worldwide triumph. However, the BRICs' levels of trade protection are still much higher and they have continued to pursue *dirigiste* models of development. The combination of transnationally integrated capitalism and a commanding role reserved for state and quasi-state entities in organizing the economy lends them the character of 'integrated state capitalism', with often authoritarian, illiberal political systems (Stephen 2014). As international institutions may come to reflect the preferences of the emerging powers, 'the liberal content of global governance is being challenged from within' (ibid.: 914). China has become the world's most targeted country in anti-dumping investigations and still lacks recognition as market economy by major trade powers. In December 2016, the Chinese government launched WTO disputes against the EU and the US for continuing to treat it as a non-market economy despite the expiry of certain clauses of its Accession Protocol. Furthermore, China has engaged in the creation of new international institutions such as the New Development Bank, the Asian Infrastructure Investment Bank, RCEP or the Belt and Road Initiative. These China-led initiatives can be seen as parallel structures and potential rivals to existing multilateral institutions.

The global trade agenda shifted from traditional 'at-the-border' measures such as tariffs or quotas to 'behind-the-border' issues that regulate competition (for instance competition policy, FDI or government procurement) and address market failure (for instance core labour standards or environmental protection). With the establishment of the WTO, the GATT was, among others, supplemented by the General Agreement on Trade in Services (GATS), the Agreement on Trade-related Aspects of Intellectual Property Rights (TRIPs), a first Agreement on Agriculture and agreements dealing with technical barriers to trade or sanitary and phytosanitary rules. For the EU and the US, these achievements were not far-reaching enough and they sought to promote 'WTO+' issues by other means. Their FTAs have progressively incorporated human rights, social and environmental norms that do not seem directly related to trade. Since the EU perceives itself not only as an economic community but also as a community of values, it has developed the most far-reaching policy of linking trade instruments to non-trade concerns, such as political conditionality. Yet, developing countries and emerging economies have not much appreciated these issue linkages in most cases, and the EU has hardly enforced them on big powers. Unlike the EU and the US, China pursues an unconditional aid, investment and trade policy as far as political values are concerned. This is in line with its foreign policy principles regarding the respect for sovereignty and non-interference in domestic affairs.

On a bilateral level, EU and US regulatory influence in emerging economies is mainly based on co-optation, for instance through transgovernmental networks, rather than conditionality (Lavenex et al. 2017: 7–8). Yet, if mega-regional trade agreements like TPP, TTIP or the less ambitious RCEP and plurilateral agreements like the Trade in Services Agreement (TiSA) were successfully concluded, they would likely change the multilateral trading system by setting rules for a substantial part of world trade. Moreover, in the new millennium, a new thinking about global value chains has been gaining ground to grasp the changing re-import/re-export patterns of 'supply-chain trade' (Gereffi 2014). The traditional interest competition between export-oriented and import-competing sectors has been expanded to import-dependent firms, raising new challenges for trade policy as well as consumer concerns over production standards abroad. By contrast, some of the emerging powers have been pursuing rather neo-mercantilist policies, characterized by selective multilateralism and protectionism. Such a competitive perspective views foreign economic relations more as a 'zero-sum game' in which one side's gain is another's relative loss and in which the idea of geo-economics – the geostrategic use of economic power – easily gains popularity (Wigell 2016). Under the Trump administration, US trade policy has also been shifting in this direction, both in bilateral trade relations and in WTO negotiations and disputes.

To conclude, since 1995 the international trade structure has been transformed through power-related, institutional and normative changes.

Throughout the 1990s and early 2000s, the West's economic power used to be unmatched and the ideas of free market economy and broadening trade liberalization wielded incomparable traction. Yet, the pre-eminence of the transatlantic economy has been increasingly challenged by the rise of Asia, rival coalitions and alternative visions of the world order, despite the simultaneous ascendancy of the EU as a global (trade) actor. The emerging trade structure is largely tripolar with the US, the EU and China as prevalent powers. The next section analyses how these transformations have affected the EU's trade strategy.

EU trade strategy in response to the structural changes

The development of the EU's trade strategy since the establishment of the WTO can be divided into at least three distinct phases, as set out in the subsections below. Each subsection discusses the multilateral trade relations and the EU's bilateral ties with the US and China in specific phases by highlighting power-related, institutional and ideational factors.

Managing globalization by multilateral means (1995–2003)

In the wake of the collapse of communism, the worldwide embrace of neoliberalism, followed by the spreading of anti-globalization protests, the EU pursued a policy of 'managed globalization', aiming at the adoption of global rules and the strengthening of international regimes (Abdelal & Meunier 2010). The power constellation in this period contributed to the EU's performance as a proactive, reformist leader in the WTO (Dee 2015: 72–79). At the first WTO Ministerial Conference in Singapore in 1996, the EU strongly advocated the launch of a new multilateral trade round with a comprehensive agenda. Negotiations in the field of agriculture and services were already scheduled for 2000 as part of the 'in-built agenda' of the Uruguay Round agreements. Considering this institutional constraint, the EU expected a comprehensive round to allow it to negotiate a package deal that could balance any future agricultural concessions. In line with its strategy of 'managing globalization', the EU proposed the so-called Singapore issues (competition, FDI, public procurement, trade facilitation) and rules on core labour standards, environment and consumer safety. However, most of these ideas met with fierce resistance from developing countries, and a new round failed to take off at the 1999 WTO Ministerial Conference in Seattle.

To underline the priority of multilateralism, Trade Commissioner Pascal Lamy had in 1999 announced a moratorium on new EU bilateral trade negotiations for the Round's duration (Melo Aruja 2016: 32–40). In 2001, in the shadow of the 9/11 attacks, the Ministerial Conference in Doha finally launched a new trade round, and the EU supported the development focus of the Doha Round. It propagated a 'round for free' for the LDCs and presented its 'Everything-but-Arms' initiative that unilaterally grants all LDCs duty-free and quota-free access to the EU's internal market. Moreover, and also in view of its Eastern enlargement, the EU carried out a reform of the Common Agricultural Policy (CAP) in 2003 that made farm support less trade distorting by decoupling direct payments from production requirements. The idea of agricultural exceptionalism deserving state assistance has increasingly been eroded also in the EU (Daugbjerg & Swinbank 2009). Nevertheless, the 2003 Ministerial Conference in Cancún broke up over serious divergences over agriculture and the Singapore issues. It 'marked the end of bilateral co-hegemony in multilateral trade' (Mortensen 2009: 86).

Tariffs in the transatlantic economy are generally very low and the most significant impediments to trade and investment are regulatory barriers – although in certain sectors tariff peaks may have persisted and even relatively low tariffs can have 'knock-on effects' down the value chains (Hamilton 2016: 372). Despite shared neoliberal ideas, the regulatory differences – reflecting different societal preferences and risk assessment approaches – have generated many EU-US trade disputes at the WTO. The completion of the EU's internal market served as the initial impetus for a transatlantic dialogue on regulatory standards. A series of initiatives followed, ranging from the 1990 Transatlantic Declaration, the 1995 New Transatlantic Agenda to the 1998 Transatlantic Economic Partnership and the 2007 Transatlantic Economic Council. These initiatives resulted in mutual recognition agreements and soft law instruments, but overall remained rather limited in scope (see Takács 2014).

In the 1990s, the EU's economic relations with China were still rather asymmetrical in terms of relative shares of GDP, trade and FDI (see Table 7.2). China's foreseeable ascent prompted the EU to 'set itself the overriding general objective of promoting the fullest possible Chinese involvement in the international arena', including accession to the WTO (European Commission 1995). For this purpose, the EU portrayed itself as a 'champion of multilateralism' and 'liberal trade power' (Michalski & Pan 2017: 618). This policy was also inspired by 'the well-founded belief that human rights tend to be better understood and better protected in societies open to the free flow of trade, investment, people, and ideas' (European Commission 1995). The necessity for the EU to position itself in order to enhance its global competitiveness was also emphasized (ibid.). The Chinese accession negotiations to the WTO were hampered by many setbacks, including EU sanctions in response to the 1989 massacre of Tiananmen Square.

Re-orientation from multi- to bilateralism (2004–2008)

The EU tried to accommodate China and the other new powers within the decision-making structure of the WTO as well as in other global institutions (Garcia-Duran et al. 2016). Its role became that of a defender and pusher (Dee 2015: 79–82). The EU agreed to drop the idea of the Singapore issues (except for trade facilitation) and to phase out export subsidies for agricultural products. Having reached the limits of what its member states could accept, the EU attempted to act as mediator instead of leader in the Doha Round (Ahnlid & Elgström 2014: 83–84). In July 2008, a dispute between the US, on the one hand, and India, supported by China, on the other hand, over a special safeguard mechanism for developing countries to counter import surges in food spoiled an agreement. These setbacks led the EU to question the 'Lamy doctrine' and refocus attention on the bilateral level, where it enjoys more bargaining leverage to incorporate 'WTO+' issues (such as the Singapore issues) into FTAs.

Under the George W. Bush administration, the US engaged in 'competitive liberalization' by concluding ambitious bilateral FTAs in Latin America and Asia. Since both the US and the EU have major stakes in third markets, neither can afford to ignore the other's policy. 'Competitive interdependence incorporates an inbuilt dynamic in which the US and the EU necessarily compete, whether at the multilateral or regional level or both' (Sbragia 2010: 379). By contrast, the benefits and costs of a transatlantic free trade area, in particular whether it would constitute a threat to the multilateral trading system, have long been subject to a controversial debate. The idea had been floated in 1995 by the German Minister of Foreign Affairs and then again in 2006 by the German Chancellor (Hayes 2015: 114). However, it did not find the necessary political support at the time.

As part of the EU's renewed 2005 Lisbon Strategy, trade was to primarily contribute to growth and jobs. In 2006, Trade Commissioner Peter Mandelson launched the new strategy 'Global Europe' that singled out future FTA partners based on their market potential (economic size and growth), level of protection against EU export interests and negotiations with EU competitors (European Commission 2006a: 9). 'Global Europe' envisaged in particular bloc-to-bloc agreements with ASEAN, Mercosur and the Gulf Cooperation Council, as well as bilateral deals with important trading partners such as South Korea, India and Russia. Due to their increasing integration into global value chains, FTAs with Asian countries were particularly important for import-dependent firms in Europe (Eckhardt & Poletti 2015). The EU-Korea FTA, the EU's first FTA with an Asian country, was negotiated between 2007 and 2009 after the US had concluded negotiations with Korea in spring 2007. Moreover, the EU began negotiations with India in 2007 and with individual members of ASEAN as of 2010.

The EU's relationship with China became gradually less asymmetric because of China's rapid growth, while at the same time the Chinese policy grew more self-confident. With the establishment of a strategic partnership in 2003 EU-China relations entered a short 'honeymoon period'. The EU expected 'China to contribute to global stability by gradually taking on more responsibility, commensurate with its political and economic weight, both in the bilateral and the multilateral context' (European Commission 2003: 8). The Chinese government published its first own strategic policy chapter on the EU, in which it stipulated the objective to deepen 'trade under the principles of mutual benefit, reciprocity and consultation on an equal basis' (China 2003).

The disillusionment for China came with the EU's failure to lift the 1989 arms embargo in 2005. In a separate Communication dedicated to China, issued at the same time as the 'Global Europe' trade strategy, the European Commission (2006b: 7) complained that China's incomplete implementation of WTO obligations and new barriers to market access were 'preventing a genuinely reciprocal trading relationship'. It proposed negotiations on a Partnership and Cooperation Agreement (PCA), which both sides embarked upon in 2007. However, relations soon soured over economic and human rights issue, and the PCA talks have in effect been on hold since mid-2009 (Smith 2016: 85–88).

A geo-economic turn (as of 2009) and the 'Trump effect' (as of 2017)

In the WTO, the EU reluctantly agreed to relax the 'single undertaking' practice in favour of an 'early harvest' approach. At the 2013 Bali Ministerial Conference, the Agreement on Trade Facilitation was concluded. The EU has also joined the plurilateral TiSA negotiations. The 2015 Nairobi package contained a series of decisions on agriculture, such as a commitment to abolish export subsidies, and on issues related to LDCs. As trade policy started taking place increasingly outside the WTO's institutional framework, the EU implemented a two-pronged entrenchment strategy by hardening its position in the Doha Round negotiations, while simultaneously engaging in efforts to conclude comprehensive bilateral trade agreements with key trade partners (Garcia-Duran et al. 2016: 94).

In reaction to the global economic and financial crisis, the EU adopted in 2010 the 'Europe 2020' strategy, which replaced the Lisbon Strategy for the new decade. 'Europe 2020' aimed at smart, sustainable and inclusive growth to improve Europe's competitiveness. In this context, an update of the 'Global Europe' strategy was presented by Trade Commissioner Karel De Gucht. His 'Trade, Growth and World Affairs' (TGWA) strategy emphasized reciprocity and that the EU's trade and foreign policies should be 'mutually reinforcing', encouraging partners to promote the respect of human rights, democracy, the rule of law, labour and environmental standards (European Commission 2010: 15). With the entry into force of the Lisbon Treaty at the end of 2009, the European Parliament acquired more powers in trade, FDI was added to the EU's competence and the common commercial policy was placed within the EU's broader objectives of external action.

For the first time, the US and Japan were among the target partners of TGWA (European Commission 2010: 11). Negotiations with both started in 2013 and could be interpreted as an EU 'balancing act' in view of the TPP negotiations, which the US agreed to join in 2008, as well as President Obama's 'pivot' to Asia. This geo-economic view was reinforced by

Russia's annexation of Crimea in March 2014 and the prominence gained by the so-called Islamic State in the Middle East. TTIP would strengthen the transatlantic alliance of liberal democracies with open markets and allow the West to shape the future regulatory global framework for trade and investment before the 'window of opportunity' was closing. As Hamilton (2016: 367) argues succinctly:

> For more than two centuries, either Europeans or Americans, or both together, have been accustomed to setting global rules. [...] Yet, with the rise of new powers, the resurgence of older powers and the emergence of serious challenges at home, Europeans and Americans now face the prospect of becoming rule-takers rather than rule-makers, unless they act more effectively together to ensure that high standards prevail.

However, the TTIP negotiations caused an unprecedented debate about trade policy. Domestic opposition in the EU and to a lesser extent in the US came primarily from non-traditional trade actors because of the extraordinary level of cross-investment between the two economies and the importance of global value chains (Young 2016). Concerns about regulatory differences and fears that through the investor-to-state dispute settlement (ISDS) mechanism big business could sue EU member states for compensation outside the normal judicial process, if its investor rights were curtailed by public policies, mobilized in particular civil society groups. Amid this increasing controversy over TTIP, and at the half-way juncture of the 'Europe 2020' strategy, the new Trade Commissioner Cecilia Malmström presented her 2015 'Trade for All' strategy, which has to some extent taken on board demands of critics (European Commission 2015). To increase transparency, the Commission has been publishing virtually all EU positions, and it proposed to replace the ISDS mechanism by a new Investment Court System that would work with publicly appointed judges and clear rules. The first agreements which incorporated this new approach were the Comprehensive Economic and Trade Agreement (CETA) with Canada and the EU-Vietnam FTA. Furthermore, the EU's trade policy would clearly protect the right to regulate and promote 'European and universal standards and values alongside core economic interests' (ibid.: 18).

The global power shifts led the Trump administration to consider 'a new trade policy that defends American sovereignty, enforces U.S. trade laws, uses American leverage to open markets abroad, and negotiates new trade agreements that are fairer and more effective' (United States 2017: 7). With his 'America First' approach, the President has promised to protect heavy industries, bring back manufacturing jobs to America and to fight 'unfair' trade deficits and currency manipulations. He seems to believe that exports are good for the US economy, while imports are bad, and that the US can make more effective use of its market power in bilateral trade negotiations. Such a parochial trade policy sits squarely with global value chains. In June

2018 the US began applying tariffs on certain steel and aluminium imports from the EU and other countries, claiming a potential threat to impair national security. The EU responded by retaliatory tariffs on US products and a challenge in WTO dispute settlement. In late July 2018, both sides agreed to negotiate (*Financial Times* 2018a), and the US continued its 'tit-for-tat' tariff escalation with China instead. Four months later, at the margins of the G20 summit in Buenos Aires, the American and Chinese Presidents agreed to suspend new tariffs in a temporary truce and to enter negotiations as well (*Financial Times* 2018b).

The US President's 'economic nationalist' rhetoric and seemingly suspicious views of the WTO, which includes blocking the appointment of judges to the appellate body over concerns of 'judicial activism', contrast with the EU's multilateral, rules-based approach as well as with China's new, more pronounced pro-globalization discourse. The US withdrawal from TPP, the renegotiation of NAFTA and other FTAs as well as the 'freezing' of TTIP have had the side effect of speeding up other EU trade negotiations, for instance the conclusion of an FTA with Japan and the modernization of the agreement with Mexico. Moreover, together with a group of like-minded countries, the EU started working towards a reform of the WTO. As a result, 'the overall direction of EU trade policy contrasts sharply with the defensive and destructive attitude taken by the US' and opens the opportunity for 'the EU to claim the title of leader of the world trading system' (*Financial Times* 2017). However, whether in the future the EU will instead cooperate more closely with China to potentially replace the former transatlantic leadership remains doubtful.

The European Commission's TGWA strategy pointed to the persistence of important market access barriers in China: 'in standards and regulations, services, investment and public procurement, as well as insufficient enforcement of intellectual property rights, [...] forced transfers of technology and granting local producers preferential access to raw materials' (European Commission 2010: 11). Not surprisingly, China has become the EU's most frequent target for trade defence measures. In 2015 the Chinese government released its state-led industrial policy plan 'Made in China 2025' that seeks to make China dominant in global high-tech manufacturing, leading developed countries to push back against certain practices (McBride 2018).

As the PCA negotiations with China reached a dead-end, talks on a Comprehensive Agreement on Investment, the EU's first investment-only agreement, were instead launched in 2013. These negotiations may well serve as a test case for an FTA in the longer run, but the big differences in legal frameworks, economic models and values pose considerable challenges (Hallinan 2016). The Organization for Economic Cooperation and Development (OECD) ranks China the fourth-most restrictive country in 2016 in an index which measures restrictions on FDI in 62 countries, including all OECD and G20 countries (see OECD 2018). The rapid surge of Chinese FDI in Europe and the US has stirred additional concerns, for instance about sensitive technology disclosures (Meunier 2014), and the EU has recently set up a screening mechanism for incoming FDI.

Furthermore, as a self-declared developing country, for many years China had been the biggest beneficiary of the EU's unilateral Generalized System of Preferences. As of 2015, the EU removed China from this list, considering that it no longer needed preferential market access. The 'Trade for All' strategy issued in the same year remains silent about how the EU intends to further engage with China. Instead, the European Commission and High Representative (2016: 2) proposed elements for a new strategy on China which promotes the idea of 'reciprocity, a level playing field and fair competition across all areas of co-operation'. Moreover, they encourage China to play a more active role at the WTO, 'assuming responsibilities in line with the benefits it draws from an open trading system and strengthening the ambition of these initiatives', including respect for international law and universal values (ibid.: 14–15).

China updated its EU strategy in 2014, referring to the Union as a 'strategic partner in China's efforts to pursue peaceful development and multipolarity of the world' and underlining that 'disagreements and frictions on issues of value such as human rights as well as economic and trade issues ... should be properly handled through dialogue in the spirit of equality and mutual respect' (China 2014). Hence, the EU and China are also competing on whose values and norms will shape the international order (Michalski & Pan 2017: 625) as well as on regulatory preferences (Lavenex et al. 2017: 17).

Conclusions: a more assertive EU trade strategy

This chapter asked to what extent changes in the international trade structure since the 1990s have contributed to adaptations of the EU's trade strategy. It showed that in the 21st century, shifts in power, institutions and ideas have been transforming the international trade structure into an emerging order that is largely tripolar, although the EU, the US and China are not pursuing a shared agenda. In response, the EU's trade strategy has changed from 'managed globalization' putting the WTO first, to a competitiveness-driven re-orientation from multilateralism to bilateralism, culminating more recently in a geo-economic turn. This approach puts more stress on the conclusion of strategically important trade agreements and on reciprocity, enforcement of commitments and promotion of rules and values. The jury is still out on how the seemingly neo-mercantilist trade policy of US President Trump will play out in bilateral relations as well as in the WTO. Despite a gradual diffusion of power away from the West, there seem to be no grand alternatives to an international liberal order led by authoritarian capitalist states like China or Russia that would appeal to the rest of the world (Ikenberry 2018: 23). The future order might well become more volatile, reflecting multiple voices and values.

Taking a system-centred approach, this chapter found that all three factors derived from mainstream IR theories – power, institutions and ideas – help explain the transformation of the international trade structure and the EU's changing strategy. Ideas of trade liberalization persist as drivers of EU trade policy, while in the post-Cold War era its strategy has primarily been shaped by relative power constellations, moderated by the institutional constraints of the WTO. Given that trade policy is embedded in global rules and international negotiations are essential for market access, this finding may be less surprising.

Regarding continuity, the transatlantic economy is still the EU's most important trade relationship. Paradoxically, today the EU wants to conclude an FTA with the US but the US seems no longer interested in TTIP, while China wants to negotiate an FTA with the EU but not vice versa. Regarding discontinuity, US-EU leadership in the WTO has waned and the Quad has not yet been replaced by a new coalition able and willing to steer multilateral negotiations. The global trade regime has come to rely more on bilateral (as well as plurilateral and mega-regional) FTAs. In the emerging tripolar trade structure, the EU has adopted a more geo-economic approach with a stronger pursuit of both interests and values at the same time, in line with the 'principled pragmatism' of its Global Strategy (European External Action Service 2016). The transformation of power structures might well require more flexible formats of cooperation in the future.

References

Abdelal, R. & S. Meunier (2010) 'Managed Globalization: Doctrine, Practice and Promise', *Journal of European Public Policy* 17(3), 350–367.

Ahnlid, A. & O. Elgström (2014) 'Challenging the European Union: The Rising Powers and the USA in the Doha Round', *Contemporary Politics* 20(1), 77–89.

Anderson, J., G.J. Ikenberry & T. Risse (eds.) (2009) *The End of the West? Crisis and Change in the Atlantic Order*, Ithaca: Cornell University Press.

China (2003) 'China's EU Policy Chapter', Beijing, Ministry of Foreign Affairs, October. Available at: http://china.org.cn/e-white/20050817/index.htm.

——— (2014) 'China's Policy Chapter on the EU: Deepen the China-EU Strategic Partnership for Mutual Benefit and Win-win Cooperation', Beijing, Ministry of Foreign Affairs, 4 April. Available at: www.fmprc.gov.cn/mfa_eng/wjdt_665385/wjzcs/t1143406.shtml.

——— (2016) *The 13th Five-Year Plan for Economic and Social Development of the People's Republic of China (2016–2020)*, Central Committee of the Communist Party of China, Beijing. Available at: http://en.ndrc.gov.cn/newsrelease/201612/P020161207645765233498.pdf.

Daugbjerg, C. & A. Swinbank (2009) *Ideas, Institutions and Trade: The WTO and the Curious Role of EU Farm Policy in Trade Liberalization*, Oxford: Oxford University Press.

Dee, M. (2015) *The European Union in a Multipolar World: World Trade, Global Governance and the Case of the WTO*, London: Palgrave Macmillan.

Eckhardt, J. & A. Poletti (2016) 'The Politics of Global Value Chains: Import-dependent Firms and EU-Asia Trade Agreements', *Journal of European Public Policy* 23(10), 1543–1562.

European Commission (1995) *A Long-Term Policy for China Europe Relations*, COM(1995) 279 final, Brussels, 5 July.

——— (2003) *A Maturing Partnership – Shared Interests and Challenges in EU-China Relations*, COM(2003) 533 final, 10 September.

——— (2006a) *Global Europe: Competing in the World: A Contribution to the EU's Growth and Jobs Strategy*, COM(2006) 567 final, Brussels, 4 October.

——— (2006b) *EU-China: Closer Partners, Growing Responsibilities*, COM(2006) 631 final, Brussels, 24 October.

——— (2010) *Trade, Growth and World Affairs: Trade Policy as a Core Component of the EU's 2020 Strategy*, COM(2010) 612 final, Brussels, 9 November.

——— (2015) *Trade for All: Towards a More Responsible Trade and Investment Policy*, COM(2015) 497, Brussels, 14 October.

——— (2016a) *DG Trade Statistical Guide*, Brussels.

——— (2016b) 'Top Trading Partners', *DG Trade*, Brussels. Available at: http://trade.ec.europa.eu/doclib/docs/2006/september/tradoc_122530.pdf.

——— (2017) *DG Trade Statistical Guide*, Brussels, June.

European Commission & High Representative (2016) *Elements for a New EU Strategy on China*, JOIN(2016) 30 final, Brussels, 22 June.

European External Action Service (2016) *Shared Vision, Common Action: A Stronger Europe – A Global Strategy for the European Union's Foreign and Security Policy*, Brussels, June.

Financial Times (2017) 'Trump's Trade Follies Give Brussels an Open Door', 6 September.

——— (2018a) 'US and EU Declare Ceasefire to Trade War', 26 July.

——— (2018b) 'Trump Offers Xi Tariffs Reprieve in Trade War Ceasefire', 2 December.

Garcia-Duran, P., M. Millet & J. Orbie (2016) 'EU Trade Policy Reaction to the BIC: From Accommodation to Entrenchment', in E. Barbé Izuel, O. Costa & R. Kissack (eds.), *EU Policy Responses to a Shifting Multilateral System*, Basingstoke: Palgrave Macmillan, 93–114.

Gereffi, G. (2014) 'Global Value Chains in a post-Washington Consensus World', *Review of International Political Economy* 21(1), 9–37.

Goldstein, J. (1989) 'The Impact of Ideas on Trade Policy', *International Organization* 43(1), 31–71.

Hallinan, D. (2016) 'The EU-China Bilateral Investment Treaty: A Challenging First Test of the EU's Evolving BIT Model', *China-EU Law Journal* 5(1–2), 31–53.

Hamilton, D. (2016) 'Rule-Makers or Rule-Takers? An American Perspective on Transatlantic Trade and Investment Partnership', *European Foreign Affairs Review* 21(3), 365–382.

Hayes, E. (2015) 'TTIP: Transatlantic Free Trade at Last?' *Global Affairs* 1(2), 113–120.

Hoekman, B.M. & P.C. Mavroidis (2015) 'WTO 'à la carte' or 'menu du jour'? Assessing the Case for More Plurilateral Agreements', *The European Journal of International Law* 26(2), 319–343.

Ikenberry, G.J. (2018) 'The End of Liberal International Order?' *International Affairs* 94(1), 7–23.

Keohane, R.O. (1988) 'International Institutions: Two Approaches', *International Studies Quarterly* 32(4), 379–396.

Kupchan, C.A. (2012) *No One's World: The West, the Rising Rest, and the Coming Global Turn*, New York: Oxford University Press.

Lavenex, S., I. Krizic & O. Serrano (2017) 'EU and US Regulatory Power under Strain? Emerging Countries and the Limits of External Governance', *European Foreign Affairs Review* 22(2/1), 1–18.

Leitner, K. & S. Lester (2017) 'WTO Dispute Settlement 1995–2016: A Statistical Analysis', *Journal of International Economic Law* 20(1), 171–182.

McBride, J. (2018) 'Is "Made in China 2025" a Threat to Global Trade?' New York, Council on Foreign Relations, 2 August. Available at: www.cfr.org/backgrounder/made-china-2025-threat-global-trade.

Melo Aruja, B.A. (2016) *The EU Deep Trade Agenda*, Oxford: Oxford University Press.

Meunier, S. (2014) 'A Faustian Bargain or Just a Good Bargain? Chinese Foreign Direct Investment and Politics in Europe', *Asia Europe Journal* 12(1), 143–158.

Michalski, A. & Z. Pan (2017) 'Role Dynamics in a Structured Relationship: The EU-China Strategic Partnership', *Journal of Common Market Studies* 55(3), 611–627.

Mortensen, J.L. (2009) 'The World Trade Organization and the European Union', in K.E. Jørgensen (ed.), *The European Union and International Organizations*, London: Routledge, 80–100.

OECD (2018) *FDI Regulatory Restrictiveness Index*. Available at: www.oecd.org/investment/fdiindex.htm.

Oriol, C., R. Kissack & E. Barbé (2016) 'Accommodating or Entrenching? How the EU Is Dealing with Changes in the Multilateral System', in E. Barbé, C. Costa & R. Kissack (eds.), *EU Policy Responses to a Shifting Multilateral System*, London: Palgrave Macmillan, 1–23.

Poletti, A. & D. De Bièvre (2016) *From Disputes to Cooperation at the World Trade Organization*, Essex: European Consortium for Political Research Press.

Ruggie, J.G. (1982) 'International Regimes, Transactions, and Change: Embedded Liberalism in the Postwar Economic Order', *International Organization* 36(2), 379–415.

Sbragia, A. (2010) 'The EU, the US, and Trade Policy: Competitive Interdependence in the Management of Globalization', *Journal of European Public Policy* 17(3), 368–382.

Smith, M. (2016) 'EU Diplomacy and the EU-China Strategic Relationship: Framing, Negotiation and Management', *Cambridge Review of International Affairs* 29(1), 78–98.

Song, G. & Yuan, W. (2012) 'China's Free Trade Agreement Strategies', *The Washington Quarterly* 35(4), 107–119.

Stephen, M.D. (2014) 'Rising Powers, Global Capitalism and Liberal Global Governance: A Historical Materialist Account of the BRICs Challenge', *European Journal of International Relations* 20(4), 912–938.

Takács, T. (2014) 'Transatlantic Regulatory Cooperation in Trade: Objectives, Challenges and Instruments for Economic Governance', in E. Fahey & D. Curtin (eds.), *A Transatlantic Community of Law: Legal Perspectives on the Relationship between the EU and US Legal Orders*, Cambridge: Cambridge University Press, 158–185.

United States (2017) *2017 Trade Policy Agenda and 2016 Annual Report of the President of the United States on the Trade Agreements Program*, Washington, Office of the United States Trade Representative.
Waltz, K.N. (1979) *Theory of International Politics*, New York: Random House.
Wendt, A. (1999) *Social Theory of International Politics*, Cambridge: Cambridge University Press.
Wigell, M. (2016) "Conceptualizing Regional Powers' Geoeconomic Strategies: Neo-imperialism, Neo-mercantilism, Hegemony, and Liberal Institutionalism', *Asia Europe Journal* 14(2), 135–151.
Woods, N. (1995) 'Economic Ideas and International Relations: Beyond Rational Neglect', *International Studies Quarterly* 39(2), 161–180.
World Bank. (database) *World Development Indicators*.
Xi, J. (2017) 'President Xi's Speech to Davos in Full', *World Economic Forum*, 17 January. Available at: www.weforum.org/agenda/2017/01/full-text-of-xi-jinping-keynote-at-the-world-economic-forum.
Young, A.R. (2016) "Not Your Parents' Trade Politics: The Transatlantic Trade and Investment Partnership Negotiations', *Review of International Political Economy* 21(3), 345–378.

8 A disorderly retreat from global governance? US trade and investment policies in the Trump era

Sophie Meunier

Introduction

The election of a new President of the United States (US) usually brings about reset in a variety of policy domains, particularly when the President hails from the opposing party to his predecessor. Reset, however, is most often accompanied by continuity, especially in foreign relations. More so than on domestic issues, there has traditionally been bipartisan consensus on the need to preserve the role of the United States in the world and the desirability, at least rhetorically, of promoting democracy and human rights abroad. When it comes to international economic relations, the central tenets of American strategy have been to open and safeguard the world for American companies and to design and defend a rules-based liberal international economic order built on governance by multilateral institutions.

The presidency of Donald J. Trump, however, has been anything but traditional. He was elected in part thanks to his blustering, norm-shattering populist nationalist rhetoric on international economic relations. A clear, consistent trade policy strategy proved difficult to decipher in his first year in office, in part because of the competition between two factions of advisers – the 'globalists' and the 'nationalists'. This uncertainty was also created by Trump's seemingly impulsive positions, often at odds with established policies of the State Department and United States Trade Representative office (USTR), which have rattled long-standing alliances and sometimes contradicted one another. Trump's second year in office, however, revealed the stark protectionist turn taken by American trade policy, in rhetoric as well as in action.

The populist nationalist strategy has created major discontinuities in postwar American policy toward trade and investment by challenging the multilateral trade order and even the value of trade openness, resorting instead to a transactional zero-sum view of a world where trade gains are achieved only by tit-for-tat reciprocity on a bilateral basis. Some of the early actions by the Trump administration have included withdrawing the US

An earlier version was prepared for the Conference 'A New Order or No Order? Continuity and Discontinuity in the EU-China-US Relationship', College of Europe, Bruges, 29 September 2017. Thank you to Saori Shibata and to workshop participants for comments, and to Duncan Freeman for great suggestions. Thanks also to Lori Bougher for research assistance.

from the Trans-Pacific Partnership (TPP) negotiations, suspending the negotiations for the Transatlantic Trade and Investment Partnership (TTIP), renegotiating the North American Free Trade Agreement (NAFTA), and even suggesting the cancellation of existing agreements, such as the United States-Korea Free Trade Agreement (KORUS). The Trump administration also unilaterally imposed tariffs, floated the idea of leaving the World Trade Organization (WTO), and furthered restrictions of foreign direct investment (FDI). The rhetoric has been particularly harsh toward China but combative as well toward the European Union (EU).

The contemporary international trade and investment policy of the United States has proven challenging to analyze through traditional political economy models emphasizing cleavages along factoral and sectoral lines and the influence of particular interest groups (e.g. Milner 1989; Rogowski 1989; Busch & Reinhardt 2000; Hiscox 2002). According to these models, trade policy usually reflects the preferences of diverse domestic groups, such as exporters and trade unions, which are balanced and aggregated through a variety of institutional and political structures. Having defined its preferred policy positions, the US administration then bargains with other countries, both bilaterally and multilaterally through the WTO. The final agreements are the product of these bargains, which involve some give-and-take and some reciprocity. For the first two years of the Trump administration, however, neither the politics, nor the institutions through which this aggregation takes place reveal which preferences are driving policy. Many US businesses, big and small, have been startled by changes they did not lobby for. Republicans have usually been more pro-trade, pro-big business, and more anti-unions than their Democratic counterparts. The nationalist, protectionist turn of a faction of the Republican Party has taken many by surprise and has put traditional domestic alliances and coalitions in disarray.

This chapter takes stock of how US trade policy fits within a more uncertain, more anti-globalization, and more multipolar world where the EU and China are now almost equal actors. The first section examines the structural power of the US in international economic relations. The second explores the recent populist American backlash against globalization, the protectionist impulses of President Trump, and the growing bipartisan consensus on protectionism. The third section analyzes the complex challenges of a trade war with China. The last section questions the evolution of the liberal international economic order and asks whether the apparent retreat of the US from global governance will result in the EU or China or a combination of both to take over the management of the international trade and investment system.

American structural power in the world economy

Since World War II (WWII), the United States has been the leading player in the international economy. For several decades it acted as a hegemon in setting up and sustaining the postwar international economic regimes, from the

Bretton Woods institutions to the WTO, driven by US-initiated agreements and the pressure of American multinational companies (Keohane 1984).

Today the American economy is still the largest as measured by nominal gross domestic product (GDP) (second largest in Purchasing Power Parity). The rapid growth of the BRIC countries (Brazil, Russia, India and China) at the turn of the 21st century reduced the relative share of American GDP in global GDP. Yet the US remains for now the leading innovator in the world, and its large technology corporations – such as Apple, Google, and Facebook – are dominant, especially in the 'new economy'. As for the dollar, it remains the world's primary reserve currency.

In trade, the US is one of the world's three main players, alongside China and the EU, as shown in Table 8.1. In 2016, the US was the first importer of goods and services in the world, and the first exporter of services and second exporter of goods (World Trade Organization 2017). Its main trade partners are China, the EU, and Canada. In FDI, the US was the world's top host and home country of FDI flows in 2016 (UNCTAD 2017). The US Commerce Department estimated in 2016 that inward FDI was responsible for 12 million jobs in the US – 8.5 per cent of the labor force (Richards & Schaefer 2016).

The transatlantic economic relationship, in terms of both trade and investment, is the backbone of the world economy. It is the largest and wealthiest market in the world, accounting for 50 per cent of the world's GDP and 30 per cent of world trade (European Union External Action Service 2017). The EU is a particularly important market for the American economy: 44 out of the 50 US states export more to the EU than to China. The transatlantic economy is also an overall balanced relationship, as shown in the table above. By contrast, the relationship between the US and China is very imbalanced and characterized by a massive American trade deficit of over USD 275 billion as of October 2017.

Moreover, the US economy is far less dependent on trade than China or the EU, as shown in Table 8.2. The share of trade as percentage of GDP has decreased in recent years, with only a quarter of the American economy dependent on trade by 2016. This relative closure may enhance the bargaining position of the US vis-à-vis other economies more exposed to trade in international commercial negotiations.

Table 8.1 Shares and ranking of leading US trade and investment partners (2016)

US shares of	*China (per cent)*	*EU (per cent)*
Exports of goods to	8.0 (rank 4)	18.6 (rank 1)
Imports of goods from	21.1 (rank 1)	19.0 (rank 2)
Exports of services to	7.2 (rank 2)	30.7 (rank 1)
Imports of services from	3.2 (rank 7)	35.0 (rank 1)
FDI inward stocks	0.7 (rank 8)	60.2 (rank 1)
FDI outward stocks	1.7 (rank 9)	54.8 (rank 1)

Source: Bureau of Economic Analysis, US Department of Commerce.

able 8.2 Trade dependence: imports and exports as share of GDP (2016)

rade (M + X) s percentage f GDP	*2012*	*2013*	*2014*	*2015*	*2016*
hina	22.70 + 25.41 = 48.11%	22.06 + 24.50 = 46.56%	21.38 + 23.50 = 4.88%	18.10 + 21.35 = 39.45%	17.38 + 19.66 = 37.03%
uropean Union (extra-EU)	17.2 + 17.6 = 34.8%	16.4 + 18.1 = 34.5%	16.3 + 17.6 = 33.9%	16.4 + 17.8 = 34.2%	16.2 + 17.3 = 33.5%
nited States	17.11 + 13.61 = 30.72%	16.59 + 13.64 = 30.23%	16.54 + 13.62 = 30.16%	15.39 + 12.50 = 27.89%	14.69 + 11.89 = 26.58%

ource: World Bank National Accounts Data, OECD National Accounts Data, and Eurostat.

The populist American backlash against globalization

Like all other advanced industrialized economies, the United States has profited from, but also been hurt by, globalization, which has created losers in addition to winners (Rodrik 2018). The losers' grievances were echoed loudly in the 2016 American presidential election by populist candidates – mostly Donald Trump and Bernie Sanders. This section examines the current populist American backlash against globalization by focusing on the changing balance of losers vs. winners, the protectionist impulses of Trump, and the rise of a bipartisan protectionist consensus that may result in an American trade policy increasingly on the defensive against globalization.

The globalization backlash

The gradual deregulation that has occurred in many economic sectors since the 1980s as a result of successive international trade agreements and the accession of China to the WTO in 2001 has ushered in creative as well as destructive forces for the American economy. It resulted in the opening of new markets abroad, increased outsourcing, and the rise of global value chains. Coupled with technological gains from automation, it decimated some traditional, labor-intensive, and polluting industries in the Rust Belt, such as steel. It also enabled American consumers to purchase cheaper goods and allowed the emergence of new, highly skilled jobs, notably in the tech sector. At the collective level, the US made important absolute gains as a result of the explosion of globalization. Other countries made higher relative gains. At the individual level, globalization had strong redistributive implications that were, for the most part, not compensated through welfare policies. It was therefore accompanied by a spectacular rise of economic inequalities in the United States (e.g. Rodrik 2018).

Under the presidencies of George W. Bush and Barack Obama, US trade and investment policy had followed a similar set of goals: opening up markets abroad for American exports, raising global standards, and protecting rights and obligations through dispute settlement mechanisms. With an increasingly divided and cumbersome multilateral trade opening process, the US embarked instead on an agenda of 'competitive liberalization' resulting in the proliferation of negotiations of bilateral and plurilateral trade and investment agreements, including the KORUS entered into force in 2012, the TPP with 11 other Pacific nations, the TTIP with the EU, and a Bilateral Investment Treaty (BIT) with China.

The asymmetrical redistributive impact of trade opening was not addressed through compensatory social policies, creating resentment from those who feel that globalization has threatened their current situation and future prospects. Donald Trump capitalized on this resentment, campaigning explicitly on anti-trade, anti-globalization issues and a suspicion of multilateral institutions designed to rein in sovereignty and open up borders. He articulated that America had been 'taken advantage of' through these trade agreements and promised to bring back coal and manufacturing jobs to the US His campaign rallies, which claimed to give a voice to the forgotten losers of the 'bad' trade deals, ranted against China, demonized the WTO, and focused on fair trade with Mexico (e.g. Trump 2017a).

In this dimension, the American election resembled the Brexit referendum that had occurred four months earlier in the United Kingdom. In both cases, angry voters expressed populist frustration at the loss of traditional manufacturing jobs, growing inequalities, eroding national sovereignty, and the general feeling that they were under existential threat from 'others'. In both the UK and the US, the effects of deindustrialization, dislocation, and cultural alienation were particularly pronounced because of the absence of welfare safety nets (Rodrik 2018).

'Trade is bad': a President with protectionist impulses

Trump has long exhibited protectionist impulses, as evidenced by his public pronouncements against Japanese trade and investment already in the 1980s (Fisher 2018). His blustering, bordering on bullying, promotion of unilateralism in international economic affairs seems to be more deep-seated than just political strategy. In all walks-of-life, political and personal, Trump has a 'zero-sum' and transactional worldview. This view is particularly pronounced in trade, where he sees deficits and imports as a sign of inherent weakness. He sums up his view in the simplest way: 'TRADE is BAD' (Woodward 2018).

Trump's mercantilist rhetoric and deep suspicions about multilateralism have squared well with the nationalist trade agenda of the populist sovereigntist 'Breitbart' camp represented among others by White House adviser Stephen Miller, former adviser Steve Bannon, Commerce Secretary Wilbur Ross, and White House National Trade Council Director Peter Navarro. Together, these trade 'hawks' are arguing for a strategy putting 'America First', which includes high tariffs, a border tax, and 'Buy American' proposals. Their focus is on bringing back manufacturing jobs, especially in heavy industries such as steel and aluminum, and on curbing multilateralism. This means suspending the negotiation of new agreements and renegotiating old agreements. Moreover, President Trump believes that as a self-proclaimed master of the art of the deal, he can obtain better deals by leveraging American power than did his predecessors.

Trump's very first action in office was to sign an Executive Order withdrawing the United States from the TPP, a deal concluded between the US and 11 other Pacific nations during the Obama administration. The agreement, which included environmental and labor rights protections, was due to cover 40 per cent of the world's economy. American businesses backed it overwhelmingly.

Trump also ordered the suspension of the TTIP negotiations between the US and the EU. He complained loudly, in tweets and speeches, about the 'bad' and 'unfair' trade deficit of the US with Germany (Schoen 2017). He decried the EU as the 'biggest foe' of the US in trade (*BBC News* 2018). He also criticized the process of European integration, which he claimed was 'set up to take advantage of' the US, as evidenced by the EU 'cheating' the US in trade (Galindo 2018). He suggested, therefore, that other member states should follow in the footsteps of the UK and exit the EU (Herszenhorn 2017). He started a trade war with the EU in March 2018 with the imposition of unilateral tariffs on steel and aluminum, which have remained in effect (as of writing) despite a truce in retaliation and counter-retaliation and the promise to work toward zero tariffs reached in July 2018.

Trump also followed through on his campaign promise to overhaul the 'worse trade deal ever made' – the 1994 NAFTA between the US, Canada, and Mexico (Trump 2017b). Though he had initially promised to pull out of NAFTA altogether, he then instructed his administration to renegotiate the terms of the deal. A revised version of the agreement, renamed the United States-Mexico-Canada Agreement (USMCA), was signed in October 2018. The changes – including on dairy exports, labor provisions, and investment disputes – were not major, leading many analysts to dub the new agreement NAFTA 2.0 (Kirby 2018).

In spite of the escalating military crisis with North Korea, Trump also intended to withdraw from the 'horrible' KORUS, which has been in force since 2012, after an overwhelming majority ratification in the US Senate (Rucker 2017). However, he was prevented from doing so by several members of his administration (Lee 2017; Woodward 2018). Instead, a new version of the treaty was signed in September 2018 with minor changes regarding exports of American cars and South Korean steel.

The protectionist impulses of the American President seem similar when it comes to foreign investment. During his September 2017 speech at the United Nations, Trump mentioned the unfairness of multilateral trade deals, in part because of what he called the existence of 'unaccountable international tribunals' responsible for 'millions of jobs vanished' (Trump 2017c). In spite of the insistence of large American corporations to keep the NAFTA

Chapter 11 in the new USMCA, the Trump administration removed the clauses providing for investor-state dispute settlement (ISDS), which in the past had served mostly for American businesses to sue Canada.

A bipartisan protectionist trade policy?

The Trump administration was deeply split during its first year between the 'nationalists' and the 'globalists'. On one side, the 'nationalists' were pushing the President's protectionist instincts. On the other side, the 'globalists', led by former National Economic Council Chairman Gary Cohn, were educating him on the virtues of free trade and cautioning him against brinkmanship. For instance, it was reported that Trump decided eventually not to pull the US from NAFTA, as he had promised during the campaign, after his Secretary of Agriculture Sonny Perdue showed him a map highlighting trade-dependent farmers, who happen to be his electoral base (Scher 2017). In March 2018, the nationalist faction won the fight, with Cohn's resignation, triggered by his disagreement over tariffs.

These divisions between a nationalist and a globalist faction in the Trump White House mirror existing divisions in the country on the issue of open economic borders. Remarkably, the divisions do not run along the traditional partisan lines of cleavage. To the contrary, the anti-globalization message seems increasingly to be a bipartisan issue.

Many Democrats have pushed back against the Bill Clinton and Barack Obama pro-free trade agenda. During the 2016 campaign, the 'progressive' Democrats, such as Bernie Sanders and Elizabeth Warren, railed against the TPP and other trade agreements endangering the jobs of American workers. Even Hillary Clinton criticized NAFTA, negotiated by her husband, and came out against TPP, which she herself had helped shepherd through as Secretary of State. Since the 2016 election, many Democrats are embracing their own protectionist past.

In July 2017, the Senate Democrats unveiled a new protectionist trade platform under the helm of New York Senator Chuck Schumer titled 'A Better Deal on Trade and Jobs: Fighting Back Against Corporations that Outsource American Jobs and Countries that Manipulate Trade Laws' (Senate Democrats 2017) As put by the *New York Times*, 'Senate democrats seek to outdo Trump on trade' with this new platform (Appelbaum 2017). Proposals include:

- 'An Independent Trade Prosecutor to Combat Trade Cheating' to challenge unfair trade practices by foreign countries (especially China), which have been ignored for too long without relying on the WTO process.
- The creation of the 'American Jobs Security Council' composed of independent experts who would review a potential purchase by a foreign company of an American company on economic grounds and have the authority to stop the deal if it could have detrimental economic impacts.

- A renegotiated NAFTA to support more American jobs and higher wages, including the presence of American workers representatives at the bargaining table, strong and enforceable labor standards, and greater market access for US exports, especially agricultural exports.
- 'Buy America Requirements for All Taxpayer-Funded Projects': taxpayer dollars would be required to be spent on US companies and US jobs for all federal public works and infrastructure projects.
- 'An Outsourcing Tax for Companies Leaving the US': companies would be punished for shipping jobs and factories overseas, while companies that relocate foreign jobs back to the US would receive tax incentives.

Thus, the policies implemented by Trump administration, though upending the status quo, reflect a growing bipartisan consensus on protectionist trade policies. The majority of Americans, however, still seems to support free trade, though this usually does not factor much in policy-making. A Morning Consult/ Bloomberg poll conducted in the United States in September 2017 found 52 per cent of respondents in favor of expansion of free trade across borders, vs. 25 per cent in opposition to free trade and 23 per cent with no opinion (Mark 2017).

A looming trade and investment war with China

The Trump administration has embarked on a belligerent economic policy of trade wars with allies and foes alike, which the President has claimed are 'easy to win' (Trump 2018). In March 2018, the US imposed 25 per cent tariffs on steel and 10 per cent on aluminum imports based on Section 232 of Trade Expansion Act of 1962, leading to a scrambled response for exemptions and retaliation by US trade partners, as well as demands for compensation for American industries hurt by such retaliation. The Trump administration does not seem to have given much thought to its largest trade partner, the EU – except for demonizing it as the biggest foe of the US, criticizing the American trade deficit with Germany, and vowing counter-retaliation against the EU's retaliatory tariffs and WTO complaint. The TTIP negotiations, which were frozen immediately after the inauguration, have not resumed as of writing, though Trump has indicated that his administration might launch new bilateral trade negotiations with the EU – this may end up as a TTIP agreement under a new name, much as the USMCA replaced NAFTA. China, by contrast, has loomed large in the elaboration of a new American doctrine on trade and investment. This section explores in turn Trump's anti-China rhetoric, the launch of a trade war with China, and the recent evolution toward increased restrictiveness on inbound investment.

Anti-China economic rhetoric during the Presidential campaign and beyond

Blustering rhetoric against China on trade was a central element of Trump's Presidential campaign. He pledged at electoral rallies to 'get China to stop ripping us off'. He called China 'an economic enemy' who wants to 'beat us and own our country', is 'raping our country', and has perpetrated one of the 'greatest thefts in the history of the world' (Stracqualursi 2017). He threatened to impose unilaterally a broad 45 per cent tariff against China. He promised that he would label China a currency manipulator on Day 1 of his presidency.

Previous administrations had hoped and assumed that China's spectacular economic growth, made possible by its integration in world trade, would lead to peaceful convergence toward pluralistic, liberal political norms and practices. But China's rise did not result in democratic liberalization and it did happen through implicit and explicit rule-breaking of the liberal international economic order (*The Economist* 2018). Trump's economic nationalist advisers are indeed convinced that China represents an existential threat to the US and that America should therefore declare an economic war on China. For Steven Bannon, 'the economic war with China is everything. And we have to be maniacally focused on that' (Interview with American Prospect, 2017). The newly created White House Trade Council director, economist Peter Navarro, wrote in his 2011 book *Death by China* that American companies cannot compete against a country that engages in abusive trade policies (Navarro & Autry 2011). Taking a more aggressive and pro-active stance toward China's perceived unfair rise to economic power has become bipartisan.

Robert Lighthizer, the Trump administration US Trade Representative, sums up the challenges posed by China, which has taken advantage of its membership in the WTO to become fully integrated in industrial and logistical global value chains while not playing by the rules of fair competition:

> The sheer scale of [China's] coordinated efforts to develop their economy, to subsidize, to create national champions, to force technology transfer, and to distort markets in China and throughout the world is a threat to the world trading system that is unprecedented. Unfortunately, the World Trade Organization is not equipped to deal with this problem. The WTO and its predecessor, the General Agreement on Tariffs and Trade, were not designed to successfully manage mercantilism on this scale. We must find other ways to defend our companies, workers, farmers, and indeed our economic system. We must find new ways to ensure that a market-based economy prevails.
>
> (Lighthizer 2017)

The trade war against China

It has therefore become official US policy to renegotiate terms of trade without naiveté in order to compensate for China's blurring of the lines between state and market. But if branding China as an economic enemy during the campaign may have been politically expedient and made for a catchy sound bite, renegotiating the terms of trade with China is difficult to achieve for a variety of reasons. First, China is so enmeshed in global value chains that limiting Chinese imports would hurt American manufacturers. The difficulties of dealing with Chinese dumping solar panels provide an example of the many constituencies with diverse, often opposite, interests in the US (manufacturers vs. installers, workers vs. consumers, coal lobby vs. environmentalist groups, etc.). Second, reducing the trade deficit with China would also hurt the purchasing power of American consumers who got used to buying cheap goods in large American stores such as Walmart. The geopolitical instability in North Korea also contributed to a softening toward China in the first months of the Trump administration.

Initially, the American administration tried to work with China to renegotiate productively the economic relationship between the two countries. When Presidents Trump and Xi Jinping met at Mar-a-Lago in April 2017, they agreed to take 100 days to promote the 'healthy development of bilateral trade and investment'. This was followed in May 2017 by the negotiation of a small deal, announced with great fanfare, which eased market access for American companies in China notably on beef and financial services in exchange for Chinese exports of poultry.

However, the US did not get China to acquiesce to any of its demands, including access to China's financial services markets, a reduction of excess Chinese steel capacity and auto tariffs, cutting subsidies for state-owned enterprises, and lifting ownership caps for foreign firms in China. In December 2017 the Trump administration unveiled its National Security Strategy, based on the assumption that China represents an existential threat to the United States, which branded China as a 'strategic competitor' accused of 'economic aggression' (Sevastopulo & Donnan 2017).

In January 2018, the Trump administration launched a trade war, starting with the imposition of a 30 per cent tariff on imported solar panels, in which China is the world leader, and 20 per cent on washing machines. In March the USTR launched an investigation of China's unfair trade practices using Section 301 of the Trade Act of 1974, a statute unused since the WTO's creation in 1995. China responded by imposing tariffs on over a hundred American exports. In June the Trump administration imposed a 25 per cent tariff on USD 50 billion of Chinese goods with 'industrially significant technology'. China retaliated with tariffs on American goods of a similar value and filed a complaint at the WTO. In September, the US added a 10 per cent tariff on another USD 200 billion worth of Chinese goods, prompting immediate Chinese retaliation with a 10 per cent tariff on USD 60 billion of US imports.

This trade war could have negative consequences for China, the global economy, and American businesses. China is more vulnerable than the US because of the asymmetry in the trade relationship: its exports to the US are over four times higher than US exports to China. Indeed, it has already imposed tariffs on almost all its American imports, but the US can still impose more tariffs on its end. China, however, could retaliate on other things than goods, for instance by cutting off supply of crucial inputs or selling its US Treasury bonds. For the world economy, this trade war could prove disruptive, resulting in slower growth and prompting companies to reconfigure their supply chains. As for American businesses, many industry associations – for instance representatives of soybean producers and retailers – have approached the administration to protest the tariffs, express their fears about their consequences in the short run, and ask for compensation. The trade war has prompted China to accelerate and deepen its investment in Research and Development and new technologies, which could hurt the competitiveness of American businesses in the long run.

Toward increased restrictiveness of inbound investment

In parallel to its rise as one of the world's three largest traders, China has also risen as a major international investor over the past decade. From a non-existent player 15 years ago, China has now become one of the largest senders of FDI flows in the world (UNCTAD 2017). In the United States, the stock of Chinese investment grew from almost zero in 2005 to close to USD 150 billion by the end of 2016. The evolution of flows is even more momentous than the progression of stocks: Chinese FDI flows into the US tripled between 2015 and 2016, surpassing USD 50 billion in 2016 (Baker McKenzie 2017), though they have slowed down spectacularly since the second half of 2017. This Chinese investment in the US has taken place in every economic sector, including healthcare, information technology, infrastructure, food products, tourism, industrial machinery, financial services, entertainment, and real estate.

While Chinese investments have been overall welcomed for their economic benefits, such as a chance to create local jobs through greenfield and acquisitions and an opportunity to tap into the coveted Chinese market, they have also posed political challenges in the US (Meunier 2018). Chinese FDI is viewed at the national level with bipartisan consensus with suspicion because of American concerns about the national security implications of some acquisitions.

The executive branch is required to screen incoming foreign investments and potentially suspend or prohibit mergers and acquisitions. This is accomplished through a review process done by the Committee on Foreign Investment in the United States (CFIUS), an interagency committee including officials from the departments of Commerce, Defense, Homeland Security, State, and USTR, among others (Jackson 2018). According to the latest official CFIUS records for 2012–2014, China was the home country of the largest number of deals that went through the CFIUS process, followed by the United Kingdom, Canada, Japan, and France (CFIUS 2016). In 2016, CFIUS blocked, among others, the acquisition of Philips' Lumileds by Chinese private equity investors and of German chip-maker Aixtron by

China's Fujian Grand Chip Investment on national security grounds. In 2017, President Trump signed an Executive Order prohibiting the acquisition of US computer chip-maker Lattice Semiconductor Corporation by a Chinese investor on national security grounds after a negative recommendation by CFIUS. In March 2018, also on the recommendation of CFIUS, he blocked the hostile takeover of wireless telecom company Qualcomm by Singapore-based Broadcom, with ties to China.

The heightened rhetoric about the dangers of Chinese investment has accelerated CFIUS reform. As a result of rare bipartisan efforts, Congress adopted in August 2018 the Foreign Investment Risk Review Act (FIRRMA), which reinforces the institutional structure of CFIUS and broadens the jurisdictional scope of the scrutiny of foreign investments into the US, for instance with special provisions for high-technology deals. In October 2018, the Treasury Department enacted a pilot program implementing portions of FIRRMA sooner than expected for transactions including minority stakes and joint ventures in technology and telecommunications – targeting implicitly Chinese transactions. The increased restrictiveness of the FDI review process is happening in parallel with similar efforts in Europe, both at the member state level (especially in Germany) and at the EU level, with a proposal for a regulation establishing a framework for screening inbound FDI on grounds of security or public order to protect the EU's essential interests adopted by the European Parliament in June 2018 (European Parliament 2018).

The increased restrictiveness of FDI review is also happening as the US and China are renegotiating the terms of investment. Americans (and Europeans) have long complained about the unfair lack of reciprocity: many American companies are forced into joint ventures with Chinese partners and have to transfer proprietary technology in order to do business in China, which might endanger their competitive advantage in the long term. The US and China started in 2008 to negotiate a BIT, which had been close to completion at the end of the Obama administration. According to Treasury Secretary Mnuchin, the US is still considering a BIT with China but the issue has not been revived under the Trump administration as of writing (Talley 2017).

Beyond a US-led liberal international economic order?

Both as the result of structural evolution and policy choices, the United States has become less central to the governance of the liberal international economic order, with potentially major implications for the rest of the world. This section explores in turn how the American-led postwar liberal international economic order has come under challenge, how the lack of global ambition by the current administration is accelerating this American retreat from global governance, and whether China or the EU can step into this breach.

An American-led liberal international economic order under challenge

The liberal international economic order was created under American impulse in the aftermath of WWII. Its core trade principles have included liberalization, non-discrimination, reciprocity, and mechanisms for dispute resolution. They have been embedded in the General Agreement on Tariffs and Trade (GATT), which enabled gradual trade opening over decades of multilateral rounds. They were reinforced with the creation of the WTO in 1995. The rules for investment are different from trade, as the regime is polycentric and made up of thousands of bilateral agreements instead of administered by a central multilateral organization, but the core principles are similar.

For decades the US acted as a hegemon and bore the costs of preserving an open trading system, which is a public good. The implementation of strong international economic regimes enabled cooperation to continue even after the US lost its hegemonic position (Ruggie 1982; Keohane 1984; Ikenberry 2011, 2018).

In a way, this American-led order became victim of its own success; American hegemony was bound to decline. As the countries of Europe gradually integrated in the region, the EU became an equal to the US in setting the rules of the game (Meunier 2005). Trade openness then enabled the economic growth and political emergence of developing countries, especially the BRICs, in the early 2000s. The membership of China into the WTO in 2001 catapulted the country as a trade behemoth. The 'rise of the rest' (Zakaria 2009) contested the dominance of the US and the EU in setting world trade rules, as exemplified during the unsuccessful Doha Round negotiations, especially at the time of the failure at Cancun in 2003. Some analysts interpreted this as the 'decline of the west' (Ikenberry 2008).

Growing American disengagement from global governance

This secular trend of a loss of relative economic power by the US does not necessarily imply a loss of political power. It has proven costly to set and enforce the rules of the liberal international order, even if it comes with privileges, and is not a task that emerging economies can easily take on board (Stokes 2018). The erosion of US leadership in global governance started under previous American administrations, but they continued, often in partnership with the EU, to work toward shaping and preserving global governance, even as American structural economic power was in relative decline.

By contrast, the Trump administration has an explicit 'America First', zero-sum nationalist approach to trade and foreign policy based on a cost-benefit analysis (Stokes 2018). The goal is not to provide the public good of governance or lead in this domain. Rather, the goal is to restore primacy to the nation-state and to deal with other countries on a reciprocal bilateral basis. US policy objectives are, as President Trump articulated his doctrine in his first United Nations speech in September 2017, to look out for Americans and engage other nations in a tit-for-tat relationship (Trump 2017c). In order to achieve these objectives, the US government is ready, at least in rhetoric, to risk trade wars if it does not respect its WTO obligations through unilateral action and other countries retaliate by imposing their own punitive tariffs.

Indeed, the Trump administration seems intent not only to disengage from the WTO but also to weaken the WTO regime altogether. As a *New York Times* article headline stated in December 2017, 'Once the WTO's biggest supporter, the US is its biggest skeptic' (Swanson 2017). The American philosophy regarding the necessity of a global free trade regime has shifted. The WTO is now viewed as an instrument to cheat American workers and compromise American sovereignty. Instead of strengthening the regime, as his predecessors did, President Trump wants to undermine it, starting with the WTO dispute settlement system. The Obama administration had blocked the re-appointment of a judge to the WTO's Dispute Settlement Body. The Trump administration has taken this further, refusing to accept the appointment of any new judges to the Appellate Body, which currently has three vacancies out of seven judges. Such a personnel vacuum would slow down, weaken, and even paralyze the dispute settlement process, which is apparently the intended objective. Going further, Trump has even suggested that the US could quit the WTO, 'the single worst trade deal ever made' (Micklethwait, Talev & Jacobs 2018).

By choosing to disengage and retreat now, the US is accelerating the secular trend toward smaller relative American political power caused in part by the growth of other economies but also by the increasing reliance on regional deals, at the expense of the multilateral system: the more trade is covered by agreements taking place outside the WTO framework, the less the US is able to shape the rules. By disengaging voluntarily, the US may miss out more on shaping the rules of the future. It is also changing the geometry of global governance to the benefit of the world's other two largest traders, China and the EU – but are they ready to take on more of the political burden and power?

China or the EU as new sheriffs of global governance?

It has become commonplace in the Western media to assume that China, given the size of its economy, population, and military power, is becoming the new hegemon. Indeed, as Chinese President Xi Jinping expressed in his 2017 Party Congress report, being more active in global governance has been an open ambition of China for a variety of reasons, such as enhanced decision-making power, adoption of international norms reflecting Chinese characteristics, and great power status (Xi 2017b). Some of this governance activity has taken place precisely outside of the Bretton Woods liberal international institutions set up by the US after WWII. China has started to build for years now a parallel network of governance institutions – for instance the Shanghai Cooperation Organization (SCO), the Silk Road Fund, and the Asian Infrastructure Investment Bank (AIIB).

The American disengagement signaled by Trump's election is now projecting the spotlight on China. The US withdrawal from TPP led the other partners to conclude the Comprehensive and Progressive Agreement for Trans-Pacific Partnership (CPTPP) in March 2018, while also giving new blood to the negotiations for the Regional Comprehensive Economic Partnership (RCEP), a proposed free trade agreement between most of the same members as TPP minus the US, but plus China and India.

Indeed, it looks like China is now openly defending global governance, presented as under attack from the US President Xi gave a remarkable speech in January 2017 at the World Economic Forum in Davos where he was interpreted as extolling the virtues of globalization and free trade and promising to defend them (Xi 2017a). As the *Financial Times* headlined in October 2017, 'China moves in as US pulls back from global institutions' (Donnan 2017). However, as often argued by Chinese analysts, this American disengagement is arriving too early for China, which might not be ready yet to provide the public goods of global leadership while having to deal simultaneously with pressing domestic issues (Chen 2017).

The EU, by contrast, already possesses many tools of global governance but often cannot translate them into actual power and leadership (Meunier & Vachudova 2018). The EU has long exerted strong power in trade policy, both as a formidable bargainer and as a world regulator. It has wielded foreign policy power through trade by using notably normative power and conditionality (Meunier & Nicolaidis 2017). Indeed, as Andrew Moravcsik has long argued, the EU has been the world's 'second superpower', albeit a quiet one (Moravcsik 2017). However, a series of internal crises in recent years – from the euro crisis to the massive influx of refugees, Brexit, and fundamental challenges to the rule of law in some member states – have affected the EU's ability to project global power.

The American disengagement has created a diplomatic opening for Europe. In his speech at the General Assembly of the United Nations in September 2017, French President Emmanuel Macron presented an alternative to the vision offered by Trump on the same occasion, heralding multilateralism, the respect of agreements, and the primacy of diplomacy as only possible answers to global challenges (Macron 2017). Similarly, EU foreign policy chief Federica Mogherini indirectly attacked the Trump administration's retreat from global governance by arguing that the EU is currently the 'only credible and predictable' global power. 'There is an alternative to the foreign policy of isolation, fear, protectionism and confrontation, and this is the European way', she said. This European way is made of cooperation and partnership, respect for international law and standards of multilateralism as well as a constant search for win-win solutions (Michalopoulos 2017).

Indeed, the Trump administration's nationalist protectionist policies have resulted in an acceleration of the pace with which the EU negotiates trade agreements with rest of the world. Since Trump's inauguration, the EU has signed an economic partnership agreement with Japan, started negotiations with Australia and New Zealand, negotiated to modernize the agreement with Mexico and finish talks with Mercosur, and implemented the provisional entry into force of the CETA agreement with Canada. When it comes to the investment regime, the EU has ambitiously proposed the creation of a multilateral investment court to replace the oft-decried ISDS process (Meunier & Morin 2017). The EU is also continuing talks for a BIT with China. These are not a comprehensive global response, however, as argued in the *Financial Times*:

> Certainly, compared with the shambles on the other side of the Atlantic, in which Donald Trump is threatening to tear up deals and start trade wars every other week, Brussels has a clear and mainly constructive plan. Unfortunately, despite the EU's ambitions, it is too narrow and shallow to qualify as assuming the role of global trade leadership from the US.
> (Beattie 2017)

Conclusion

To be sure, the United States is still at the center of the governance of the world economy – whether through the role of the dollar, primacy in the Bretton Woods institutions, or the strength of its multinational companies. More so than in the military sphere, however, its relative power in economic governance has declined, which has precipitated the radical shift toward a new American strategy based on transactional reciprocity.

Like all Western democracies, the US is in the midst of a political partisan realignment along the globalization cleavage. Unions and workers tended to form the base of the Democratic Party, while the Republicans supported free trade; the lines of cleavage are now shifting with the extremes increasingly supporting nationalism and protection, while the center favors openness. It has become more difficult for the US to continue providing the public good of global governance for a free world economy while its political realignment is not complete.

Some of the challenges are also created by the relative rise of other economic powers, especially China. One central challenge for US policy-makers moving forward, whether Republican or Democratic, will be to address the market distortions introduced by the subsidization of national champions in China and to reintroduce some reciprocity in foreign investment. A related challenge, also faced by the EU, is to figure out how trade and investment are connected to foreign policy and security, especially in a world where technological interdependence makes countries vulnerable.

References

Appelbaum, B. (2017) 'Senate Democrats Seek to Outdo Trump on Trade', *The New York Times*, 2 August 2017. Available at: www.nytimes.com/2017/08/02/us/politics/senate-democrats-seek-to-outdo-trump-on-trade.html.

Baker McKenzie (2017) 'Chinese Investment Tripled in US in 2016, Doubled in Europe', 6 February 2017. Available at: www.bakermckenzie.com/en/newsroom/2017/02/chinafdi.

BBC News (2018) 'Donald Trump: European Union Is a Foe on Trade – BBC News', 15 July 2018. Available at: www.bbc.com/news/world-us-canada-44837311.

Beattie, A. (2017) 'EU Trade Sacrifices Substance for Speed', *Financial Times*, 25 September 2017. Available at: www.ft.com/content/dd8426a8-a1da-11e7-b797-b61809486fe2.

Busch, M.L. & E. Reinhardt (2000) 'Geography, International Trade, and Political Mobilization in US Industries', *American Journal of Political Science* 44(4), 703–719. Available at: doi:10.2307/2669276.

CFIUS (2016) 'Committee on Foreign Investment in the United States Annual Report to Congress CY2014'.

Chen, D. (2017) 'Is China Ready for Global Leadership?' *The Diplomat*, 27 February 2017. Available at: https://thediplomat.com/2017/02/is-china-ready-for-global-leadership/.

Donnan, S. (2017) 'China Moves in as US Pulls Back from Global Institutions', *Financial Times*, 13 October 2017. Available at: www.ft.com/content/fcbf3ba2-afcc-11e7-aab9-abaa44b1e130.

European Parliament (2018) 'EU Framework for FDI Screening' PE 614.667. Available at: www.europarl.europa.eu/RegData/etudes/BRIE/2018/614667/EPRS_BRI(2018)614667_EN.pdf.

European Union External Action Service (2017) 'EU-US Trade'. Available at: https://eeas.europa.eu/delegations/united-states-america_en/36758/EU-US Trade.

Fisher, M. (2018) 'Over Four Decades, Trump's One Solid Stance: A Hard Line on Trade', *Washington Post*, 7 March 2018. Available at: www.washingtonpost.com/business/over-four-decades-trumps-one-solid-stance-a-hard-line-on-trade/2018/03/07/4b1ed250-2172-11e8-badd-7c9f29a55815_story.html?noredirect=on&utm_term=.080b793d34e2.

Galindo, G. (2018) 'Trump: EU Was 'Set up to Take Advantage' of US', *Politico*, 28 June 2018. Available at: www.politico.eu/article/donald-trump-eu-was-set-up-to-take-advantage-of-us-trade-tariffs-protectionism/.

Herszenhorn, D.M. (2017) 'Trump Officials Ask Which Country Will Be next to Exit EU', *Politico*, 13 January 2017. Available at: www.politico.eu/article/donald-trump-officials-ask-which-country-will-be-next-to-eu-exit/.

Hiscox, M.J. (2002) *International Trade and Political Conflict: Commerce, Coalitions, and Mobility*, Princeton: Princeton University Press.

Ikenberry, G.J. (2008) 'The Rise of China and the Future of the West', *Foreign Affairs*, 1 January 2008. Available at: www.foreignaffairs.com/articles/asia/2008-01-01/rise-china-and-future-west.

——— (2011) *Liberal Leviathan: The Origins, Crisis, and Transformation of the American World Order*, Princeton: Princeton University Press.

——— (2018) 'The End of Liberal International Order?' *International Affairs* 94(1), 7–23. Available at: doi:10.1093/ia/iix241.

Jackson, J.K. (2018) 'The Committee on Foreign Investment in the United States (CFIUS)', *Congressional Research Service*, 70. Available at: https://fas.org/sgp/crs/natsec/RL33388.pdf.

Keohane, R. (1984) *After Hegemony: Cooperation and Discord in the World Political Economy*, Princeton: Princeton University Press. Available at: http://press.princeton.edu/titles/1322.html.

Kirby, J. (2018) 'USMCA, Trump's New NAFTA Deal, Explained in 500 Words', *Vox*, 3 October 2018. Available at: www.vox.com/2018/10/3/17930092/usmca-nafta-trump-trade-deal-explained.

Lee, M.Y.H. (2017) 'Trump Wants to End 'Horrible' South Korea-US Trade Deal. Koreans Disagree', *Washington Post*, 14 September 2017, sec. Asia & Pacific. Available at: www.washingtonpost.com/world/trump-wants-to-end-horrible-south-korea-us-trade-deal-koreans-disagree/2017/09/13/fb528b3e-9627-11e7-a527-3573bd073e02_story.html.

Lighthizer, R. (2017) 'US Trade Policy Priorities: Robert Lighthizer, United States Trade Representative | Center for Strategic and International Studies', *CSIS Center for Strategic and International Studies*. Available at: www.csis.org/analysis/us-trade-policy-priorities-robert-lighthizer-united-states-trade-representative.

Macron, E. (2017) 'United Nations General Assembly – Speech by M. Emmanuel Macron, President of the Republic (19 September 2017)', *France Diplomatie: Ministry for Europe and Foreign Affairs*, 19 September 2017. Available at: www.diplomatie.gouv.fr/en/french-foreign-policy/united-nations/events/united-nations-general-assembly-sessions/unga-s-72nd-session/article/united-nations-general-assembly-speech-by-m-emmanuel-macron-President-of-the.

Mark, D. (2017) 'US Support for Free Trade Endures in Trump Era, Poll Shows', *Morning Consult*, 17 September 2017. Available at: https://morningconsult.com/2017/09/17/support-for-free-trade-endures-in-trump-era-poll-shows/.

Meunier, S. (2005) *Trading Voices: The European Union in International Commercial Negotiations*, Princeton: Princeton University Press.

——— (2018) 'Beware of Chinese Bearing Gifts: Why China's Direct Investment Poses Political Problems in Europe and the United States', in J. Chaisse (ed.), *China's Investment Three-Prong Strategy: Bilateral, Regional, and Global Tracks*, Oxford: Oxford University Press, 345–359.

Meunier, S. & J.-F. Morin (2017) 'The European Union and the Space-Time Continuum of Investment Agreements', *Journal of European Integration* 39(7), 891–907.

Meunier, S. & K. Nicolaidis (2017) 'The European Union as a Trade Power', in C. Hill & M. Smith (eds.), *International Relations and the European Union*, Oxford: Oxford University Press, 275–298.

Meunier, S. & M.A. Vachudova (2018) 'Liberal Intergovernmentalism, Illiberalism and the Potential Superpower of the European Union', *Journal of Common Market Studies*, September. Available at: https://onlinelibrary.wiley.com/doi/full/10.1111/jcms.12793.

Michalopoulos, S. (2017) 'Mogherini Lashes Out at Trump, Says EU Is the 'Only Credible' Global Power', *EURACTIV*, 19 October 2017. Available at: www.euractiv.com/section/defence-policy/news/mogherini-lashes-out-at-trump-says-eu-is-the-only-credible-global-power/.

Micklethwait, J., M. Talev & J. Jacobs (2018) 'Trump Threatens to Pull US Out of WTO If It Doesn't "Shape Up"', *Bloomberg*, 30 August 2018. Available at:

www.bloomberg.com/news/articles/2018-08-30/trump-says-he-will-pull-u-s-out-of-wto-if-they-don-t-shape-up?srnd=premium.

Milner, H.V. (1989) *Resisting Protectionism: Global Industries and the Politics of International Trade*, Princeton: Princeton University Press.

Moravcsik, A. (2017) 'Europe Is Still a Superpower', *Foreign Policy*, 13 April 2017. Available at: https://foreignpolicy.com/2017/04/13/europe-is-still-a-superpower/.

Navarro, P. & G. Autry (2011) *Death by China: Confronting the Dragon -A Global Call to Action*, Upper Saddle River: Pearson Prentice Hall.

Richards, J. & E. Schaefer (2016) 'Jobs Attributable to Foreign Direct Investment in the United States', *International Trade Administration*. Available at: www.trade.gov/mas/ian/build/groups/public/@tg_ian/documents/webcontent/tg_ian_005496.pdf.

Rodrik, D. (2018) 'Populism and the Economics of Globalization', *Journal of International Business Policy* 1(1), 12–33. Available at: doi:10.1057/s42214-018-0001-4.

Rogowski, R. (1989) *Commerce and Coalitions: How Trade Affects Domestic Political Alignments*, Princeton: Princeton University Press.

Rucker, P. (2017) 'Trump: 'We May Terminate' US-South Korea Trade Agreement', *Washington Post*, 28 April 2017. Available at: www.washingtonpost.com/politics/trump-we-may-terminate-us-south-korea-trade-agreement/2017/04/27/75ad1218-2bad-11e7-a616-d7c8a68c1a66_story.html.

Ruggie, J. (1982) 'International Regimes, Transactions, and Change: Embedded Liberalism in the Postwar Economic Order | International Organization | Cambridge Core', *International Organization* 36(2), 379–415. Available at: www.cambridge.org/core/journals/international-organization/article/international-regimes-transactions-and-change-embedded-liberalism-in-the-postwar-economic-order/238A600FEFE7EDBC2DDAB30E6A28B4D9.

Scher, B. (2017) 'Why Bannon Lost and the Globalists Won', *POLITICO Magazine*, 18 August 2017. Available at: http://politi.co/2uZ2wLd.

Schoen, J.W. (2017) 'Trump's Tweet Tirade against Germany Could Backfire on US', 30 May 2017. Available at: www.cnbc.com/2017/05/30/trumps-tweet-tirade-against-germany-could-backfire-on-us.html.

Senate Democrats (2017) 'A Better Deal on Trade and Jobs'. Available at: https://democrats.senate.gov/wp-content/uploads/2017/07/A-Better-Deal-on-Trade-and-Jobs-FINAL.pdf.

Sevastopulo, D. & S. Donnan (2017) 'Trump to Accuse China of "Economic Aggression"', *Financial Times*, 16 December 2017. Available at: www.ft.com/content/1801d4f4-e201-11e7-8f9f-de1c2175f5ce.

Stokes, D. (2018) 'Trump, American Hegemony and the Future of the Liberal International Order', *International Affairs* 94(1), 133–150. Available at: doi:10.1093/ia/iix238.

Stracqualursi, V. (2017) '10 Times Trump Attacked China', *ABC News*, 6 April 2017. Available at: http://abcnews.go.com/Politics/10-times-trump-attacked-china-trade-relations-us/story?id=46572567.

Swanson, A. (2017) 'Once the W.T.O.'s Biggest Supporter, US Is Its Biggest Skeptic', *The New York Times*, 10 December 2017, sec. Business Day. Available at: www.nytimes.com/2017/12/10/business/wto-united-states-trade.html.

Talley, I. (2017) 'White House Warns against Chinese Investment in US Semiconductor Industry', *Wall Street Journal*, 6 January 2017, sec. Politics. Available at: www.wsj.com/articles/white-house-warns-against-chinese-investment-in-u-s-semiconductor-industry-1483721973.

The Economist (2018) 'The End of Engagement – China v America', 18 October 2018. Available at: www.economist.com/leaders/2018/10/18/the-end-of-engagement?cid1=cust/ednew/n/bl/n/2018/10/18n/owned/n/n/nwl/n/n/na/159594/n.

Trump, D. (2017a) 'Full Transcripts of Trump's Calls with Mexico and Australia', *Washington Post*, 3 August 2017. Available at: www.washingtonpost.com/graphics/2017/politics/australia-mexico-transcripts/.

——— (2017b) 'Donald J. Trump on Twitter: "We Are in the NAFTA (Worst Trade Deal Ever Made) Renegotiation Process with Mexico & Canada. Both Being Very Difficult, May Have to Terminate?"', 27 August 2017. Available at: https://twitter.com/realdonaldtrump/status/901804388649500672?lang=en.

——— (2017c) 'Full Text of Trump's Speech to United Nations General Assembly', *Ora TV*, 19 September 2017. Available at: www.ora.tv/homepage/2018/1/16/1?break_aspect_ratio=true.

——— (2018) 'When a Country (USA)…' Tweet. *@realDonaldTrump* (blog), 2 March 2018. Available at: https://twitter.com/realdonaldtrump/status/969525362580484098?lang=en.

UNCTAD (2017) 'World Investment Report 2017: Investment and the Digital Economy', *Geneva*. Available at: http://unctad.org/en/pages/PublicationWebflyer.aspx?publicationid=1782.

Woodward, B. (2018) *Fear: Trump in the White House*, New York: Simon and Schuster.

World Trade Organization (2017) 'Trade Profiles'. Available at: http://stat.wto.org/CountryProfile/WSDBCountryPFView.aspx?Language=E&Country=US.

Xi, J. (2017a) 'President Xi's Speech to Davos in Full', *World Economic Forum*, 17 January 2017. Available at: www.weforum.org/agenda/2017/01/full-text-of-xi-jinping-keynote-at-the-world-economic-forum/.

——— (2017b) 'Full Text of Xi Jinping's Report at 19th CPC National Congress', *Xinhua*, 3 November 2017. Available at: www.xinhuanet.com/english/special/2017-11/03/c_136725942.htm.

Zakaria, F. (2009) *The Post-American World and the Rise of the Rest*. London: Penguin Books.

Part IV

Climate change and energy

9 The EU-China-US trilateral relations in global climate governance

The perspective of China

Bo Yan

Introduction

Climate change represents one of the most far-reaching challenges of global governance. To address the adverse impacts of climate change collectively, a global climate order has been built and evolved in the last three decades through the efforts of a series of actors. The central component of this global climate order is the climate regime built around three key agreements, namely the United Nations Framework Convention on Climate Change (UNFCCC), the Kyoto Protocol and the Paris Agreement. The Paris Agreement was adopted at the Conference of the Parties (COP) 21 in 2015 and entered into force in November 2016. While setting forth aspirational goals to limit global temperature rise well below 2 degrees Celsius above pre-industrial levels and to pursue efforts to limit the temperature increase even further to 1.5 degrees Celsius, it establishes a basic framework for enhanced international climate cooperation post-2020, starting a new phase of global climate governance.

Among the nearly 200 members of the global climate regime, the European Union (EU), China and the United States (US) are the three key players who performed central roles in the establishment and development of the global climate order. The interrelations among the three have had a significant impact on global climate governance. Most recently, however, this relationship has been challenged when US President Donald Trump announced on 1 June 2017 that he would withdraw the US from the Paris Agreement. This step not only acutely dampened global efforts to curb climate change but also brings about change to the trilateral relationship.

Given this context, what sort of trilateral relationship are we witnessing in the field of climate change and how has this changed in the post-Paris era? How has the trilateral relationship impacted on the global climate order in the past and how might it impact on this order in the future? By answering these central questions, this chapter will argue that the trilateral relations between the EU, China and the US on climate change represent a typical example of a co-opetitive (a hybrid of concurrent cooperative and competitive) international relationship with high fluidity. A scenario depicted as '*ménage à trois*' has been and will be the predominant pattern of the trilateral relations in global climate governance.

This chapter proceeds as follows. The next section explains the choice of the analytical framework to explore the trilateral relations through the prism of both cooperation and competition. The third section describes the EU-China-US trilateral relationship on climate change in the past and at present. The fourth section zooms in on the impact of the trilateral relations on global climate order, while the fifth section explores the future development trends of the trilateral relations in the context of the evolving global climate order. The conclusion offers a preliminary assessment of the trilateral relationship, especially from the perspective of China.

Cooperation and competition within the trilateral relationship: an analytical framework

The notion of a 'strategic triangle' was originally used in discussing the relationship between the United States (US), the Soviet Union and the People's Republic of China (PRC), particularly since the Sino-American rapprochement in the early 1970s. The theoretical research on the strategic triangle was first developed by Lowell Dittmer. Defining the 'strategic triangle' as a sort of transactional game among three players, he identified four different systemic patterns of this triangle during the Cold War: the '*ménage à trois*', consisting of symmetrical amities among all three players; the 'romantic triangle', consisting of amity between one 'pivot' player and two 'wing' players, but enmity between the two latter; the 'stable marriage', consisting of amity between two of the players and enmity between each and the third; and 'unit veto', which depicts enmity among all three actors (Dittmer 1981: 485–515, 1987: 29–47).

According to Dittmer, in the zero-sum game among the US, China and the Soviet Union, if the objective was to optimize the interests of all players of the game, the most desirable pattern would be the *ménage à trois*. It would preserve a balance and provide incentives to all three for continued cooperation at minimal cost. However, from the point of view of each individual player, the *ménage à trois* is not maximally secure since each individual player may be able to ascertain the motives and goals of its immediate negotiating partner, but it can never be sure whether the relationship between the second and third parties is in its interest, unless it is visibly negative. Therefore, from the perspective of each individual player, the most desirable arrangement is the romantic triangle (Dittmer 1981: 485–515).

Womack (2016) builds on Dittmer (1981) to show how asymmetry affects triangular dynamics. Different configurations of friendly or unfriendly bilateral relations and (a)symmetry between states can produce four different types of triangles. These may involve entirely positive relations (*ménage à trois*), two positive and one negative relations (romantic), two negative and one positive relations (marriage) or all negative relations (unit veto). According to Womack, because of the disproportionate costs and benefits caused by asymmetry, 'the most stable types of triangles are the romantic triangles ..., followed by the ménage à trois and marriage' (Womack 2016: 104).

With respect to the trilateral relations between the EU, the US and China, which is different from those of the US, China and the Soviet Union, Chen Zhimin expanded upon Dittmer's theory by defining the relations as a trilateral game simultaneously involving competition and cooperation (Chen 2011: 9–10). According to Chen, while competitive relations still follow the rules of a zero-sum game, cooperative relations follow the rules of a positive-sum game. By giving a value to the benefits and costs of each player, the total score of each player's benefits in a competitive game is equal to the score of the relations between this player and the other two players minus the score of the relations between the other two players. In a cooperative game, the total score of each player's benefit is equal to the score of the relations between this player and the other two, plus the score of the relations between the other two. In this way, by calculating the cooperative benefits and competitive benefits of each player, one can investigate the benefits configuration of each pattern from a novel perspective (Chen 2010: 9).

Thus, in the *ménage à trois*, although competitive benefits are small, each player has huge cooperative benefits. In the romantic triangle, although the cooperative benefits are not big, the pivot has huge competitive benefits while the two wing players have obvious negative returns of competitions. In the pattern of marriage, although the couple have certain competitive benefits, each player has obvious negative returns from competition with the third player. In the pattern of unit veto, each actor has huge negative returns from cooperation and competition. Therefore, if each actor is concerned with the cooperative benefits of the trilateral game, the three should pursue the pattern of *ménage à trois* (Chen 2010: 10).

On climate change, while there is a competitive game among China, the EU and the US, the significance of the cooperative game is increasing. The competition aspect refers to the games among the three on how to fairly distribute their responsibilities and commitments within climate governance and their divergences on the principles and rules of such governance. By contrast, they have strong motivations for cooperation due to their common interests in protecting the environment as a global public good. Different from the zero-game among the US, USSR and China in the Cold War, any one player among the US, EU and China would benefit from its cooperation with the other two on climate change, as well as from cooperation between them. Therefore, Chen's framework recognizes both competition and cooperation of trilateral relations and is thus complementary to Dittmer's and Womack's theories. It will be applied to describe and explain the patterns of the trilateral relations among the US, China and the EU on climate change in the following part.

The development of EU-China-US trilateral relations on climate change

The past nearly three decades have witnessed the emergence of the EU-China-US trilateral relationship on climate change, which has developed across four distinct periods: the early developments and the Kyoto period (1990s–1997), the post-Kyoto-period (1998–2007), the Copenhagen period (2007–2011), the Paris period (2011–2015) and the post-Paris period (2016–today).

The emergence of the trilateral relationship

The EU-China-US trilateral relationship on climate change initially emerged in the early 1990s, when international climate negotiations proceeded on a broadly triangular basis among the (then) European Community (EC), the US and developing countries (Djoghlaf 1994: 97). However, the pattern of the trilateral relations was not so clear since China itself was not an important player for the US and the EU yet, but fully participated to the works of the Group of 77 of now about 130 developing countries, while simultaneously maintaining its independent status (Bo, Romano & Chen 2014: 200).

The trilateral relationship began to take shape during the early period of the Kyoto process. Between 1995 and 1997, with the common goal of reaching a binding protocol to strengthen the commitments made with the 1992 UNFCCC, the EU and the US shared more common stances than China and the US or China and the EU. In that period, China enjoyed enhanced national power in terms of economic growth and political influence, while also observing an increase in its emissions. Although China maintained a low profile, the EU joined the US in exerting pressure upon it to accept proposals favouring their own positions, namely new commitments for developing countries, which were immediately refused by China. However, the EU and China had similar positions on the protocol being negotiated in terms of differentiation, targets for developed countries and flexible mechanisms (Schunz 2014: 67–112). In terms of Dittmer's and Chen's framework, there was thus a general romantic triangle among the three in this period, with two positive relations between the EU and the US, the EU and China, respectively, and one negative relations between the US and China.

Post-Kyoto period

Following the Kyoto summit, the EU began to regard China as a more important player on the basis of its rapid growth in both emissions and power, which coincided with the irreconcilable divergence of the US and the EU on the issue of carbon sinks and the withdrawal of the US from the Kyoto Protocol in March 2001. In this context, the EU and other developing countries, including China, closely collaborated in international climate negotiations and jointly contributed to the adoption of the Marrakesh Accords at COP 7 in November 2001, which included detailed rules for the implementation of the Kyoto Protocol (Bo, Romano & Chen 2014: 200).

Since the entry into force of the Kyoto Protocol in 2005, relations between the EU and China on climate change have been greatly enhanced. Especially at the multilateral level, the EU as a leader and China as an important player started to share common positions in the approaches and framework of the post-Kyoto process. The EU also decided to strengthen its cooperation with China (and other partners) on climate change on a bilateral basis. The EU-China Partnership on climate change is one of these initiatives. Hailed as one of the major outcomes of the 2005 China-EU Summit, the Partnership is committed to strengthening cooperation and dialogue on climate change and energy between the EU and China and provides for a robust follow-up process, which includes a regular review of progress in the context of annual summits (China-EU 2006). At the 10th China-EU Summit, held on 28 November 2007, the two sides agreed to increase their efforts to further enhance bilateral cooperation, including their cooperation on technology development and transfer (Council of the European Union 2007). Although it is a bilateral cooperation partnership, it underlines both the EU's and China's adherence and commitments to working within the UN framework (ibid.). In terms of Dittmer's and Chen's framework, the basic pattern of the triangle in this period is 'marriage', with a positive relationship between the EU and China and negative relationships between the US and the EU, and the US and China, respectively.

Copenhagen period

Since 2007, China has become the world's largest emitter of greenhouse gases (GHGs) (IEA 2009). This development pushed the issue of emissions by developing countries onto the centre-stage of international climate negotiations.

At the bilateral level, climate relations between China and the US achieved rapid progress. Following the election of Barack Obama as President, the US sent several delegations to China in 2009, with climate change as the key issue in meetings with Chinese leaders. The two players attempted to strengthen their dialogue and coordination in climate negotiations and to promote their understandings and cooperation on climate and energy. A memo to promote the cooperation on climate change, clean energy and environment was signed in the first meeting of the US-China Strategic and Economic Dialogue in July 2009 (Xie 2009). Meanwhile, China and the EU continued to consult on institutional guarantees, funding arrangements, technical cooperation and other issues for enhancing capacities to address climate change (Wen 2009). In the Joint Statement of the 12th China-EU Summit held on 30 November 2009, 'the two sides recognized the comprehensive cooperation in the field of climate change between the EU and China, and agreed to enhance coordination and cooperation to further implement the EU-China Joint Declaration on Climate Change', and 'to upgrade the current Partnership on Climate Change' (Council of the European Union 2009). The EU and China also tried to coordinate their positions on a bilateral basis before the Copenhagen Conference (COP 15). It seemed at the time that the pattern of a romantic triangle had emerged among the three.

However, the Copenhagen Conference at the end of 2009 saw a different pattern unfold. During the first half of the conference, the EU adopted the strategy of imposing pressure on China and intensively linked negotiations to the trilateral relationship among the US, China and the EU. The EU believed that the US would not take on additional commitments without major emerging countries, especially China, doing the same. Therefore, with the help of the US, the EU attempted to urge developing countries to take on more commitments and, in return, expected to gain greater commitments from the US. In the second half of the conference, the EU continued to urge both China and the US to make more commitments. However, the EU's strategy did not succeed. On the contrary, it led to a certain degree of convergence between the US and China and other BASIC countries (Brazil, South Africa, India). During the final stages of the summit, the US and BASIC countries held a joint meeting to reach an agreement, with the EU on the sidelines (Schunz 2014: 220). As a result, the points that were most important to the Europeans were removed from the draft agreement, in particular the concrete emissions reduction targets (Bo, Romano & Chen 2014: 204–205).

Paris period

Since 2010, the three players have developed overall cooperative relations, although their competition persisted. During the negotiations leading to the 2015 Paris Agreement, the divergence between the US, China and the EU especially pertained to differentiation. While both the EU and the US insisted on the reinterpretation and reapplication of the principle of Common but Differentiated Responsibilities and Respective Capabilities (CBDRRC), China argued that this principle should continue to be applied between Annex I and Non-Annex I countries under the UNFCCC. Divergences also included the question whether and how the new rules of mitigation burden-sharing and transparency should be guided by the CBDRRC principle. This brought the UN climate negotiations into an impasse of sorts.

It was the US and China who broke this impasse by bridging their divergences on the principle of CBDRRC. Their Joint Announcement on Climate Change of 12 November 2014 stated that '[t]hey are committed to reaching an ambitious 2015 agreement that reflects the principle of common but differentiated responsibilities and respective capabilities, in light of different national circumstances'. The same expression was re-used in the Joint US-China Presidential Statement on Climate Change issued on 25 September 2015, thereby reaffirming the consensus. The EU and China echoed this consensus in their Joint Statement on Climate Change of 26 June 2015. This implies that the three reconciled their divergences on the principle of CBDRRC, which paved the way for the outcome by achieving collective leadership to promote the adoption of the Paris Agreement. Moreover, the US and China also reached consensus on the issues of transparency and finance, which was not against the positions of the EU, even though the latter was not entirely satisfied with the rules (Bo 2018: 200–202). A pattern of *ménage à trois* for the trilateral relations thus clearly emerged during this period.

Post-Paris period

This *ménage à trois* continued in the immediate post-COP 21 period when all three players rapidly ratified the Paris Agreement. A disruption came with the ascent to power of US President Donald Trump. On 1 June 2017, he announced that he would withdraw the US from the Paris Agreement. The possible US withdrawal from the Paris Agreement would not only have an adverse impact on the agreement's universality and effectiveness but also weaken the coordination and cooperation among the three crucial players. Since then, the general cooperation between the three players has been declining.

Bilaterally, climate change has become less important in the US-China relationship, at least in the short term. When President Xi Jinping visited the US in April 2017, climate change, which had previously been a key issue, was not mentioned at all. In almost every meeting, President Obama and President Xi had talked about climate change governance, which was regarded as an important issue for their bilateral relations and global governance. Although China still attaches importance to climate change and has confirmed its commitment to the Paris Agreement after Trump's decision, the US retreat makes it impossible for the two biggest emitters to jointly promote the UN climate change negotiations in the post-Paris era as they used to.

In transatlantic relations, climate change has also become one of the most controversial issues. At the G7 summit in May 2017, while the other G7 leaders pledged to 'reaffirm their strong commitment to swiftly implement the Paris Agreement', President Trump refused to endorse the agreement, saying he needed more time to decide even under pressure from allies. The final G7 communiqué stated that the US 'is in the process of reviewing its policies on climate change and on the Paris Agreement and thus is not in a position to join the consensus on these topics'. German Chancellor Angela Merkel said the discussion on climate change had been 'very difficult, if not to say very dissatisfying', adding 'we have a situation of six against one' (*BBC* 2017).

Trump's later decision proved that his allies' persuasion attempts and pressures had failed. After Trump's announcement, European Climate Action Commissioner Arias Cañete stated that, '[t]he EU deeply regrets the unilateral decision by the Trump administration to withdraw the US from the Paris Agreement' (Cañete 2017). The leaders of France, Germany and Italy issued a joint statement rejecting Trump's proposal of a renegotiation of the Agreement. 'We deem the momentum generated in Paris in December 2015 irreversible and we firmly believe that the Paris agreement cannot be renegotiated, since it is a vital instrument for our planet, societies and economies' (Watts & Connolly 2017). Speaking to the European Parliament,

Commission President Juncker ruled out any renegotiation of the Paris Agreement (McGrath 2017). In July 2017, the German hosts of the G20 summit also failed to find common ground with the US on climate change.

Since neither China nor the EU has been successful in convincing Trump to continue US engagement on climate change, expectations were raised of a possible joint leadership from China and the EU. Climate action was a key topic during the meeting between Jean-Claude Juncker and Premier Li Keqiang at the 19th EU-China Summit on 2 June 2017. As Trump had initially showed a negative attitude towards the Paris Agreement, China and Europe conceived new cooperative steps to defend the Agreement. Negotiations between the two sides were initiated during the UN climate negotiations in Marrakesh in 2017, involving the Chinese special representative on climate change Xie Zhenhua and EU Commissioner Arias Cañete. For more than a year, Chinese and EU officials were working behind the scenes to agree on a joint statement on climate change and clean energy. Although this statement failed to be endorsed by the 19th China-EU summit due to the fact that they did not agree on China's categorization as a market economy, the EU-China Leaders' Statement on Climate Change and Clean Energy came out in July 2018 as an annex to the Joint Statement of the 20th EU-China Summit. The EU and China underlined their highest political commitment to the effective implementation of the Paris Agreement in all its aspects and committed to contributing actively to the conclusion of the Paris Agreement Work Programme at COP 24 in Katowice in order to ensure full and effective implementation of the Paris Agreement.

In light of these developments, the trilateral relations in the post-Paris era have so far resembled to the pattern of 'marriage', with the US having negative relations with both the EU and China, while the EU and China have positive relations.

The impact of the trilateral relations on the global climate order

In the past three decades, various actors and institutions at different levels have made efforts to collectively address climate change. While a diverse range of institutions have taken up the issue, the climate regime within the UN, especially the UNFCCC, is globally recognized as the leading institutional arrangement on the matter. Although the EU, China and the US are also important players in climate institutions outside the UN system such as the Major Economies Forum on Climate and Energy (MEF), they especially play a key role within the UN system, which forms the core of the global climate order.

The global climate regime

To explore the impact of the trilateral relations on the global climate order, a brief introduction to the global climate regime is needed. As the core of the global climate order, this regime was developed through three milestones: the UNFCCC, the Kyoto Protocol and the Paris Agreement.

The UNFCCC entered into force on 21 March 1994. Today, it has near-universal membership. The Convention recognized that climate change posed a problem and set a lofty but specific goal, which is to stabilize GHG concentrations 'at a level that would prevent dangerous anthropogenic (human induced) interference with the climate system' (Art. 2). It stated that, 'such a level should be achieved within a time-frame sufficient to allow ecosystems to adapt naturally to climate change, to ensure that food production is not threatened, and to enable economic development to proceed in a sustainable manner' (ibid.). It also set the principles, the foremost of which states that

> [t]he Parties should protect the climate system for the benefit of present and future generations of humankind, on the basis of equity and in accordance with their common but differentiated responsibilities and respective capabilities. Accordingly, the developed country Parties should take the lead in combating climate change and the adverse effects thereof.
>
> (ibid.)

With the idea that industrialized countries are the source of most past and current GHG emissions, they are expected to do the most to cut emissions domestically under the Convention and support developing countries by providing financial support for action on climate change, above and beyond any financial assistance they already provide to these countries. Industrialized countries also agreed to share technology with less-advanced nations.

The Kyoto Protocol is an international agreement linked to the UNFCCC, which commits its Parties by setting internationally binding emission reduction targets. The Protocol places a heavier burden on developed nations under the principle of common but differentiated responsibilities. Its major feature is that it set mandatory targets on GHG emissions for the world's leading economies. These targets range from −8 per cent to +10 per cent of the countries' individual 1990 emissions levels 'with a view to reducing their overall emissions of such gases by at least 5 per cent below existing 1990 levels in the commitment period 2008 to 2012'. In Doha, Qatar, on 8 December 2012, the Doha Amendment to the Kyoto Protocol was adopted with new commitments for those Annex I Parties to the Kyoto Protocol who agreed to take on commitments for a second commitment period running from 1 January 2013 to 31 December 2020.

Under the Protocol, countries must meet their targets primarily through national measures. However, the Protocol also offers them additional means to meet their targets by way of three market-based mechanisms (emissions trading, clean development mechanism, joint implementation). The mechanisms help to stimulate green investment and help Parties meet their emission targets in a cost-effective way.

Adopted at the COP at the end of 2015, the Paris Agreement entered into force in November 2016 and marks a milestone for global climate governance under the UNFCCC. As well as establishing aspirational goals to limit global temperature rise to well below 2 degrees Celsius above pre-industrial levels and to pursue efforts to limit the temperature increase even further to 1.5 degrees Celsius, it establishes a basic framework for enhanced international climate cooperation post-2020.

More specifically, the principle of CBDRRC is an essential element of the Paris Agreement and continues to be a guiding principle for the post-2020 climate regime when distinguishing the responsibilities and commitments of developed and developing countries. Additionally, the Paris Agreement added a specification to the principle of CBDRRC, namely that differentiation has to be seen 'in the light of different national circumstances', which means the Agreement introduced some dynamic elements into the interpretation and application of the CBDRRC. Applying the principle, the Kyoto Protocol had originally stipulated binding commitments of mitigation and timetables for Annex I countries and voluntary mitigation actions for non-Annex I countries with support from developed countries in terms of finance and technology. However, 'in the light of different national circumstances' implies more varied and new approaches to distinguish Parties and the need to take into account the differences of subgroups among developing countries, especially the least developed countries and small-island developing countries.

The Paris Agreement also addressed specific and crucial areas necessary to combat climate change, including mitigation, adaptation, loss and damage, finance, technology, transparency, etc. In relation to mitigation, the Paris Agreement established binding commitments by all Parties to prepare, communicate and maintain a nationally determined contribution (NDC) and to pursue domestic measures to achieve it. Developed countries should continue to take the lead by setting absolute, economy-wide reduction targets, while developing countries should continue to enhance their mitigation efforts and are encouraged to move towards economy-wide targets over time in the light of their specific national circumstances.

The impact of the trilateral relations on global order

The establishment and evolution of the global climate regime are the outcome of a series of efforts through the multilateral process under the UNFCCC as well as countries' bilateral and unilateral contributions. Among the more than 190 parties, the EU, China and the US are the most crucial players due to their level of emissions and influence in the process of UN climate negotiations.

First, China, the US and the EU are the top three emitters, covering 52 per cent of global emissions, with China 28 per cent, the US 15 per cent, the EU28 10 per cent in 2016 (Global Carbon Budget 2017). In terms of emissions of carbon dioxide per capita, while the world average level is 4.2 tons, the US was at 16.5, China at 7.2 and the EU at 6.9 in 2016 (ibid.). Cumulative emissions from fossil-fuel use and industry (1870–2016) were distributed as follows: US 26 per cent, EU 22 per cent and China 13 per cent, while cumulative emissions for the more recent period 1990–2016 amounted to China 20 per cent, US 20 per cent and the EU 14 per cent (ibid.).

Second, the three players have a significant impact on the process and outcome of UN climate negotiations. The EU has displayed the strongest and most stable political will to play a leading role in global climate governance. It has shown directional leadership since the mid-1990s and played leading roles in the establishment of the Durban Platform in 2011 and the adoption of a series of decisions in COPs after that. The EU and its member states, building on their strong track record of domestic climate action, have also demonstrated instrumental leadership ahead of and during COP 21, engaging, together with many other partners, in a broad High Ambition Coalition across different regional groupings of developed and developing countries. This coalition played a critical role in shifting negotiation dynamics at a decisive stage of COP 21 (European Council 2016).

The US has played crucial roles as a double-faced player by promoting or obstructing UN climate negotiations. The Clinton and Obama administrations showed global leadership regarding the Kyoto Protocol and the Paris Agreement. The US had especially become more actively involved in UNFCCC negotiations after 2011 and also succeeded in generating credibility through its domestic climate policy. In his second term, President Obama became increasingly active on climate policy through the adoption of Environmental Protection Agency (EPA)-level regulation. By contrast, George W. Bush and Donald Trump announced their withdrawal from the Kyoto Protocol and the Paris Agreement, respectively, having negative impacts on global climate governance.

China has played a more central role in global climate negotiations since the 2009 Copenhagen Conference. At the Paris Conference, China actively engaged with both developing and developed countries. While playing constructive and leading roles among developing countries through the negotiation groups of BASIC, Like-Minded Developing Countries (LMD) and Group of 77 plus China to maintain the solidarity and common interests of developing countries, China maintained close ties with developed countries, especially the US and EU, to seek consensus, and supported the host country and the United Nations to drive the process.

Against this backdrop, the three players and their trilateral relations have exerted great influence on the global climate regime. In the early 1990s, the adoption of the UNFCCC was a compromise between developed countries and developing countries aimed at addressing climate change and pursuing economic development at the same time. Whereas the principle of CBDRRC was a compromise which reflected the concerns of developing countries, especially China, the Convention had been close to finalization with a common US-EC formulation of their commitments regarding emissions (Dasgupta 1994: 143). At the same time, China tended neither to oppose nor to overemphasize the binding target for developed countries to limit GHGs proposed by the EC for inclusion in the Convention, while firmly rejecting any specific target of limiting GHGs for developing countries.

Despite these divergences among major players, the Kyoto Protocol was finally adopted at COP 3 in December 1997 and entered into force in February 2005. Following the withdrawal of the US from the Kyoto Protocol in 2001, especially the EU, but also China played their leadership roles in saving this protocol. They promoted its entry into force as well as the extension of its commitment period until 2020 so as to guarantee the continuity of the global climate regime.

Although there were divergences among China, the US and the EU on the elements of the 2015 global climate agreement, their divergences were reconciled in a flexible way, which contributed to the adoption of the Paris Agreement. Most importantly, the Paris Agreement keeps the principle of CBDRRC, which is the outcome of the collective leadership of the US, China and the EU (as well as France, holding the presidency at the summit). The US and China together played crucial roles in bridging their divergences on the principle of CBDRRC by issuing the US-China Joint Announcement on Climate Change in November 2014, stating that, '[t]hey are committed to reaching an ambitious 2015 agreement that reflects the principle of common but differentiated responsibilities and respective capabilities, in light of different national circumstances'. Their bilateral consensus on CBDRRC gave positive signals to the COP organized in late 2014 when the Lima Call to Climate Action was adopted and provided strong political momentum for the 2015 Paris Conference. Moreover, the US and China also reached consensus on the rules on transparency and finance. The China and France Joint Statement not only reflects the consensus of the US and China but also makes a breakthrough on the mitigation rules (China-France 2015). Comparing the paragraphs of the Paris Agreement on transparency, finance and mitigation with those of the joint statements between China and the US, China and France, the former reflects the contents of the latter to a large extent (Bo 2018: 200–202).

In brief, although the competitiveness of the trilateral relationship has sometimes brought about deadlock in international climate negotiations, the cooperation of the three players has contributed more substantially to the global climate order, especially the evolution of the global climate regime under the UN framework. Moreover, their national climate governance has also demonstrated positive spillover effects on the global climate order.

The future global climate order in light of the changing trilateral relationship

Although President Trump has long been sceptical of climate change and has not even acknowledged it as a problem, the topic will remain an important issue in global governance and also for the trilateral EU-China-US relationship. Moreover, scientists are now more convinced than ever that human activities seriously affect the global climate. The common interests of the three to deal with climate change thus persist, as they continue to be interdependent in this issue area.

Since the Paris Agreement has already entered into force, with or without the US, it will act as an important arrangement for the global climate order for the post-2020 period. In fact, after Trump's announcement, the US still made it clear that it will continue to participate in international climate change negotiations and meetings, and such participation included ongoing negotiations related to guidance for implementing the Paris Agreement (Office of the Spokesperson 2017). The US participated in the 23rd Conference of the Parties (COP 23) of the UNFCCC in late 2017 in order to protect US interests and ensure all future policy options remain open to the administration. Furthermore, it remains a party to the UNFCCC. Therefore, interactions between the three players continue within the UN climate regime.

Meanwhile, the withdrawal of the US from the Paris Agreement exacerbates the leadership deficit in global climate governance, making a pattern of collective leadership of the three nearly impossible in the near future. With its 'America First' policy, the Trump administration will shed the responsibilities which the US shouldered before, such as its support for free trade and climate change governance. Quite apparently, the administration has no political will to exercise leadership on the issue of climate change globally and domestically. The EU may have a leadership ambition, but it faces internal constraints regarding the adoption of more ambitious climate policies geared towards the 1.5 degrees Celsius target. With Trump's decision to pull the US out of the Paris Agreement, there were voices both at home and abroad arguing that China was prepared to fill the leadership vacuum left by the US in the post-Paris era. However, although China confirmed its commitments to the Paris Agreement and climate governance globally and domestically, it seems that it is reluctant to accept the concept of 'international leader' or to label itself as a leader in climate governance. This reluctance may be due to the following reasons. First, in Chinese, the concept of international leader tends to make a distinction between leading countries and those who are led, and this dichotomy is contrary to China's principle that all countries are equal in law. Second, China worries that it may take on disproportionate responsibilities which are beyond its capabilities with the label of 'international leader'. Third, China is still not confident enough in its diplomatic resources and means to lead global climate governance alone.

Having said that, the practical cooperation among the EU, China and the US in areas such as clean energy and carbon markets will continue. All three have a consensus and plan to develop clean energy. China is the leading country in terms of investment and application of clean energy. Its cumulative installed capacity of wind power and photovoltaic power ranks first in the world. According to Vice-Premier Zhang Gaoli, China will continue to develop a large amount of low-carbon clean energy in the future and actively carry out international cooperation in this field and will promote international cooperation in clean energy and build a community of clean energy (Zhang 2017).

Europe is on the brink of a clean energy revolution and the Commission has cleared the way to a more competitive, modern and cleaner energy system (Geropoulos 2016). At the end of November 2016, the European Commission presented a package of measures to keep the EU competitive as the clean energy transition is changing global energy markets. The Commission's 'Clean Energy for All Europeans' legislative proposals cover energy efficiency, renewable energy, the design of the electricity market, security of electricity supply and governance rules for the Energy Union. These proposals are designed to demonstrate that the clean energy transition is the growth sector of the future, turning this transition into an industrial opportunity.

The US has made it clear that it supports a balanced approach to climate policy that lowers emissions while promoting economic growth and ensuring energy security:

> We will continue to reduce our greenhouse gas emissions through innovation and technology breakthroughs, and work with other countries to help them access and use fossil fuels more cleanly and efficiently and deploy renewable and other clean energy sources, given the importance of energy access and security in many nationally determined contributions.
>
> (Office of the Spokesperson 2017)

Carbon trading is another issue for pragmatic cooperation among the three. For China's construction and operation of the national carbon emissions trading market, the experience and lessons of the EU and the state of California have been very valuable. Whereas there was already cooperation in this field between China and the EU, in 2018 the EU and China agreed to further enhance and reinforce bilateral cooperation activities on emissions trading in the context of reforming the EU-Emissions Trading System and the launch of the national Emissions Trading System in China in 2017, allowing for the sharing of experience and expertise among the two largest carbon markets in the world. Meanwhile, California's Governor Brown discussed the possibility of linking California's carbon market to China's when he met with Chinese officials in June 2017. The following month, the Californian Legislature passed AB 398, a bill to extend the state's centrepiece cap-and-trade programme to 2030 (Ruairí 2017). This has provided further space for the two sides to cooperate on carbon trade.

Last but not least, the global climate order is so much embedded in international society that American sub-state actors have been actively engaging

China and Europe and adding new levels to the trilateral relations on climate change. Domestically, President Trump's decision to withdraw from the Paris Agreement has produced an extraordinary reaction from a group of US states, cities and corporations opposed to the move. They have joined forces in a loose coalition that intends to try and meet US GHG emission targets set by the Paris Agreement (Hill 2017). In this context, these sub-state actors also seek active engagement with China and the EU.

As previously mentioned, California Governor Brown met with Chinese officials during his visit to China in June 2017, including the Minister of Science and Technology, Wan Gang, and Special Representative of Climate Change Xie Zhenhua. But the climax of his stay in China was the meeting with Chinese President Xi Jinping on 6 June 2017 in a rare diplomatic coup. California was even portrayed as a quasi-national negotiator with China on climate change (Meyers 2017). Xi spent nearly an hour talking to Brown and encouraged California to promote ties at the local level in science, innovation and green development. It is highly significant that the governor of California met with the Chinese president and talked about climate change after Trump's announcement. According to Brown, President Xi welcomed an increased role on the part of California and gave the green light for more collaboration between China and California and other US states through this subnational-level arrangement. Moreover, Brown signed an agreement with China's Ministry of Science and Technology and similar collaboration agreements with leaders in two Chinese provinces, Jiangsu and Sichuan, which called for investments in low-carbon energy sources, cooperation on climate research and the commercialization of cleaner technologies (Xinhua 2017).

Almost at the same time, former mayor of New York Michael Bloomberg made an unannounced visit to Paris and on 2 June 2017 met French President Macron, who had been leading Europe's charge to defend the Paris Agreement. Mr. Bloomberg said at a joint press conference,

> [t]oday I want the world to know the US will meet our Paris commit – through a partnership among cities, states, and businesses, we will seek to remain part of the Paris agreement process – The American government may have pulled out of the agreement, but the American people remain committed to it. We will meet our targets.
>
> (*Agence France-Presse* 2017)

In some sense, the US sub-state actors could fill the gap left by the federal government's decision to abdicate leadership on this issue and play big roles within the trilateral relations in implementing the Paris Agreement and maintaining diplomatic contact. If this scenario were to come true and the EU and China were to make more progress on climate governance by strengthening bilateral coordination, a romantic trilateral relationship might emerge again among the EU, China and the US in the future.

Conclusion

The trilateral relations between the EU, China and the US represent a typical example of a co-opetitive international relationship. While having divergences on the principles and rules of the UN climate regime, which forms the core of global climate order, they achieved generally cooperative relations in the multilateral negotiations of climate change, which were crucial to the adoption of the UNFCCC, the Kyoto Protocol and the Paris Agreement. Their divergences on the institutional design of the global climate regime, especially on how to distribute responsibilities and costs, have led to a stalemate in international climate negotiations, but they have always maintained dialogue and coordination for further cooperation. Moreover, much closer and more cooperative relations have existed between the EU and the US or the EU and China in certain periods or on certain issues, while in others they have even established a romantic triangle, which indicates the high fluidity of this relationship.

Complementary to Dittmer's theory, Chen's framework proves to be applicable to describe and explain the trilateral relations of the EU, China and the US on climate change governance. However, since this framework is state-centric, it could not include the increasingly important interactions among sub-state actors from the EU, China and the US. Therefore, the framework may need to be further adapted if it wants to have greater explanatory power in the new constellation of global climate politics.

The trilateral relations on climate change have a great impact on the global climate order. Although their competition on certain issues caused an impasse in UN climate negotiations at several points in time (such as at COP 15), at others their effective cooperation or even collective leadership has promoted the development of the global climate regime in a substantial sense, for instance at COP 21.

Having said that, the impact of the trilateral relations on global climate order should not be exaggerated. Above all, climate change is a global issue and requires the participation of all countries. Although multilateral cooperation outside the UN framework is meaningful for global climate governance, the UNFCCC is still the leading and central institution of global climate governance. The EU-China-US trilateral cooperation on climate change can therefore only be complementary to the UN framework. Furthermore, even if the competitiveness between the three is more prominent in certain periods, its impact on UN climate negotiations would only be limited.

The three players achieve their interactions mainly within the multilateral UN climate regime or at a bilateral level. Although there is a coordination mechanism for each pair, there is no trilateral mechanism among the three on climate change yet. There is little chance of a trilateral mechanism emerging in the near future because China, at least, still prefers bilateral interactions with either the EU or the US.

At the bilateral level, China thinks highly of the roles of both the US and the EU in the global climate order, although it maintains cooperation with other emerging countries like India, Brazil and South Africa. The bilateral cooperation between China and the EU has been long and productive, contributing especially to the existence and extension of the Kyoto Protocol. The bilateral cooperation between China and the US has made possible substantial breakthroughs in global institution-building on climate change, especially with regard to the Copenhagen Accord and Paris Agreement by settling the divergences on the role of CBDRRC. Compared with these two bilateral cooperative relations, the transatlantic cooperation on climate change has in the past seemed less fruitful and proactive (Schunz 2016).

If all three continue to pay attention to the cooperative benefits of the trilateral game on climate change, a *ménage à trois* would be the ideal pattern for the future. Meanwhile, although a collective leadership by all three might not be possible in the near future, a new pattern of leadership in global climate governance might emerge in the post-Paris era. It could be called 'shared leadership' shown by a group of actors, including China, the EU, European countries, other major economies like Canada and individual US states. They could show their leadership in a concerted institutional way, like they have done in UN climate negotiations in the past, in a complementary way, like on the clean energy issue, or in a parallel way, i.e. simultaneously taking leadership responsibility in different geographical regions.

References

Agence France-Presse (2017) 'Michael Bloomberg meets Emmanuel Macron as His Drive to Honour Paris Climate Change Pact Gathers Pace', 3 June. Available at: www.telegraph.co.uk/news/2017/06/02/michael-bloomberg-meets-emmanuel-macron-drive-honour-paris-climate/.

BBC (2017) 'G7Ttalks: Trump Isolated over Paris Climate Change Deal', 28 May. Available at: www.bbc.com/news/world-europe-40069636.

Bo, Y. (2018) 'Divergences and Convergences between the EU and China on post-2020 Global Climate Governance', in M. Telo (ed.), *Deepening the EU-China Partnership: Bridging Institutional and Ideational Differences in an Unstable World*, Abingdon: Routledge, 193–203.

Bo, Y., G.C. Romano & Z. Chen (2014) 'The EU's Engagement with China in Global Climate Governance', in C. Bouchard, J. Peterson & N. Tocci (eds.), *Multilateralism in the 21st Century: Europe's Quest for Effectiveness*, Abingdon: Routledge, 198–224.

Cañete, M.A. (2017) 'Statement by EU Climate Action and Energy Commissioner on the US Announcement to Withdraw from the Paris Agreement', 1 June. Available at: https://ec.europa.eu/clima/news/statement-eu-climate-action-and-energy-commissioner-miguel-arias-ca per centC3 per centBlete-us-announcement_en.

Chen, Z. (2010) 'China the US and Europe: The Cooperation and Competition in the new Trilateral Relation', *World Economy and Politics* 1, 5–22.

——— (2011) *China, the US and Europe: The Cooperation and Competition in the New Trilateral Relations*, Shanghai: Shanghai People's Press.

China-EU (2006) 'Partnership on Climate Change Rolling Work Plan', 19 October. Available at: www.fmprc.gov.cn/eng/wjb/zzjg/tyfls/tfsxw/t283051.htm.

Council of the European Union (2007) PRESSE [279], Joint Statement of 10th EU-China Summit – Beijing, 28 November, Brussels.

——— (2009) PRESSE [353], Joint Statement of the 12th EU-China Summit – Nanjing, 30 November, Brussels.

Dasgupta, C. (1994) 'The Climate Change Negotiations', in I.M. Mintzer & J.A. Leonard (eds.), *Negotiating Climate Change: The Inside Story of the Rio Convention*, Cambridge: Cambridge University Press, 129–148.

Dittmer, L. (1981) 'The Strategic Triangle: An Elementary Game-Theoretical Analysis', *World Politics*, 33(4), 485–515.

——— (1987) 'The Strategic Triangle: A Critical Review', in I. Kim (ed.), *The Strategic Triangle: China, the United States and the Soviet Union*, New York: Paragon House Publisher, 29–47.

Djoghlaf, A. (1994) 'The Beginning of an International Climate Law', in I.M. Mintzer & J.A. Leonard (eds.), *Negotiating Climate Change: The Inside Story of the Rio Convention*, Cambridge: Cambridge University Press, 97–112.

European Council (2016) 'European Climate Diplomacy after COP21' Council Conclusions, 15 February. Available at: http://data.consilium.europa.eu/doc/document/ST-6061-2016-INIT/en/pdf.

Geropoulos, K. (2016) 'New Europe Goals Include Energy Efficiency, Renewables, Innovation, Benefits for Consumers', *New Europe*, 30 November. Available at: www.neweurope.eu/article/eu-commission-package-targets-clean-energy-transition/.

Global Carbon Project (2017) 'Global Carbon Budget 2017', *Earth System Science Data Discussions*. Available at: doi:10.5194/essdd-2017–123.

Hill, J.S. (2017) 'Jerry Brown & Michael Bloomberg Launch "America's Pledge" Paris Agreement Initiative', *Cleantechnica*, 18 July. Available at: https://cleantechnica.com/2017/07/18/jerry-brown-michael-bloomberg-launch-americas-pledge-paris-agreement-initiative/.

IEA (2009) 'CO2 Emissions from Fuel Combustion', *Statistics Highlights*. Available at: www.iea.org/co2highlights/co2highlights.pdf.

McGrath, M. (2017) 'Juncker Rejects US Climate Deal Re-negotiation', *BBC News*. Available at: www.bbc.com/news/science-environment-40274234.

Meyers, J. (2017) 'China is Now Looking to California – Not Trump – To Help Lead the Fight against Climate Change', *The Los Angeles Times*, June 6. Available at: www.latimes.com/world/asia/la-fg-china-global-climate-20170606-story.html.

Office of the Spokesperson (2017) 'Communication Regarding Intent to Withdraw From Paris Agreement', Washington, August 4. Available at: www.state.gov/r/pa/prs/ps/2017/08/273050.htm.

Ruairí, A.-K. (2017) 'California Just Got Bipartisan Support to Extend Its Cap and Trade Program to 2030', *Vox*, 18 July. Available at: https://www.vox.com/energy-and-environment/2017/7/15/15955756/california-climate-brown-ab398-cap-and-trade.

Schunz, S. (2014) *European Union Foreign Policy and the Global Climate Regime*, Brussels: Peter Lang.

——— (2016) 'The Prospects for Transatlantic Leadership in an Evolving Multipolar World', *European Foreign Affairs Review* 21(3), 431–448.

Watts, J. & K. Connolly (2017) 'World Leaders React after Trump Rejects Paris Climate Deal', *The Guardian*, 1 June. Available at: www.theguardian.com/environment/2017/jun/01/trump-withdraw-paris-climate-deal-world-leaders-react.

Wen, J. (2009) 'Speech at the 5th China-EU Business Summit', 1 December. Available at: www.gov.cn/ldhd/2009-12/01/content_1477030.htm.

Womack, B. (2016) *Asymmetry and International Relationships*, New York: Cambridge University Press.

Xie, Z. (2009) 'China and the US Broaden Understanding and Deepen Understanding'. Available at: www.gov.cn/jrzg/2009-07/29/content_1378231.htm.

Xinhua News Agency (2017) 'Xi Jinping Meeting California State Governor Brown', 6 June. Available at: www.gov.cn/xinwen/2017-06/06/content_5200336.htm.

Zhang, G. (2017) 'Promoting Clean and Efficient Energy Sharing in the World'. Available at: www.gov.cn/guowuyuan/2017-06/07/content_5200631.htm?gs_ws=tsina_636325078269855835.

10 The EU-US-China triangles and the Paris Agreement

A clash of orders?

Duncan Freeman

Introduction

The ratification and entry into force of the Paris Agreement in 2016 was generally welcomed by its signatories as a significant step on the path to halting anthropogenic climate change. This achievement depended above all on a political consensus based first on the acceptance by governments of the science of anthropogenic climate change and the need for action to counter its effects. Among these, the US, China and the EU, representing its member states, were central, not least because they are the largest emitters of CO_2. The targets of the agreement, if they are to be reached, will be achieved largely by decarbonization of economies through adoption of technological solutions implemented under Nationally Determined Contributions (NDCs). Underlying the success of the Paris Agreement is the widespread, although not unanimous, acceptance of an additional argument that climate action is beneficial not just for the climate but also for the economy. This is in contrast to previous positions adopted by many governments and representatives of industry, where climate policy was generally considered to be an economic cost.

The Paris Agreement was global in its intended reach, but it is based on voluntary national policy commitments. Unlike the Kyoto Protocol, there is no binding distribution of a fixed carbon budget, and as yet it has weak or undefined monitoring and enforcement mechanisms (Doelle 2015; Bodansky 2016). The Paris Agreement has been described as a 'soft' form of governance in contrast to the legally binding Kyoto Protocol (Falkner 2016; Rajamani 2016). Nevertheless, it seeks to embed climate policy at the global and national levels through the NDCs, which for the most part will be achieved through policies to support the deployment of renewable energy and other technological solutions. Thus, the Paris Agreement is not just an international political commitment to global climate governance but depends primarily on national energy and economic or industrial policy. However, while the NDCs are policy commitments by states and are national in their scope, they rely to a considerable extent on economic actors, most importantly businesses, that operate in a global environment of markets for trade, investment and technology that are not purely national but have become increasingly globalized. Furthermore, the role of subsidiary sub-state governmental institutions in the parties to the agreement is also important. In the EU, member states are major actors in themselves, as are the states in the US and provinces and other local authorities in China, which also act in a global context. Furthermore, even more than in other policy areas, given its global nature, the climate and energy problem cannot be confined to the triangle of the EU, China and US, important as they may be in terms of emissions, economic size or level of technology.

The commonplace observation that climate change is global in nature encompasses its causes, consequences and solutions and accentuates interdependencies between the EU, China and the US and all other states. In climate change as in other areas such as international trade and investment, the policies of the Trump administration in the US have brought these interdependencies to the fore through its rejection of the Paris Agreement. The decision has been criticized for its potential effect on the climate, but like the previous refusal of the US to sign the Kyoto Protocol, following which its CO_2 emissions declined, the impact of a withdrawal from the Paris Agreement may not be entirely negative. Indeed, some leading figures working on climate change remained optimistic. For instance, Patricia Espinosa, Executive Secretary of the United Nations Framework Convention on Climate Change (UNFCCC), has insisted that action on climate change is unstoppable, regardless of the actions of the US (*BBC* 2017). The optimism expressed with regard to the effects of the possible withdrawal of the US, and also for the prospects of the Paris Agreement and international cooperation on climate change, rests to a considerable degree on an economic foundation that is widely accepted (Averchenkova et al. 2016; Fankhauser & Jotzo 2017). The essence of the argument, which focuses particularly on electricity generation, is that rapidly declining renewable energy costs and technological innovation will result in fossil fuels being displaced from the market (Greenpeace 2017a). Similarly, the internal combustion engine will be driven from the market by the declining cost of ever more advanced electric vehicles (EVs) (EVvolumes). According to this logic, the global order of climate policy set out in the Paris Agreement is reinforced by the economic order based on competition for the most effective technologies and the lowest costs. Even if the climate policy order is undermined by the withdrawal of the US from the Paris Agreement and its domestic policies favouring fossil fuels, the impact will be limited by the beneficial workings of the economic order. In these circumstances, the actions of the two other major economies and greenhouse gas emitters, the EU and China, play a central role, as do domestic actors in the US. Regardless of the US withdrawal from the Paris Agreement, the argument proposes that the economic logic of climate policy is inescapable.

In contrast to this argument, the triangle of the EU, the US and China in relation to climate change is not so simple in its construction that the weakening commitment of one party, and consequently its policy relationships with the other two, can necessarily be compensated for by a proportional strengthening of the commitment by the others. The formal structures of the Paris Agreement itself may be considered as less important than other aspects of the relationships between and the policies adopted by the actors. This chapter argues that the politics of economics do not necessarily reinforce the positive outcomes for climate change mitigation foreseen in the Paris Agreement and may actually undermine them. While there is considerable force to the economic argument, it relies on the assumption that effective technical solutions and falling costs are driven by actors including governments and businesses operating in an open global market economy. The economics of climate change policy is generally considered in isolation from wider questions of international trade and investment policy. It contends that a high degree of economic liberalism that has arguably been embedded in the international order (Ruggie 1982) is a precondition for effective market solutions for climate change. Positive outcomes for the Paris Agreement presuppose thus not just embedded climate policy but also embedded economic liberalism of open economies. However, this double embeddedness is threatened not just by the actions of the US at the political level through withdrawal from the Paris Agreement. Regardless of whether such a global economic order requires a hegemon in the form of the US or can be created through a cooperative regime (Keohane 1984; Krasner 2009), the policies of the Trump administration have made the economic policy area increasingly one of conflict, which has the potential to undermine the projected benefits provided by the economics of climate change policy. This is particularly the case when considering the EU, the US and China and the relationship between them. Increasing recourse to policy choices based on national priorities, or defence of national economic interests, potentially creates obstacles to positive outcomes for climate policy. In particular, national trade and investment policy priorities, including their securitization, especially under the increasing pursuit of national economic competition, may undermine international climate policy cooperation. This occurs in an environment where economic policy debates and choices focus on domestic priorities and interests in response to failures of globalization, open economies and free trade, linked to the economic order embodied by the World Trade Organization (WTO) and other multilateral institutions that themselves are under challenge. Such policies raise barriers to global trade and investment flows and bring to the fore the role of the state and markets, which are prone to impact on measures to deal with climate change.

This impact on climate policy may occur at an overall political level where national economic and other policy priorities such as security override climate policy goals to undermine joint action on climate change, for instance the rejection by President Trump of the Paris Agreement as a 'bad deal'. The second, and possibly more important, impact is at the specific level of national economic and other policy concerns related to industrial sectors, which are crucial to climate mitigation, and might override climate policy targets. The resort to economic nationalism, industrial policy or protectionism, or even legitimate trade defence measures, provides a broad set of policy options, but is often specifically used in key sectors related to climate and energy policy which are also increasingly seen as strategic industries that represent vital economic interests. These are frequently the target of trade defence or other measures that may have adverse effects such as disrupting trade and investment flows and raising the cost of renewable energy projects. Indeed, the more they are considered economically strategic, the more such sectors vital to climate change mitigation are likely to be the subject of policy interventions that prioritize national economic interests. Furthermore, the tendency to link trade and investment to issues of national security may add another set of barriers to beneficial climate outcomes in areas such as energy supply and technology. The policies adopted by the EU, China and the US diverge and conflict, creating the possibility that the mutually reinforcing relationship of climate policy and economics will be undermined. In this context, the EU has possibly a crucial role to play, both through its domestic climate policies and its commitment to global climate governance.

This chapter examines the interdependencies between the three key actors of the EU, China and the US in the area of climate change. However, it argues that climate policy is increasingly interdependent with economic policy and examines whether these are mutually reinforcing. This chapter first discusses whether the Paris Agreement is sustainable, then considers the development of the idea of green growth and that climate policy and economics are mutually reinforcing. Finally, this chapter considers recent developments which suggest that the assumption of mutual reinforcement is undermined by increasing emphasis on national economic interest that challenges the liberal international market order.

The global climate order under the Paris Agreement

Historically, the EU, the US and China have had very different roles in international climate policy. The EU has been considered a global leader on climate change, in part because of its early adoption of domestic policy on climate change but also because of its international role (Oberthür 2007; Oberthür & Roche Kelly 2008; Rayner & Jordan 2013; Skovgaard 2014). The EU began adoption of domestic policy on climate change in the 1990s, but it was instrumental first in the negotiation of the Kyoto Protocol and was central to efforts to replace it. While the role of the EU as a leader was questioned after the Copenhagen summit (Kilian & Elgström 2010), its role in negotiating the Paris Agreement has been considered important and successful, and since its conclusion the EU has reiterated its commitment to global climate diplomacy (Council of the EU 2018, 2019). Apart from diplomacy related to global governance, the EU, China and the US have developed considerable bilateral cooperation on climate change. Both the EU and US have developed cooperation with China related to energy and climate change in areas such as policy and regulation as well as research. Energy and climate have been a major element of the EU relationship with China. For instance, the EU and China established a partnership on climate change in 2005 (European Commission 2005), energy and climate change were key elements of the EU-China 2020 Strategic Cooperation Agenda agreed in 2013 (European Commission 2013a) and the EU and China concluded a roadmap on energy cooperation in 2016 (European Commission 2016b). One notable impact has been the role of the EU in the development of emissions trading in China (European Commission 2018a).

The Paris Agreement differs in its aims from the Kyoto Protocol, which preceded it. The Kyoto Protocol sought to place a global limit on CO_2 emissions, and then allocate the responsibilities for their reduction through a legally binding agreement. The implementation of the Kyoto Protocol and the attempt to extend it was fraught with conflict, not least between the developed and developing nations over the allocation of responsibility for emissions and their reduction, revealed in arguments over the split between the developed world, which had created most of historic emissions, and the developing world, the producers of current and projected future emissions. One of the key factors in this conflict was that dealing with climate change under this type of agreement was seen as placing limits on economic growth and therefore development, especially for developing countries such as China and India. There were also disputes over who would bear the costs of measures to deal with climate change, especially funding for implementation in the developing world.

The Paris Agreement adopts an entirely different bottom-up 'soft' form of governance (Falkner 2016; Rajamani 2016) that eliminates the battle over allocation of emissions and also opens a path to linking climate policy and economic growth which had previously been considered as in opposition. While powerful business and political groups, often linked to the fossil fuel sector, had argued that anthropogenic climate change did not exist, there were also those that made the argument that even if climate change did exist the cost of dealing with it would damage their national economies, especially in sectors that would suffer higher energy costs, so that competitiveness has been a central factor in discussion of the implementation of climate policy (Aldy & Pizer 2015).

The NDCs that follow from the Paris Agreement are not legally binding targets and are not sufficient to actually meet the requirements to restrict global temperature rises to the level needed to prevent 'dangerous anthropogenic interference with the climate system' (Art. 2 UNFCCC), but they nevertheless do commit governments to action which is specified by their national commitments. According to the UNFCCC, the NDCs will make a difference to projected trajectories for CO_2 emissions, even if they are still not sufficient to meet the 2°C target (UNFCCC 2016).

The Paris Agreement required the ratification of 55 countries representing 55 per cent of global emissions for it to enter into effect. In formal terms, these requirements have been exceeded so that the withdrawal of the US would not terminate the agreement. But President Trump has also begun to reverse domestic policies adopted by the Obama administration that are intended to address climate change and instead give preference to fossil fuels, including coal. Trump has expressed scepticism concerning climate change and in addition to the rejection of the science on which the Paris Agreement is based, the position of the Trump administration is a reassertion of the belief that climate policy is a cost, exemplified by his claim that 'the concept of global warming was created by and for the Chinese in order to make U.S. manufacturing non-competitive' (Jacobsen 2016).

So far, the response of both the EU and China has been to reaffirm their commitment to the Paris Agreement, and neither have shown any signs of weakening in this regard (Council of the EU 2017a, 2017b; Xi 2017). Regardless of the position of the US, as was the case for its previous withdrawal from the Kyoto Protocol under President George W. Bush, the Paris Agreement is unlikely to collapse as a result of US defection unless other significant emitters follow. The commitments of the EU and China will continue as their domestic policies will remain in place. As both have made clear statements to this effect (Council of the EU 2017a, 2017b; Xi 2017), in this political sense, the Paris Agreement has succeeded in embedding climate policy at the global and national levels.

The global legally binding framework that the EU had long preferred, along the lines of the Kyoto Protocol, was not adopted in Paris. The EU frequently states its preference for a rule-based international order, but the Paris Agreement arguably represents a compromise on the rigidity of that position in the form of soft governance (Falkner 2016; Rajamani 2016). This solution solved the problem of finding political consensus, and as a formal international agreement, the Paris Agreement is not endangered by a US withdrawal. However, its success depends on an economic order that is central to the rule-based system that the EU espouses.

Climate change and economic growth

The belief that climate change mitigation is an economic cost is one that was advanced by many climate sceptics as an argument against taking any action to address the problem. It was also a view shared even among those who argued for action on climate change. The Stern Review, which focused on the economic impacts of climate change, was based on the premise that the small economic cost to gross domestic product (GDP) of action in the short term should be paid in order to avoid the larger long-term losses in the future resulting from unconstrained climate change (Stern 2006). Although it recognized that there might be business opportunities arising from climate mitigation in sectors such as renewables, the overall analytical framework of the Stern Review considered climate mitigation primarily as an economic cost.

The question of economic cost has been central to previous failures to find consensus on climate policy. The position in the developed world has shifted, and the idea of 'green growth' has gained influence and acceptance. In this view, tackling environmental and climate issues are no longer considered as a cost but as a positive driver of economic development. The view has been espoused by influential international institutions such as the Organization for Economic Cooperation and Development (OECD 2011), and the International Finance Corporation (IFC), the private finance arm of the World Bank, has endorsed the idea (IFC 2016). The idea that climate change policy can be positive for growth is now advocated by many business groups (Global Commission 2015; *Bloomberg* 2016; Climate Trust 2017).

The EU has also incorporated this thinking into its view of economic policy. An example of this is the Agenda 2020 adopted in 2010, which included elements of green growth thinking in a wider growth strategy (European Commission 2010). The EU's previous growth strategy, the Lisbon Strategy of 2000, had not incorporated the idea of green growth. The Lisbon Strategy failed to meet most of its goals, and the results of the 2020 Agenda in terms of encouraging economic growth have so far been weak. The commitment to strong climate policy has depended on wider economic conditions. Following the advent of the financial and economic crisis in the EU in 2008, commitment to climate targets was weakened by short-term economic priorities (Skovgaard 2014). Nevertheless, the view that climate action and economic growth are positively linked has gained greater acceptance and has been incorporated in other EU policy documents. The EU climate and energy framework adopted in 2014 noted that previous action in this area was responsible for sustaining the employment of more than 4.2 million people in various eco-industries (European Commission 2014). The climate and energy framework incorporated the idea of decarbonization as a positive contributor to economic growth, and stated that

> there is a need to continue to drive progress towards a low-carbon economy which ensures competitive and affordable energy for all consumers, creates new opportunities for growth and jobs and provides greater security of energy supplies and reduced import dependence for the Union as a whole.
>
> (European Commission 2014)

The possibility of green growth was reiterated by the Commission in 2018 in its long-term plan for a climate-neutral economy (European Commission 2018b).

The idea that climate policy and economic growth were not in opposition was also recognized by the US government. President Obama's 2013 Climate

Change Action Plan incorporated this view of the positive economic potential of climate change action. The Obama administration asserted that,

> thanks in part to the Administration's success in doubling America's use of wind, solar, and geothermal energy and in establishing the toughest fuel economy standards in our history, we are creating new jobs, building new industries, and reducing dangerous carbon pollution which contributes to climate change.
>
> (White House 2014)

Furthermore, the Obama administration argued that sectors such as renewables could not be left to its competitors to dominate:

> The path towards sustainable energy sources will be long and sometimes difficult. But America cannot resist this transition, we must lead it. We cannot cede to other nations the technology that will power new jobs and new industries, we must claim its promise.
>
> (Obama 2013)

In order to achieve its goals the Obama administration adopted many policy measures, especially focusing on support for renewable energy, including the Clean Power Plan (GWEC 2016).

While the Obama administration sought to advance policy at the federal level, often against strong political opposition, the important role of states in acting on climate change has been long recognized (Peterson & Rose 2006). The experience of states in the US has been used as the basis for the argument that policy experience shows that climate policy action at local, state and federal levels could be positive for economic growth (Johns Hopkins 2010). The optimism of Patricia Espinosa was based on a belief that both states and businesses in the US would continue to pursue green growth strategies, and she argued that 'a lot of US businesses are really going into the agenda of sustainability and some are making their own commitments in emissions reductions in their own operations', and also that, '[a]n incredible amount of cities have embarked on ambitious goals; some states like California have been for many years in the forefront of this agenda' (*BBC* 2017).

While China saw efforts to place restrictions on its emissions at Copenhagen as a threat to its economic development path by limiting its future energy consumption, it did not see policy to tackle climate change in itself as an economic cost, but as an opportunity. In contrast to the EU and the US, the Chinese government was an early adopter of the idea that climate change mitigation could be a driver of economic growth. At the time when Stern still considered climate change mitigation a cost, the Chinese government saw it as an opportunity. This can be seen in the Renewable Energy Plan issued in 2007. While the Plan focuses on the question of the development of renewables as an energy source, it is also concerned with the development of the renewable sector as a question of industrial policy and a source of economic growth. Among its key aims is not only the deployment of renewable energy but also the promotion of technologies and industries, with the aim that by 2020 a 'domestic manufacturing capability based mainly on China's own intellectual property rights (IPRs) will have been established, satisfying the needs for deploying renewable energy on a large scale in China' (NDRC 2007). Chinese leaders have insisted that climate change is a development problem. At a Politburo meeting in 2010, Chinese Communist Party Secretary General Hu Jintao argued that, 'tackling climate change was a key strategy for China's social and economic development and a major opportunity to accelerate the transformation of the economic development model and adjust its economic structure' (Xinhua 2010).

This position was clearly expressed in the 12th Five-Year Plan (2011–2015), which included a section on green development and identified strategic emerging sectors as the focus for growth, including renewables and other new energy sectors, and transport sectors such as EVs. This emphasis has continued in the 13th Five-Year Plan (2016–2020), in which green development has been adopted as part of its guiding thinking. The thinking is incorporated into China's NDC, which the World Bank has noted, is not simply a means to support growth in the Chinese economy but also to foster economic transformation. 'Green growth' is at the core of the shift from the past industrial model based on heavy industry to a 'new normal', where the economy is faced with environmental and resource constraints (World Bank 2016).

Altogether, the argument that climate change mitigation is positive for economic growth has thus to varying degrees been accepted in the EU, the US and China, although how it is incorporated into policy has differed, with the latter showing the earliest and strongest commitment to putting it into practice, primarily through its industrial policy mechanisms. The position of the Trump administration reverses the argument, and reverts to the position that climate change mitigation is an economic cost that subtracts from growth. However, there is no indication that either the EU or China will abandon their current position. On the contrary, in the case of China, recent commitments to investment in the renewables sector indicate a strengthening of its position.

The viability of mitigation through adoption of renewable energy solutions will depend on its current and future economic costs, and by some measures renewables are already competitive with fossil fuels (IRENA 2016; Greenpeace 2017a). The cost of renewables has fallen significantly, and according to the International Renewable Energy Agency (IRENA), the global weighted average reductions of Levelized Cost of Electricity from 2015 to 2025 are forecast to be 59 per cent for solar PV, 26 per cent for onshore wind and 35 per cent for offshore wind (IRENA 2016). The role of global actors has been central to the reduction of costs of solar modules and one key factor has been competition from Chinese producers. As the IRENA analysis points out, there are regional variations in solar PV costs, but competitive pressures are leading to convergence (ibid.). Wind power costs have fallen from a peak in 2008–2009, and according to IRENA forecasts, there will also be greater competition among suppliers in the wind power value chain and technological advances, which will bring down costs (ibid.). In the US, wind energy accounted for 41 per cent of all new power capacity additions in 2015 and there have been significant declines in wind costs since their peak in 2008 (Department of Energy 2016). With an increased focus on export markets, Chinese manufacturers could exert significant downward pressure on prices in the future (GWEC 2016).

Thus, according to IRENA,

> renewable energy technologies can help countries meet their policy goals for secure, reliable and affordable energy; electricity access for all; reduced price volatility; and the promotion of social and economic development. Recent and expected cost reductions in renewable power generation technologies clearly show that renewables are now an increasingly cost-effective solution to achieve these goals.
>
> (IRENA 2016)

There has been a virtuous cycle of policy support for renewable power generation technologies leading to accelerated deployment, technology improvements and cost reductions, which has already had a profound effect on the power generation sector (ibid.). The International Energy Agency has asserted that

> high levels of incentives are no longer necessary for solar PV and onshore wind, but their economic attractiveness still strongly depend on the regulatory framework and market design. Meanwhile, some technologies (offshore wind, solar thermal electricity and some bioenergy) require continued policy support to bring them down the learning curve.
>
> (IEA 2015)

The economic logic of climate change policy has strengthened in recent years as renewable energy has become increasingly competitive in many regions of the world. The development of renewable deployment has become globalized, and competition among producers has driven down costs, especially in solar PV and wind power equipment, which has enabled them to compete with fossil fuels. The global nature of the market means that no one country, regardless of the policy it adopts, is isolated from these effects. It is no longer possible for one government to make policy which does not take into account the global context, and the EU and China will continue to play an influential role (Greenpeace 2017b), which will impact the US regardless of the policy choices it makes on renewables and fossil fuels. While this may be true, the relationship is more complex. As will be argued, the interdependencies of this economic dimension to the triangle are more complex and do not necessarily reinforce beneficial climate outcomes.

The national economic challenge to climate policy

The argument that technology and economics can decarbonize economies depends not just on effective global climate policy implemented through national commitments of the Paris Agreement but also on a benign international political and economic environment, especially in trade and investment. Without a supportive environment, the international economic drivers of decarbonization which depend on global trade and investment flows may be weakened or even reversed. However, in the relationship between the EU, the US and China the politics of international economics is not necessarily benign and may run counter to climate policy. The erosion of economic liberalism may also weaken the effectiveness of embedded climate policy. The increasing emphasis by governments on national economic priorities and competition in general and more specifically in sectors related to climate such as renewable energy, of which the 'America First' of the Trump administration slogan is only the most obvious example, threatens to undermine the economic assumptions of climate policy optimists. This may occur at the general policy level, where national economic interests are given priority over climate change concerns and international cooperation. It may also occur at the level of measures taken with regard to specific sectors that are central to climate policy.

Following the ratification of the Paris Agreement, the prime mover in this regard may have been the US, but wider economic outcomes will depend on the actions of the EU and China. The US has rejected not only the Paris Agreement but also the liberal international economic order, focusing on protectionism and national interest and the priority of sovereign nation states over global governance. The EU, in its policy pronouncements, remains committed to both the climate and economic orders embodied in the Paris Agreement and the WTO. Nevertheless, domestic and external pressures push the EU toward increasingly defensive economic policies. These are in part a response to developments in the US, which threaten EU interests, but also to those in China. The Chinese government has reiterated its commitment to the Paris Agreement, and also rejects a retreat from globalization and its associated economic order, and has advanced the idea of a community of common destiny (Xi 2017). However, it is precisely China's success in integrating climate and industrial policy that leads to the possibility of a reaction by other key actors such as the EU and the US seeking to protect their own commercial interests. Underlying the positions on trade and investment are fundamentally different views of the role of markets and state in economic policy, particularly in trade and investment, but they are also inseparable from climate policy. The questions of climate, domestic economic policy, trade and investment are interdependent and conflict to varying degrees on all sides of the EU-China-US triangle.

The proposed US withdrawal from the Paris Agreement is justified on grounds of its negative economic consequences as much as on the falsehood of climate science. In Trump's terms it is a 'bad deal'. At the same time as withdrawing from the Paris Agreement, the Trump administration is attempting to provide domestic support to fossil fuels and also to their exports under the slogan of 'Energy Dominance' while also reducing support for renewable deployment and other climate change policies. The economic argument in favour of renewables appears to carry little weight with President Trump. The position of the Trump administration represents a shift not just with regard to the Paris Agreement but also in US government policy toward China. The Obama administration had sought cooperation with China, culminating in the joint announcement on climate policy by Presidents Obama and Xi in 2014 (White House 2014). By contrast, the Trump administration has reverted to using China as a justification for the US withdrawal from the Paris Agreement and reduced the level of bilateral cooperation with China (Schwartz 2017).

One consequence of the Trump administration's adoption of an 'America First' economic policy is strengthened focus on protection of domestic industries, which also has the potential to undermine positive economic outcomes that support climate policy. 'America First' is not a discriminatory policy in its goals in that it is directed against all economic relations that do not serve US national interest, including with the EU, but China has been identified as a significant economic threat by Trump himself, and members of his administration (*Bloomberg* 2017a). Furthermore, the adoption of economic nationalism reinforces long-standing protectionism, especially with regard to China, which acts in contradiction to climate policy. The US has on previous occasions imposed trade defence measures on solar panels and wind turbines from China. The Trump administration has again imposed new measures on all solar panel imports, which has already forced up prices of panels in the US and resulted in investors withdrawing from development projects and increased trade tensions (*BloombergBusinessweek* 2017; Renewable Energy World 2017; *Bloomberg* 2017b; *BBC* 2018).

In addition to trade, foreign direct investment (FDI) is increasingly important to the renewables sector. In the past, trade was the main means by which renewable energy sector was globalized, but FDI has become more important as power generation in solar and wind has grown. Chinese investors have been active in the sector globally, including in the US and the EU. At the same time, FDI from China is frequently the subject of security review, particularly in the US, which in the past has included projects related to renewable energy (*Reuters* 2017b). The US government has a long-standing policy of security review of inward FDI, particularly with regard to China. Energy infrastructure and technology will continue to be central to this policy, which in addition to its domestic impact will cover global FDI that involves US entities. Proposals being currently considered will considerably expand the scope of US investment screening in these areas and potentially block investment and even wider forms of business cooperation, especially those with China in sectors of strategic interest.

The EU has reiterated its commitment to the Paris Agreement and continues to pursue climate policy as set out in its own existing policy goals. In contrast to the change in the US position, in EU policy-making the economic cost of climate policy is no longer generally considered a barrier to mitigation efforts. Unlike the US, the EU has not rejected the economic argument, and even has incorporated the positive economic view of climate policy into its mitigation efforts. At the same time, the EU has restated that it will not abandon its commitment to an open economic order. Nevertheless, the EU and its member states, while not adopting the equivalent of 'America First', have increasingly prioritized the defence of domestic economic interests in general, and specifically in relation to both the US and China.

As a result, the EU's economic priorities, especially in the bilateral relationship with China, do not necessarily support the possibility of climate cooperation between the two. The controversy over market economy status (MES) for China in 2016, which resulted in the EU failing to meet its obligations under China's WTO accession, demonstrated the strong domestic political pressure the EU was under in relation to economic policy on China. The defensive economic priorities with regard to China were made clear in the document on China issued by the European Commission in June 2016, which places a priority on reciprocity and market access (European Commission 2016a). The failure of the EU-China Summit in 2016 to issue a joint communiqué, partly as a result of differences over economic issues such as steel, demonstrated the impact of economic differences on the political relationship. More specifically, the 2017 EU-China Summit failed to produce a widely expected statement on climate change, again in part because of differences on economic issues (*Politico* 2017; *Reuters* 2017a). It was only at their bilateral summit in 2018 that the EU and China finally issued a joint statement on climate change reaffirming their commitment to the Paris Agreement (European Commission 2018c).

While this does not indicate a breakdown in the bilateral relationship or climate cooperation, it suggests that it is susceptible to the pressures of economic priorities and disputes as the EU has given precedence to bilateral economic interests. Support for R&D and even elements of industrial policy have also been part of EU policy. The element of industrial policy has increased, as for instance the EU has initiated a battery alliance in order to create industry capacity in this sector (European Commission 2019). This reflects not merely concern about energy and climate policy but also industrial competition, especially with China. The European Commission's regulation on the screening of FDI which, although officially are non-discriminatory, is directed at China and seeks to restrict investment in 'critical' infrastructure, technology and inputs including in the energy sector, where Chinese investors have been active (European Parliament and Council 2019).

Like the US, the EU also has a long history of trade defence measures (TDMs) related to renewables, generally targeting China. The most notable example of this was the solar panel dispute which resulted in the EU and China adopting a price agreement and anti-dumping duties on imports from China in 2013 (European Commission 2013b). The duties have been terminated (European Commission 2017), but this history demonstrates the disruptive effects of policy that gives precedence to trade defence over climate impacts. As in the case of the US, these potentially have a negative impact on the deployment of renewables in the EU (*China Daily* 2017; *Guardian* 2017). Investment screening may also potentially weaken Chinese investment in renewables and electricity distribution networks.

China restated its commitment to the Paris Agreement following the announcement of US withdrawal and the Chinese government also continues to implement its domestic policy on energy, climate and the environment. President Xi Jinping has called for an energy revolution that will transform China's reliance on fossil fuels. Since the 12th Five-Year Plan, the transformation of China's energy system has been deeply integrated into industrial policy, and sectors such as renewables and EVs obtain considerable government support. China now has a major impact on global climate change in both negative and positive senses through emissions but also on the energy economy, especially related to renewables. Renewable energy costs have been driven down in large part by the creation of industrial capacity in China which relies on economies of scale but is also supported by industrial policy.

The Chinese government has criticized the US intention to withdraw from the Paris Agreement and seeks to maintain cooperation at the political level with the EU on climate change. But China's desire to cooperate with the EU is complicated by the context of an increasingly competitive bilateral economic relationship. Competition occurs across many sectors, but specifically in areas related to climate policy. The integration of industrial policy with climate change and energy policy in China may be benign from the point of view of driving down renewable energy costs, but has external impacts that go beyond climate change mitigation. By consequence, trade policy often overrides climate policy in partner countries resulting in frictions and disputes as a result of overcapacity problems and the imbalance of production and market in China in the renewables sector. China's industrial policy supports domestic producers, and its FDI policy imposes restrictions on foreign investment in the energy sector. This arguably limits China's capacity to implement climate policy by denying the benefits of technology and know-how transfers from sources such as the EU and the US. China's FDI policy is itself increasingly the target of criticism by the EU in particular, which employs the language of reciprocity to justify efforts to increase market access, adding to pressures for restrictions on Chinese investment in Europe in strategic sectors such as energy. China's economic and climate priorities may be aligned through industrial policy, and it may be the key driver of global cost reductions in sectors such as renewables, but the results are often considered potential threats in other actors such as the EU and the US in these sectors and in the wider context of trade and investment.

Conclusion

The EU-US-China climate policy triangle is important in as far as it denotes three key actors, but its geometry is not simple. The climate order of the Paris Agreement is arguably incomplete as a rule-based system but nevertheless seeks to align climate and economic policy through NDCs. To the degree that it exists, the climate order will not be fundamentally undermined by the withdrawal of the US. But, a considerable burden for the success of the Paris Agreement is placed on the economics of decarbonization. The economics of decarbonization is not simply a matter determined by climate and energy policy. Assumptions of the alignment of economic and climate change policy are based on the effectiveness of global markets that implicitly assume the embedded liberal international economic order. However, even in market economies renewables and other sectors are the subject of considerable state policy intervention. Nowhere is this more so than in China, where renewables and emerging industries are a focus of industrial policy because they are considered the industries of the future. The EU, with an aspiring but less effective industrial policy, similarly supports emergent industries. In the US of the Trump administration, policy has shifted to support fossil fuel sectors of the past, but under previous administrations it has supported renewables. Nevertheless, state intervention is significantly lower than in China and the success of China as a leader in climate policy based on industrial policy is seen as an example of the threat to the liberal order through the state intervention on which it relies.

Underlying the economic priorities are differences in economic systems. The economic conflict does not just arise from business competition but from structural differences and priorities. On the surface, the conflict is between the US and the EU on the one hand, which have an ideological preference for market economies, and China on the other hand which adopts a more active state role in the economy. However, the increasing prioritization of national economic interests in not just China but increasingly also the US and the EU brings growing likelihood of interventions that raise barriers to trade and investment in sectors that in principle are supportive of climate policy. As a result, decarbonization must occur in an environment of increasing trade and investment policy disorder which has the potential to undermine climate policy outcomes rather than reinforce them.

References

Aldy, J.E. & W.A. Pizer (2015) 'The Competitiveness Impacts of Climate Change Mitigation Policies', *Journal of the Association of Environmental and Resource Economists* 2(4), 564–595.

Averchenkova, A., S. Bassi, K. Benes, F. Green, A. Lagarde, I. Neuweg & G. Zachmann (2016) 'Climate Policy in China, the European Union and the United States: Main Drivers and Prospects for the Future', Grantham Research Institute on Climate Change and the Environment, December.

BBC (2017) 'New UN Climate Chief: "Action On Warming Unstoppable"', *BBC*, 20 February.

——— (2018) 'Trump Says No Trade War Despite Asia Outcry over Tariffs', *BBC*, 23 January.

Bloomberg (2016) 'New Energy Outlook 2016: Powering a Changing World', *New Energy Finance*.

——— (2017a) 'Trump's Top Trade Negotiator Calls China "Unprecedented" Threat', 18 September.

——— (2017b) 'Trump's Tariffs on Solar Mark Biggest Blow to Renewables Yet', 22 January.

BloombergBusinessweek (2017) 'This Case Could Upend America's $29 Billion Solar Industry', 15 June.

Bodansky, D. (2016) 'The Legal Character of the Paris Agreement', *Review of European and International Environmental Law* 25(2), 142–150.

China Daily (2017) 'Ministry Welcomes EU's Moves on Solar Panel Tariffs', 19 September.

Climate Trust (2017) 'Opportunities for Business in Fighting Climate Change', *The Climate Trust*, 27 January.

Council of the EU (2017a) 'Climate Change: The Council Reaffirms that the Paris Agreement is Fit for Purpose and cannot be Renegotiated', Press release, 19 June.

——— (2017b) *Council Conclusions on Climate Change Following the United States Administration's Decision to Withdraw from the Paris Agreement*, European Council, June 19.

——— (2018) 'Council Conclusions on Climate Diplomacy', *Council of the European Union*, 26 February.

——— (2019) 'Council Conclusions on Climate Diplomacy', *Council of the European Union*, 18 February.

Department of Energy (2016) 'Wind Technologies Market Report 2015', *US Department of Energy*, August.

Doelle, M. (2015) 'The Paris Agreement: Historic Breakthrough or High Stakes Experiment?' *Climate Law* 6(1–2), 1–20.

European Commission (2005) 'Joint Declaration on Climate Change between China and the European Union', 2 September.

——— (2010) *Communication from The Commission, Europe 2020: A Strategy for Smart, Sustainable and Inclusive Growth*, COM(2010) 2020 final, 3 March.

——— (2013a) 'EU-China 2020 Strategic Agenda for Cooperation', 23 November.

——— (2013b) 'Memo 13–729', 27 July.

——— (2014) *Communication from The Commission to The European Parliament, The Council, The European Economic and Social Committee and The Committee of The Regions: A Policy Framework for Climate and Energy in The Period from 2020 to 2030*, COM/2014/015 final, 22 January.

——— (2016a) *Elements for a New EU Strategy on China*, Joint Communication to The European Parliament and The Council, European Commission, High Representative of The Union for Foreign Affairs and Security Policy, 22 June.

——— (2016b) 'EU-China Roadmap on Energy Cooperation (2016–2020)', 29 June.

——— (2017) 'Commission Implementing Regulation (EU) 2017/1570', September 2015.

——— (2018a) 'Memorandum of Understanding to Enhance Cooperation on Emissions Trading', 16 July.

——— (2018b) 'A Clean Planet for all: A European Strategic Long-Term Vision for a Prosperous, Modern', Competitive and Climate Neutral Economy.

——— (2018c) 'EU-China Leaders' Statement on Climate China and Clean Energy', 16 July.

——— (2019) *Report from the Commission to the European Parliament, the Council, the European Economic and Social Committee, the Committee of the Regions and the European Investment Bank on the Implementation of the Strategic Action Plan on Batteries: Building a Strategic Battery Value Chain in Europe*, 9 April.

European Parliament, European Council (2019) 'Regulation Establishing a Framework of the Screening of Foreign Direct Investment into the Union', 19 March.

EVvolumes.com (2017). Available at: www.ev-volumes.com.

Fankhauser, S. & J. Frank (2017) 'Economic Growth and Development with Low-carbon Energy', *Working Paper 267*, Grantham Research Institute on Climate Change and the Environment, September.

Falkner, R. (2016) 'The Paris Agreement and the New Logic of International Climate Politics', *International Affairs* 92(5), 1107–1125.

Global Commission (2015) 'Seizing the Global Opportunity: Partnerships for Better Growth and A Better Climate', *The Global Commission on The Economy and Climate*, July.

Greenpeace (2017a) 'Comparing Electricity Production Costs of Renewables to Fossil and Nuclear Power Plants in G20 Countries', *Greenpeace*, 2017.

——— (2017b) 'China Kept on Smashing Renewables Records in 2016', *Greenpeace Energydesk*, 6 January.

Guardian (2017) 'Solar Industry Says EU Tariffs On Chinese Imports Will Raise Panel Prices', 8 September.

GWEC (2016) 'Global Wind Report, Annual Market Update 2015', *Global Wind Energy Council*, April.

International Energy Agency (IEA) (2015) 'Renewable Energy Medium Term Market Report 2015', *IEA*, Paris.

International Renewable Energy Agency (IRENA) (2016) 'The Power To Change: Solar And Wind Cost Reduction Potential To 2025', *IRENA*, June.

International Finance Corporation (IFC) (2016) 'IFC: Climate Change – Threat and Opportunity for Private Sector', *Capital Finance International*, IFC, 6 January.

Jacobsen, L. (2016) 'Yes, Donald Trump Did Call Climate Change a Chinese Hoax', *Politifact*, 3 June.

Johns Hopkins (2010) 'Impacts of Comprehensive Climate and Energy Policy Options on the US Economy', Johns Hopkins University, Centre for Climate Strategies, Washington DC, June.

Keohane, R. (1984) *After Hegemony: Cooperation and Discord in the World Political Economy*, Princeton: Princeton University Press.

Kilian, B. & O. Elgström (2010) 'Still a Green Leader? The European Union's Role in International Climate Negotiations', *Cooperation and Conflict* 45(3), 255–273.

Krasner, S. (2009) *State Power and the Structure of International Trade in Power, the State and Sovereignty: Essays on International Relations*, Abingdon: Routledge.

National Development and Reform Commission (NDRC) (2007) *Medium and Long-Term Development Plan for Renewable Energy in China*, NDRC, September.

Obama, B. (2013) 'Second Inaugural Address', January.

Oberthür, S. (2007) 'The European Union in International Climate Policy: The Prospect for Leadership', *Intereconomics* 42(2), 77–83.

Oberthür, S. & C. Roche Kelly (2008) 'EU Leadership in International Climate Policy: Achievements and Challenges', *The International Spectator* 43(3), 35–50.

Organization of Economic Cooperation and Development (OECD) (2011) 'Towards Green Growth', *OECD*, July 2011.

Peterson, T.D. & A.Z. Rose (2006) 'Reducing Conflicts between Climate Policy and Energy Policy in the US: The Important Role of the States', *Energy Policy* 34(5), March, 619–631.

Politico (2017) 'EU-China Trade Tensions Undermine Climate Unity', 2 June.

Rajamani, L. (2016) 'The 2015 Paris Agreement: Interplay Between Hard, Soft and Non-Obligations', *Journal of Environmental Law* 28(2), 1 July, 337–358.

Rayner, T. & A. Jordan (2013) 'The European Union: The Polycentric Climate Policy Leader?' *Climate Change* 4(2), March/April, 75–90.

Renewable Energy World (2017) 'Rising Chinese Solar Panel Prices May Put Indian Projects at Risk', 21 August.

Reuters (2017a) 'EU, China Trade Spat Blocks Climate Statement', 2 June.

——— (2017b) 'Chinese Deals Topped US Security Reviews in 2015: Treasury Report', 21 September.

Ruggie, J. (1982) 'International Regimes, Transactions, and Change: Embedded Liberalism in the Postwar Economic Order', *International Organization* 36(2), 379–415.

Schwartz, L. (2017) 'As Trump Veers US Off-Course, China Leads on Climate Change', *Renewable Energy World*, 23 August.

Stern, N. (2006) 'The Economics of Climate Change: The Stern Review', *Her Majesty's Treasury*, October.

Skovgaard, J. (2014) 'EU Climate Policy after the Crisis', *Environmental Politics* 23(1), 1–17.

UNFCCC (2016) 'Aggregate Effect of the Intended Nationally Determined Contributions: An Update, Synthesis Report by the Secretariat', *UNFCCC*, 2 May.

White House (2014) 'US-China Joint Announcement on Climate Change', *Whitehouse*, 11 November.

World Bank (2016) 'Pursuing an Innovative Development Pathway: Understanding China's NDC', Partnership for Market Readiness, National Centre for Climate Change Strategy and International Cooperation, World Bank, Washington, November.

Xi, J. (2017) 'Work Together to Build a Community of Shared Future for Mankind', 18 January.

Xinhua (2010) 'Hu Jintao Leads Politburo Study: Emphasizes Doing Well Work on Addressing Climate Change [Hu Jintao zhudai zhengzhiju xuexi qihou bianhua gongzuo qiangdiao zuohao yingdui qihou bianhua gongzuo]', 23 February.

11 Climate change politics in the US, China, and the EU

Climate science and the framing of climate action

Miranda A. Schreurs

Introduction

The combined carbon dioxide (CO_2) emissions of China, the European Union (EU), and the United States (US) exceed half of total global emissions. This makes an analysis of their efforts to address climate change particularly important. Developments in these three powerful polities are not only important to examine in terms of their contributions to global climate emissions, however. The positions they have taken towards climate action also say much about their political and economic priorities as well as how they tick politically (Schreurs 2016; Kalantzakos 2017; Gallagher & Xuan 2018). Despite years of cooperation among their scientific communities, the three largest greenhouse gas emitters differ significantly on their domestic approaches to climate change in large part because of the varying degrees to which climate change science is accepted by their societies and political establishments. These differences have slowed global efforts to reign in greenhouse gas emissions. Although all three signed the Paris Agreement on climate change, the US government under Donald Trump has indicated the US will leave the agreement.

This chapter examines the reasons behind the different approaches of China, the EU, and the US towards climate change. In particular, it examines how science is integrated into their political processes. This chapter begins with an examination of climate change science in the three communities, explaining how the US has played a crucial role in developing this scientific field. It then compares how climate science is understood in the three countries and the role it plays in the policy-making process. Particular attention is given to the rise of climate scepticism in the US and the linking of climate action to modernization plans in China and the EU.

Puzzling realities

There are many reasons why one might expect the US to be leading the global fight on climate change. Under the Republican presidency of Ronald Reagan, the US led the global fight to address another atmospheric pollution problem: stratospheric ozone depletion, more commonly known as the ozone hole. Without US leadership, it is doubtful that the 1987 Montreal Protocol on Substances that Deplete the Ozone Layer would have been realized when it was. The US also led early scientific research into climate change and was a force in calling for the formation, in 1988, of the Intergovernmental Panel on Climate Change (IPCC), a body of the United Nations set up to provide authoritative scientific conclusions on climate change, its causes, and consequences. Scientific concern with climate change goes back decades. A study by the organization 'Carbon Brief' backs up this point. It asked the coordinating lead authors of the IPCC which articles they considered to be the most influential on climate change. The largest number of votes went to articles authored by scientists working in US institutions (Carbon Brief 2015a).[1] In a related study, Carbon Brief found the most cited article with 'climate change' in the title was by US-based scholars Camille Paremsan (University of Texas and Plymouth University) and Gary Yohe (Wesleyan University) and the most cited article with the word 'climate' in the title was by lead author Eugenia Kalnay of the National Center for Environmental Prediction at the National Oceanographic and Atmospheric Administration and her 21 co-authors (Carbon Brief 2015b).

The US, moreover, has the world's largest and richest environmental non-governmental organizations (NGOs). Memberships in the biggest NGOs number in the hundreds of thousands to millions (e.g. WWF, National Wildlife Federation, Greenpeace, Sierra Club, Natural Resources Defense Council, National Audobon Society). One would expect their political influence on climate change to be quite strong. Finally, it is increasingly clear that climate change is impacting the US in significant ways. There has been one large and destructive hurricane after the next (Katrina, Sandy, Michael), droughts in the south-west, and forest fires of historic size. And indeed, during the presidency of Barack Obama, the US and China entered into a bilateral deal on climate change. The US would cut its greenhouse gas emissions by 26–28 per cent of 2005 levels by 2028 and China would cap the increase in its CO_2 emissions by no later than 2030. This deal was critical to the successful conclusion of the Paris Agreement. The EU had already committed to reducing its emissions by 40 per cent of 1990 levels by 2030 and also to greatly expanding reliance on renewable energy and making improvements in energy efficiency. The stage was set for strengthened multilateral action on climate change. Yet, about half a year after the ratification of the Paris Agreement, in June 2017, the Trump administration announced that it would pull the US out of the Paris Agreement. Why has the US repeatedly pulled the plug on multilateral climate action?

In the case of China, one might expect the country's leaders to fend off pressure for it to take meaningful climate action as much as it did when climate negotiations first began (Harris 2011; Kopra 2019). The country is the world's most populated (although India will soon take over this position). And, while it has pulled huge numbers out of poverty, there are still many millions more eager to reach middle-class status, meaning energy demand will remain strong. Not surprisingly, economic development remains the top priority for the country. Beyond this, not only is the country heavily dependent on coal, it still has large coal reserves (according to the World Coal Institute (2009), China has the third largest known reserves in the world following the US and Russia). All of these factors would suggest that China would oppose climate action.

At the time the Kyoto Protocol was being negotiated, China stressed that responsibility for climate change lies largely with the West, and particularly the US and Europe, the largest historical emitters of greenhouse gas emissions (Harris 2011; Kopra 2019). China positioned itself as the leader of the developing countries in the negotiations arguing for technological and financial assistance in addressing climate change and against having to set a time line for reducing its own emissions. China joined the Kyoto Protocol as an Annex B country, meaning it was not obliged to reduce its emissions; instead, it could benefit significantly from technical assistance in the development of renewable energy and energy efficiency improvements through the Kyoto flexibility mechanisms.

Also, at the Copenhagen climate negotiations in 2009 when global hopes for establishing an agreement were high, China kept largely to its previous stance that it was the responsibility of developed countries to reduce their emissions. It adopted the position of 'common, but differentiated responsibilities', accepting the notion that China needed to act, but resisting the establishment of a firm date by which it would start to reduce its own emissions. China also resisted committing to a system of transparent verification of its own greenhouse gas emissions, as the US was demanding, arguing this was a matter of national sovereignty. China was blamed in the international press for the failed outcome of the negotiations (e.g. Lee 2009; Watts et al. 2009).

Fast forward a few years, and we see that in the months prior to the Paris climate negotiations, China announced that it would peak its greenhouse gas emissions by 2030 and then begin to reduce them. Why did China agree to take on a greenhouse gas emission target and sign on to the Paris Agreement? And why after the announcement of Donald Trump that he will pull the US out of the Paris Agreement, did China not take a similar decision and instead announce that it would work with the EU and others to make the Paris Agreement a success?

The third actor in this international foreign policy play is the EU. The EU has arguably been the most consistent player of the three. From the start, it has supported global climate action. It pushed hard to keep the Kyoto Protocol alive after the US abandoned the agreement. Similarly, it championed the Paris Agreement, arguing it was critical to take action for the sake of current and future generations (Oberthür & Groen 2018). The EU has consistently been the first to show its cards, introducing EU-wide energy and renewable energy agreements prior to entering into the global agreements. Thus, in 2007, prior to the Copenhagen climate negotiations, the EU announced its legally binding plan to reduce its combined greenhouse gas emissions by 20 per cent of 1990 levels by 2020 and to expand renewables to 20 per cent of the energy mix and improve energy efficiency by 20 per cent (compared to 2005 levels). In 2014, prior to the Paris Agreement, the EU announced its plans to achieve a 40 per cent reduction in greenhouse emissions by 2030 and a 27 per cent share of renewables in the energy mix and a 27 per cent improvement in energy efficiency. These latter two goals were subsequently increased in 2018, respectively, to 32 per cent and 32.5 per cent. This occurred prior to the climate negotiations in Katowice, Poland.

Why has the EU taken on this global climate leadership role? As the divide over participation in the Iraq War, differences in the response to the migration crisis linked to the war in Syria, and the British plan to leave the EU (Brexit) clearly show, the EU is not exactly united when it comes to many foreign policy and trade decisions. The member states of the EU are really quite different in terms of their political cultures and policy priorities. They also have different energy supplies available to them and differ in their positions on the use of nuclear energy. Moreover, there is no strong leadership in the EU embodied in the hands of a single powerful executive. What then binds European countries together in relation to climate change to the point that for the better part of the last two decades, the EU has maintained a willingness to take on climate change commitments even when this has not always been reciprocated by either China or the US?

Climate science and the policy-making process

One of the biggest differences among these three economies is the extent to which climate science is accepted. The US, China, and the EU all nominate scientists to participate in the IPCC. The IPCC issues periodic reports on the state of the science on climate change. The first IPCC report was issued in 1990 and already warned of a warming climate as a result of CO_2, methane, CFCs, and nitrous oxides accumulating in the atmosphere. Each subsequent report has intensified the warnings about the consequences of rising concentrations of greenhouse gases in the atmosphere and increasingly strongly connected this rise to anthropogenic activities – primarily the burning of fossil fuels, deforestation, and agricultural activities.[2] The work of the IPCC has, however, been received differently in the three major economies.

Climate scepticism in the US

In no other country in the world has the work of the IPCC been challenged in such a politically substantial way as in the US. Already in 2004, the Union of Concerned Scientists issued a report on the George W. Bush administration's misuse of science. The report criticizes the Bush administration for consistently seeking 'to undermine the public's understanding of the view held by the vast majority of climate scientists that human-caused emissions of carbon dioxide and other heat-trapping gases are making a discernible contribution to global warming' (Union of Concerned Scientists 2004: 5). The report goes on to note that even though the National Academy of Sciences rendered a strong opinion essentially confirming the findings of the IPCC, 'Bush administration spokespersons continue to contend that the uncertainties in climate projections and fossil fuel emissions are too great to warrant mandatory action to slow emissions' (ibid.).

Efforts to debunk climate science have been closely linked to efforts to downsize government. Newt Gingrich, speaker of the House of Representatives from 1995 to 1999, came in with a plan to bring conservatives back into power using polarizing political tactics. A decade-and-a-half later the conservative and populist Tea Party movement within the Republican Party largely completed the transformation of Congress from a place of partisan compromise to one of ideological extremes. These anti-big government, populist movements produced fertile breeding ground for climate scepticism and denial (Bang, Hovi & Sprinz 2012; Skjærseth, Bang & Schreurs 2013; Schreurs 2019a). In the US Congress, powerful Senators have used their positions to sow seeds of doubt in the minds of the public on climate science and block climate legislation. The US decision to abandon the Kyoto Protocol was premised on the fact that China and India were not required to take measures to reduce their growing emissions. The Kyoto Protocol was framed as a threat to American jobs and competitiveness. James Inhofe, Republican Senator from Oklahoma who served as chair of the Senate Committee on Environment and Public Works from 2003 to 2007 and from 2015 to 2017, strongly fought against climate programmes. A book he wrote while in office describes climate science as a 'hoax' perpetrated as part of a great conspiracy against the American way of life (Inhofe 2012).

During the presidency of Donald Trump, climate denial has been taken to a new level. Trump appears determined to deliver on the conservative agenda of 'smaller government through less regulation'. This means that environmental protection policies have increasingly come under attack. Both before and since becoming President, he has regularly questioned climate science, calling it a hoax perpetrated by China and tweeting 'that scientists have manipulated data on global warming. The data is unreliable' (Trump 2011). Matthews (2017) reported that Donald Trump had tweeted climate scepticism 115 times between 2011 and mid-2017. Putting words into action, he has asserted his plans to abandon the Paris Agreement, weaken fuel efficiency standards, and reverse President Obama's Clean Power Plan, an effort to reduce greenhouse gas emissions from coal-fired power plants.

There are certainly large percentages of the US population who support the work of the IPCC and accept the science that points to a warming planet and link this to human industrial activities. Gallup has conducted opinion polls on climate change/global warming since 1990. Asked about whether they believe global warming has already begun, close to half or more of those surveyed responded positively over the years (48 per cent in 1998, 61 per cent in 2008, 49 per cent in 2011, 62 per cent in 2017). Respondents also linked global warming to human activities (61 per cent in 2001, 50 per cent in 2010, 68 per cent in 2017) (Saad 2017).

Still, there are differences in support by political party and by geographical region. To the question, 'do you think the seriousness of global warming is generally exaggerated?', a large percentage of Republicans answered affirmatively (66 per cent in 2017, 69 per cent in 2018) compared with 10 per cent of Democrats in 2017 and 4 per cent in 2018. Asked if they agree with the statement, 'most scientists believe global warming is occurring', 53 per cent of Republicans responded positively in 2017, but only 42 per cent in 2018. In comparison, in both years 86 per cent of Democrats agreed (Brenan & Saad 2018).

Yale University researchers detailed climate opinions down to the district and state level for 2016. A clear difference can be seen by state as to whether respondents believe most scientists agree climate change is happening. In Washington, Oregon, California, New Mexico, Colorado, Wisconsin, Illinois, New York – states which lean blue (Democrat) or purple (partly Democrat), the majority of respondents agreed that most scientists think global warming is happening. In contrast, in many of the Republican or Republican-leaning states there were far higher percentages who responded that there was some or even a lot of disagreement among scientists (Marlon et al. 2016).

China: from climate scepticism to an embrace of climate science

Western scientists dominated the IPCC in its early years and this appears to have fed into nationalist sentiments and to raise some concerns in China about the neutrality of the IPCC findings, at least until sometime after the Copenhagen climate negotiations. Climate conspiracy theorists in a handful of books and on social media argued that climate change was a Western plot intended to keep the country from developing further (Watts 2010; Liu 2015; Dembicki 2017). They questioned the speed and severity of climate change, the motivations behind developed countries pushing for a legally binding agreement, whether the scientific case for climate action was strong, and if climate change could also be beneficial for China (Nadin & Painter 2011; Liu 2015; Dembicki 2017).

Still, it was perhaps more a case of power politics and national interests that swayed Chinese leaders' positions on climate change than scepticism of the IPCC findings. Rebecca Nadin and James Painter (2011) made a comparative study of climate scepticism in the media in five countries covering the periods of 2007 and 2009–2010. They found very little sceptical reporting in the Chinese media compared to very large amounts in the US and the United Kingdom (UK). John Chung-En Liu's study of the Chinese newspaper *People's Daily* also found almost no signs of climate scepticism, although he did find instances of climate scepticism in social media (Liu 2015).

Chinese negotiators both at Kyoto and Copenhagen thus focused attention on the country's share of cumulative global emissions (the sum of annual emissions starting from 1751) rather than on its rising annual emissions. They pointed out that it was the US and the EU that were responsible for the bulk of historical emissions. Indeed, in 1990, the US was responsible for about 31 per cent and the EU-28 for about 29 per cent of cumulative (historical) CO_2 emissions compared with only about 5 per cent for China (Ritchie & Roser 2017). China's leadership thus argued that it was the responsibility of rich countries to take measures to sharply reduce their greenhouse gas emissions and to assist developing countries with financial and technical assistance.

China's position on climate change began to change in the 2010s as the impacts of global warming on the economy became increasingly apparent and China's emissions continued to climb, making it harder to escape international scrutiny. Having become the world's largest emitter of greenhouse gases in 2006, China's credibility as a leader of the third world on climate matters also increasingly came into question. Air pollution, moreover, had reached crisis proportions and was causing societal unrest (Schreurs 2019b).

Chinese climate science was also progressing. China's Third National Assessment Report on Climate Change of November 2015, put together by over 500 experts from government ministries, the Chinese Academy of Sciences, and universities, found that average temperatures in China had increased by 0.9 degrees Celsius to 1.5 degrees Celsius between 1909 and 2011 and that the country was highly vulnerable to sea-level rise (Sandalow 2018).

Today, the work of the IPCC is widely accepted in China. In contrast with the situation in the US, there is little evidence of climate scepticism among the Chinese public or leadership. Chinese media reports on climate change, but primarily in relationship to specific events like the international climate negotiations or domestic policies. Science news also comes largely from the government, and the media tends to praise Chinese achievements.

The EU's embrace of IPCC findings

In contrast with the situation in the US, the EU bases its climate policy and energy decisions on the findings of the IPCC. The EU's goal to reduce emissions by 80–95 per cent of 1990 levels by 2050 aligns with IPCC estimates of the reductions which will be needed by developed countries to keep average temperatures from rising above 2 degrees Celsius above pre-industrial levels.

While there are some climate sceptics in Europe, their numbers are limited and their political influence has been held in check (Schreurs 2019a). Where they have made some inroads is in some of the Central European countries (e.g. the Czech Republic and Poland), with free market supporters in the United Kingdom, and the far right party Alternative for Germany (*Alternative für Deutschland*, AfD). These sceptics have not, however, managed to raise substantial doubts in the broader European public towards climate science.

Concerns about climate change remain very strong in Europe. According to a 2017 Eurobarometer survey, nine in ten Europeans view climate change as a serious or very serious problem. Close to four in five (79 per cent) agreed that taking action on climate change and using energy more efficiently can lead to more jobs and strengthen the economy and that promoting EU expertise in new clean technologies internationally (77 per cent) and reducing fossil fuel imports from outside the EU (64 per cent) can benefit the EU economically (Eurobarometer 2017).

Climate policy: an economic burden or an economic opportunity?

Another major difference between the US, on the one hand, and China and the EU, on the other, is the extent to which environmental protection, renewable energies, and climate action are embedded into visions and policy programmes for the future. In the EU, policies for climate mitigation and adaptation and sustainability are viewed as important vehicles for achieving modernization. Similarly, in China, climate change action is viewed not only as necessary to deal with the threats posed by a warming climate but also as an opportunity to further economic modernization and develop new competitive industries. While this view is held in many regions in the US, is embedded in some state-level policies and programmes, and was supported by the Obama administration, it was not embraced at the federal level by the George W. Bush administration and has also been largely rejected by the Trump administration.

Efforts to frame climate change action as an opportunity in the US

Although politicians in Congress and the White House have repeatedly questioned the science and cast doubt that climate change is real, many states and cities are formulating their own climate plans, programmes, and regulations. California has positioned itself as a global leader with its call to achieve 50 per cent renewable electricity by 2025 and 100 per cent by 2045. It set a carbon neutrality target for 2050, an ambitious move for an economy, which is one of the largest in the world. With the support of successive governors, and with the innovative, creative potential of Silicon Valley, the state has become a powerhouse in clean technology development (Karapin 2016). Other states are acting, too. The Climate Alliance of US States was launched by the governors of New York, Washington, and California. The alliance has grown from its initial 15 members to 22 with the addition of several more states in early 2019. These states are committed to implementing policies that advance the goals the US pledged to under the Paris Agreement, including the reduction of greenhouse gas emissions by 26–28 per cent below 2005 levels by 2025, tracking and reporting their progress to the international community, and accelerating new and current policies to reduce greenhouse gas emissions and promote clean energy deployment (United States Climate Alliance 2019). Even some Republican-dominated states, like Iowa and Texas, which are not part of the alliance, have become leaders in renewable energy development, largely because it has proven economically beneficial to do so. Furthermore, several hundred mayors have joined the Climate Mayors initiative, which commits their cities to adopt, honour, and uphold the goals of the Paris Agreement.[3]

United States climate emissions were slightly higher (about 1 per cent) in 2016 than in 1990 but well below their peak around 2005 (about 14 per cent lower) (U.S. Environmental Protection Agency 2018). The reasons are multiple. They include initiatives at the state level as well as some federal programmes, such as energy efficiency programmes in government buildings initiated during the Obama administration. The main reason, however, has been the shift from coal to unconventional sources of natural gas, which carry with them their own set of problems. To be consistent with the IPCC warnings, moreover, would require far deeper emission reductions (Gamper-Rabindran 2018).

Soon after being elected to Congress, Alexandria Ocasio-Cortez, a Democrat from New York, submitted a resolution to Congress calling upon the federal government to create a 'Green New Deal'. The resolution opens with a reference to the IPCC's Special Report on Global Warming of 1.5 degrees Celsius (IPCC 2018) and its warnings about the limited time frame available to still prevent serious climate change and the high costs that will be associated with delayed action. The resolution embodies many ideas already embraced in Europe: achieving net-zero greenhouse gas emissions, creating high-wage jobs, investing in infrastructure, securing a clean and healthy environment, making a rapid transition to renewable energy, and enhancing energy efficiency. It is a call for the development of a fairer, more socially just, and environmentally responsible economic structure. Its 89 co-sponsors are all from the Democratic Party (H. Res. 109, 116th Congress 2019–2020). The resolution builds on a call that President Barack Obama had made a decade earlier during his 2008 election campaign, to create a Green New Deal in order to stimulate new jobs and infrastructure while protecting the planet (Schreurs 2010; Bang & Schreurs 2011).

The challenge that this resolution and related types of bills are likely to have is that it jumps into the midst of a larger economic debate regarding the role the government should play in the economy. Much like Conservatives attacked Obama for his climate initiatives, Ocasio-Cortez's plan is being labelled as dangerous, a threat to American jobs, and socialist (e.g. Haskins 2019). Essentially, US climate politics have been hijacked by a larger and highly polarized debate regarding how much the state should intervene in the economy. This affects not only climate change policy but also other issues, such as healthcare, social welfare, and education. Climate scepticism in the US has less to do with an acceptance or rejection of climate science than it does with the question of acceptance or rejection of a larger role for the government in mediating the economy.

While polarization remains strong, there are some signs of efforts to find a means to action. While the Republicans controlled the House of Representatives, Lamar Smith, a climate denier from Texas, led the House Committee on Science for six years. No actions were taken. With Democrats back in charge of the House of Representatives since 2018, the House Science Committee is again dealing with climate change.[4] The new senior Republican on the committee, Frank Lucas of Oklahoma, has signalled that he recognizes that human activities are contributing to climate change (Banerjee 2019). Perhaps as a new generation of younger representatives in both parties emerges, climate science will achieve a firmer foothold once again in policy debates and the voices of climate sceptics and deniers will weaken and those of scientists and climate experts will strengthen.

China: aiming at climate leadership?

In the mid-2000s, Chinese leaders increasingly began to recognize that there were many opportunities in pursuing climate action. For one, environmental protection could be used as a means to modernize the economy and justify the shutting down of highly polluting and inefficient factories and mines. Relatedly, moving aggressively on environmental technologies could give China a chance to gain dominance in sectors that can be expected to grow substantially in the years ahead, such as renewable energy and electric mobility (Conrad 2012; Wübbeke & Ting 2017).

Important legislative and programmatic changes institutionalized the leadership's growing concern with climate change and promoted clean tech research, development, and deployment. In 2007, China launched its first National Climate Change Programme aiming to develop low carbon and renewable energy, reforest vast regions of the country for them both to act as a carbon sink and to slow desertification, strengthen climate change research, and enhance research capacity. The programme set 2010 goals for improvements in the energy intensity of the economy, growth in renewable energy, and expansion of the share of forest coverage. It also discussed areas for technological advancement: clean coal, nuclear power, modernization of the electricity grid, and energy conservation.

China's five-year development plans also began to emphasize energy efficiency improvements and renewable energy development starting with the 10th Five-Year plan (2001–2005). Each successive plan set increasingly ambitious targets. China's 13th Five-Year Plan (2016–2020) set a goal of reducing the emissions intensity of the economy by 40–45 per cent of 2005 levels and a 15 per cent share of renewables in the energy mix by 2020. It called for changing the heavily resource-based economy towards a service-oriented, more diversified, and less carbon-intensive economy, and decoupling economic growth from emissions (Schreurs 2019b).

The central government also opened opportunities for provincial and local climate policy experimentation. Low-carbon pilot projects and regional carbon emissions trading programmes were started to encourage climate innovation at the local level and to test the effectiveness of various policy models (Wang, Engels &Wang 2018). Although there are still problems with the system, the career advancement performance evaluation system for local government cadres was altered to include environmental criteria so as to heighten the priority given to environmental matters in local government planning and to incentivize government officials to take environmental protection seriously (Ran 2014).

The National Energy Administration and the National Development and Reform Commission (NDRC) imposed restrictions on capacity expansions in the coal sector and took measures to modernize the coal industry. While coal-powered generation increased again in 2018, there is good reason to believe this is a temporary reversal of a downward trend (Ye & Lu 2018).

Renewable energy sources are rapidly expanding and accounted for over a quarter of electricity production in 2017 (most of this is from hydropower, with wind and solar combined accounting for over 5 per cent) (REN 21 2018). China now leads globally in overall investment in renewable power and fuels and has the highest levels of installed capacity in hydropower, solar PV, wind power, and solar water and geothermal heating capacity (REN 21 2018). Furthermore, as a result of policies adopted for energy efficiency and renewable energy, in the five years from 2010 to 2015, energy intensity dropped by an impressive 18.2 per cent even while the economy was growing at an average annual rate of 7.8 per cent (Voïta 2018).

In 2018, in a major administrative shake up, responsibility for climate change was moved from the NDRC to the Ministry of Environment. This can be read as an effort to strengthen the authority of the Ministry of Environment relative to that of powerful economic actors in the government.

The programme 'Made in China 2025', which was launched by Prime Minister Li Kejiang in 2015, spelled out China's plans to leap frog the US in advanced technologies. According to the programme, China aims to become a global leader in a variety of fields, including robotics, artificial intelligence, clean energy, and clean energy vehicles. As a result of global and especially US critique that China is unfairly protecting and subsidizing its industries, this particular programme is being downplayed (Cyrill 2018). Nevertheless, China has a clear interest in gaining technological leadership in clean energy and environmental industries.

Of course, China is still facing a challenging several decades ahead. The population is expected to peak at 1.44 billion in 2029 (up from 1.38 billion in 2019) (Stanway 2019). This means that at least for the next decade or more, the focus will need to be on how to provide sufficient resources for the still expanding population and growing economy (growth rates ranged between 6 and 7 per cent at the end of the 2010s) (Dong et al. 2017). China's Nationally Determined Contribution under the Paris Agreement, consisting in peaking emissions by 2030 (with the best intentions to peak earlier), reducing emissions intensity of the economy by 60–65 per cent of 2005 levels and obtaining a 20 per cent share of renewables by 2030, correlates with the anticipated population peak (Government of China 2015).

With the Trump administration's decision to pull the US out of the Paris Agreement, the EU and China have stepped up their cooperation on climate change, including with plans to aid developing countries. Their joint understandings and plans can be found in the EU-China Joint Statement on Climate Change (2015), the EU-China Roadmap on Energy Cooperation (2016), and the EU-China Leaders' Statement (2018). They have also agreed to discuss cooperation as the two largest emission-trading systems in the world. The risk to the US is that it could be left behind in the sustainability transitions that are underway in both Europe and China.

The EU: promoting a vision of a climate-neutral, societally just, and modern economy

Various factors are driving EU action on climate change. These include a high level of public concern with climate change across much of Europe and concerns about energy security and Europe's high and growing dependency on fossil fuel imports. The EU supports action on climate change as an important foreign policy area that promotes global environmental and social justice at the same time that it is good for the EU's image and its industries (Oberthür & Dupont 2015; Afionis 2017).

Other important perspectives for Europe are the opportunities that can arise from a low-carbon energy transition and greater sustainability. In the past, modernization efforts were based on the extraction of natural resources. In the future, the development of new industrial strengths and jobs are to be based on sustainable forms of energy and resource use. An added benefit of a clean energy transition is that it can lead to the development of a more just and democratic economic system. Thus, rather than seeing environmental protection as a threat to economic growth and jobs as seems to be the case with climate sceptics in the US, there is a general recognition in Europe that developing more energy and resource-efficient economic systems will be critical for not only the environment but also the long-term competitiveness of the continent. Substantial changes can already be seen in terms of expanded renewable energy capacity across much of Europe, increased recycling rates, and the enhanced energy efficiency performance of industries. Beyond this, new research institutions for climate, energy, and green industry have been established along with many new government departments within Europe's multi-level governance system. In many other areas, change is likely to appear soon, including in terms of electric mobility climate and environment-related digitalization, new materials, and batteries.

The European Commission has placed a high priority on climate policy, issuing communications on climate change and sustainable development intended to provide visions for future policy direction. In November 2018, the Commission issued a vision for 2050 that calls for a planet-friendly, climate-neutral European economy by the middle of the century (European Commission 2018). The European Parliament has also been a driving force, pushing the European Council to strengthen its climate initiatives on a number of occasions. In March 2019, the European Parliament and the European Council agreed to target 35 per cent of the 'Horizon Europe' programme for research and innovation on clean tech research and innovation (Simon 2019). Under the 2018 'Clean Energy for All Europeans' package, governments were mandated to prepare integrated national energy and climate plans for the period from 2021 through 2030 (European Commission 2019).

The push for change also comes from various member states. Three-quarters of EU emissions in 2016 were produced by seven states: Germany (21.1 per cent), Spain (7.7 per cent), France (10.7 per cent), Italy (9.9 per cent), the Netherlands (4.7 per cent), Poland (9.0 per cent), and the UK (11.6 per cent) (European Environment Agency 2018). These states have a particularly strong stake in EU climate policy decisions. Significantly, within this group, there have been no strong veto players on climate matters other than perhaps Poland, which is the EU member state with the strongest dependency on coal. Poland's veto threats have, however, been surmountable. Poland has agreed to increases in the EU's climate targets in exchange for assurances of financial and technical assistance to modernize its coal industry and develop renewable energies (Ceglarz & Ancygier 2015; Jankowska 2017).

Various factors are at play at the domestic level to explain individual EU member states' interests in strong climate action. Most significant because of its position as the largest economy and largest greenhouse gas emitter in Europe is Germany, which has embarked on an *Energiewende*, an energy transition away from both nuclear energy and fossil fuels and an embrace of renewable energy, energy efficiency, and clean technologies. This is a strategy that links innovation to the creation of clean tech jobs and industries. The nuclear phaseout is to be completed by 2022. Renewable energy had obtained a share of approximately 40 per cent of the electricity sector at the end of 2018. The next step in the process will be the shutting down of the country's hard coal and lignite-fuelled power plants, still about 42 per cent of electricity at the end of 2018. The Commission for Growth, Structural Change, and Employment, which was set up by the government to make recommendations on how to phase out coal, released its report in February 2019. The report calls for the complete phaseout of coal by 2038 at the latest (*Kommission Wachstum, Strukturwandel und Beschäftigung* 2019). In the meantime, the government has set up a Climate Change Cabinet in order to come to an agreement on a Climate Change Law. With its domestic energy transition, Germany has strongly supported EU climate leadership (Quitzow, Roehrkasten & Jaenicke 2016; Jaenicke 2016).

France, which has a heavy dependency on nuclear energy, already has a relatively low per capita CO_2 emission level. Yet, with many of its nuclear plants nearing the end of their operating life span, new sources of energy will be needed. Diversification of electricity production to make the country less reliant on nuclear energy requires improvements in energy efficiency and development of renewable energies (*Ministère de la Transition Ecologique et Solidaire* 2019; Bocquillon & Evrard 2017). The 2015 Energy Transition for Green Growth Act envisions greater energy autonomy, lowered greenhouse gas emissions, the development of circular economies, and the expansion of the renewables, clean transport, and green construction sectors. France has been one of the countries that have taken on the leadership baton for climate action within the EU.

The UK began to shift from a reliance on coal to gas already during the time of Margaret Thatcher in the 1980s. While this initially had little to do with climate concerns, a carbon tax on electricity has helped speed the shift away from coal and enabled the country to sharply reduce its emissions. In the meantime, and especially in the last few years, renewable energy production has expanded considerably and energy efficiency improvements have been prioritized (Rayner & Jordan 2017). The UK's Department for Business, Energy and Industrial Strategy released a 'Clean Growth Strategy' in 2017 as part of its climate mitigation efforts (Timperley 2018).

The Netherlands, with its large fossil fuel industry, was a somewhat reluctant supporter of strong climate action, but citizens there have successfully made use of the courts in a case known as *Urgenda Foundation v. The Netherlands* to force the government to do more to address climate change, arguing that the government has a responsibility to protect its citizens from threats like climate change (Liefferink, Boezeman & De Coninck 2017).

The changes in energy systems in Europe are quite impressive. Belgium has been coal-free since 2016; France plans to shut its last coal-fired power plant by 2021 and Sweden by 2022; Austria, Ireland, Italy, and the UK aim to phase out of coal by 2025 and Finland by 2029, and Denmark, the Netherlands, and Portugal are targeting 2030.[5] The expansion of renewable energy in Europe has been strong. Denmark was an early leader demonstrating the potential for development of on-shore and offshore wind power (Danish Government 2018). Portugal has pushed ahead strongly on wind power and rivals Denmark in terms of electricity produced from wind.

Given the quite strong support for climate action within individual member states, the European Commission has been able to continue a process of notching climate targets upward. The effects are visible. There have been substantial reductions in greenhouse gas emissions across most, albeit not all, EU member states. Between 1990 and 2006 emissions in Germany dropped by 27.3 per cent, France by 16.1 per cent, Sweden by 26 per cent, and the UK by 39.4 per cent. Portugal and Spain were exceptions with increases of 13.1 per cent and 12.9 per cent, respectively, in their emissions.

Austria also experienced a small increase of 1.2 per cent and Cyprus a large increase of 56.9 per cent (European Environment Agency 2018).

This is not to say that all is well in the EU when it comes to climate action. Germany has repeatedly sought to block moves by other countries to raise automobile emission standards, a clear indication of the power of the automobile industry. It has also been forced to admit that it will not meet its 2020 goal to reduce greenhouse gas emissions by 40 per cent of 1990 levels. Poland, being concerned about the impact of an energy transition on its powerful coal industry has pushed back against high renewable energy targets. While this push back has slowed progress in some areas, it has been insufficient to stop or reverse the agreement on the need for a relatively rapid transition in Europe's energy structures.

Conclusion

Although US scientists have been at the forefront of climate science, the US failed to ratify the Kyoto Protocol and has announced its intent to leave the Paris Agreement. Conservative interests, financed at least in part by the fossil fuel industry, and convinced that environmental protection equates to big government, have fought for the better part of the last two decades against climate policy initiatives. There are many actors in the US who support stronger climate policy action, but their calls for policy change have been ridiculed and attacked by anti-climate zealots, carbon-intensive industries, and conservative politicians from the local level to the national level. This has made it difficult to pursue climate legislation at the federal level. Instead, climate policies and programmes have been pushed down to the local and state levels. The risk for the US is that this policy gridlock will mean a loss not only of US international climate leadership but also of US clean energy and clean technology competitiveness.

The EU stepped into the leadership vacuum created by the US when it pulled out of the Kyoto Protocol. At least since this time, the EU has been the most consistent driving force behind multilateral climate negotiations. Domestically, the EU publics and policy-makers view climate change as a threat to its economies and the well-being of citizens. At the same time, EU institutions and member states see potential for many co-benefits from weaning the continent off of fossil fuels, developing a renewable energy-based economy, and supporting research and development into clean energy, transport, and building technologies. Unlike in the US where conservatives have portrayed climate change policy as a threat to jobs and the American way of life, in the EU political parties across the spectrum have by and large embraced the need to reduce greenhouse gas emissions and to implement the Sustainable Development Goals. They have accepted the warnings of the IPCC and oriented policy towards meeting the 2 degrees Celsius target. Environmentalists and young people (like the Fridays for Future movement) still criticize that the EU and its member states are not doing enough, but the debate is not about whether or not to act, rather about how quickly and with which policy measures and instruments. Increasingly, energy and resource efficiency improvements and clean energy are discussed in tandem with digitalization, artificial intelligence, and self-driving cars in national and European vision statements.

In China, concerns with climate change have grown with time as the country has been exposed to more extreme weather events. The Chinese leadership is also concerned about energy security and pollution. Climate policy has been closely linked to efforts to modernize the economy, develop new industrial sectors, and improve living conditions. Once a laggard in climate policy that used to vocalize climate nationalist views, China has in the meantime become a test bed of new climate policy ideas, smart city concepts, and low-carbon living initiatives. It has also become a world leader in the production and increasingly also in the development of climate and clean energy technologies.

The Paris Agreement is an important step towards the development of global initiatives on climate change. Dealing with climate change will require changes on multiple fronts across the globe. China and the EU have demonstrated that they will move ahead together to implement the Paris Agreement with or without the US. This means that Chinese and EU influence on the global climate order is likely to grow even more in the future. Interestingly, many sub-national actors in the US are willing to join them. The important question for the long term will be whether it will be possible to overcome the climate sceptic voices in the US and move forward with broader and more substantial policy change which would certainly aid global efforts to address what will perhaps become the single most important challenge facing human settlements in the century to come.

Notes

1 The authors were Syukuro Manabe and Richart T. Wetherald of the Geophysical Fluid Dynamics Laboratory, ESSA; Charles Keeling and his co-authors from the Scripps Institution of Oceanography, University of California at San Diego, and the National Oceanic and Atmospheric Administration (NOAA)'s Mauna Loa Observatory; and Isaac M. Held and Brian J. Sodan from NOAA's Geophysical Fluid Dynamics Laboratory, Princeton, and the Rosenstiel School of Marine and Atmospheric Science, University of Miami.

2 The numerous reports issued by the Intergovernmental Panel on Climate Change can be accessed at: www.ipcc.ch/reports/.

3 Climate Mayors, http://climatemayors.org.

4 The author was invited to speak to a group of Congressional representatives on the German energy transition. Her speech took place on 2 April 2019. The meeting was initiated by Congressman Lloyd Doggett (D-Texas).

5 See the website of the Powering Past Coal Alliance: https://poweringpastcoal.org.

References

Afionis, S. (2017) *The European Union in International Climate Negotiations*, New York: Routledge.

Banerjee, N. (2019) 'With Democrats in Charge, House Science Committee Talks about Climate Science', *Inside Climate News*, 14 February.

Bang, G., J. Hovi & D.F. Sprinz (2012) 'US Presidents and the Failure to Ratify Multilateral Environmental Agreements', *Climate Policy* 12, 755–763.

Bang, G. & M. Schreurs (2011) 'A Green New Deal: Framing U.S. Climate Leadership', in R.K.W. Wurzel & J. Connelly (eds.), *The European Union as a Leader in International Climate Change Politics*, London: Routledge, 235–251.

Bocquillon, P. & A. Evrard (2017) 'French Climate Policy: Diplomacy in the Service of Symbolic Leadership', in R.K.W. Wurzel, J. Connelly & D. Liefferink (eds.), *The European Union in International Climate Change Politics: Still Taking a Lead?* New York: Routledge, 98–113.

Brenan, M. & L. Saad (2018) 'Global Warming Concern Steady Despite Some Partisan Shifts', *Gallup*, 28 March. Available at: https://news.gallup.com/poll/231530/global-warming-concern-steady-despite-partisan-shifts.aspx.

Carbon Brief (2015a). 'The Most Influential Climate Change Papers of All Time', 6 July. Available at: www.carbonbrief.org/the-most-influential-climate-change-papers-of-all-time.

——— (2015b) 'Analysis: The Most 'cited' Climate Change Papers', 8 July. Available at: www.carbonbrief.org/analysis-the-most-cited-climate-change-papers.

Ceglarz, A. & A. Ancygier (2015) 'The Polish Renewable Energy and Climate Policies under the Impact of the EU', in I.P. Karolewski & M. Su (eds.), *The Transformative Power of Europe: The Case of Poland*, Baden-Baden: Nomos, 137–168.

Conrad, B. (2012) 'China in Copenhagen: Reconciling the 'Beijing Climate Revolution' and the Copenhagen Climate Obstinancy', *China Quarterly* 210, June, 435–455.

Cyrill, M. (2018) 'What is Made in China 2025 and Why Has It Made the World So Nervous', *China Briefing*, 28 December. Available at: www.china-briefing.com/news/made-in-china-2025-explained/.

Danish Government (2018) 'Denmark: Energy and Climate Pioneer: Status of the Green Transition', Copenhagen: Danish Ministry of Energy, Utilities and Climate. April. Available at: https://en.efkm.dk/media/12032/denmark_energy_and_climate_pioneer_pdfa.pdf.

Dembicki, G. (2017) 'The Convenient Disappearance of Climate Change Denial in China: From Western Plot to Party Line, How China Embraced Climate Science to Become a Green-Energy Powerhouse', *Foreign Policy*, May/June.

Dong, K.Y., R.J. Sun, H. Li & H.D. Jiang (2017) 'A Review of China's Energy Consumption Structure and Outlook based on a Long-range Energy Alternatives Modeling Tool', *Petroleum* 14(1), 214–227.

EU-China Joint Leaders' Statement on Climate Change and Clean Energy, Beijing 16 July 2018. Available at: https://ec.europa.eu/clima/sites/clima/files/news/20180713_statement_en.pdf.

EU-China Joint Statement on Climate Change, 29 June 2015. Available at: www.consilium.europa.eu/media/23733/150629-eu-china-climate-statement-doc.pdf.

EU-China Roadmap on Energy Cooperation (2016–2020). Available at: https://ec.europa.eu/energy/sites/ener/files/documents/FINAL_EU_CHINA_ENERGY_ROADMAP_EN.pdf.

Eurobarometer (2017) Climate Change. Special Eurobarometer 459 – Wave EB87.1 –TNS Opinion & Social, March.

European Commission (2018) 'A Clean Planet for All: A European Strategic Long-term Vision for a Prosperous, Modern, Competitive and Climate Neutral Economy', Brussels, COM(2018)773 final, 28 November.

——— (2019) *Clean Energy for All Europeans*. Available at: https://ec.europa.eu/energy/en/topics/energy-strategy-and-energy-union/clean-energy-all-europeans.

European Environment Agency (2018) Annual European Union Greenhouse Gas Inventory 1990–2016 and Inventory Report 2018: Submission to the UNFCCC Secretariat, EEA Report Nr 5/2018, 27 May.

Gallagher, K.S. & X. Xuan (2018) *Titans of the Climate: Explaining Policy Process in the United States and China*, Cambridge: MIT Press.

Gamper-Rabindran, S. (ed.) (2018) *The Shale Dilemma*, Pittsburgh: Pittsburgh University Press.

Government of the People's Republic of China (2015) 'Enhanced Actions on Climate Change: China's Intended Nationally Determined Contributions'. Available at: www4.unfccc.int/sites/submissions/INDC/Published%20Documents/China/1/China's%20INDC%20-%20on%2030%20June%202015.pdf.

H. Res. 109 – Recognizing the duty of the Federal Government to create a Green New Deal, 116th Congress (2019–2020). Sponsor: Rep. Ocasio-Cortez, Alexandria (Introduced 7 February 2019).

Harris, P.G. (2011) *China's Responsibility for Climate Change: Ethics, Fairness, and Environmental Policy*, Bristol: Bristol University Press/Polity Press.

Haskins, J. (2019) 'Alexandria Ocasio-Cortez's "Green New Deal" is Actually an Old Socialist Plan from Canada', *Fox News*, 19 January. Available at: www.foxnews.com/opinion/alexandria-ocasio-cortezs-green-new-deal-is-actually-an-old-socialist-plan-from-canada.

Inhofe, J. (2012) *The Greatest Hoax: How the Global Warming Conspiracy Threatens Your Future*, Washington: WND Books.

IPCC (Intergovernmental Panel on Climate Change) (2018) *Special Report: Global Warming of 1.5 degrees Celsius*, Switzerland: IPCC. Available at: https://report.ipcc.ch/sr15/pdf/sr15_spm_final.pdf.

Jaenicke, M. (2016) 'Germany: Innovation and Climate Leadership', in R.K.W. Wurzel, J. Connelly & D. Liefferink (eds.), *The European Union in International Climate Change Politics: Still Taking a Lead?* New York: Routledge, 114–130.

Jankowska, K. (2017) 'Poland's Clash over Energy and Climate Policy: Green Economy or Green Status Quo', in R.K.W. Wurzel, J. Connelly & D. Liefferink (eds.), *The European Union in International Climate Change Politics: Still Taking a Lead?* New York: Routledge, 145–158.

Kalantzakos, S. (2017) *The EU, US and China Tackling Climate Change: An Alliance for the Anthropocene*, New York: Routledge.

Karapin, R. (2016) *Political Opportunities for Climate Policy: California, New York, and the Federal Government*, Cambridge: Cambridge University Press.

Kommission Wachstum, Strukturwandel und Beschäftigung (2019) 'Abschlussbericht', January 2019, Bundesministerium für Wirtschaft und Energie, Frankfurt am Main: Druck- und Verlagshaus Zarbock GmbH & Co. KG.

Kopra, S. (2019) *China and Great Power Responsibility for Climate Change*, New York: Routledge.

Lee, J. (2009) 'How China Stiffed the World in Copenhagen', *Foreign Policy*, 21 December. Available at: https://foreignpolicy.com/2009/12/21/how-china-stiffed-the-world-in-copenhagen/.

Liefferink, D., D. Boezeman & H. De Coninck (2017) 'The Netherlands: A Case of Fading Leadership', in R.K.W. Wurzel, J. Connelly & D. Liefferink (eds.), *The*

European Union in International Climate Change Politics: Still Taking a Lead? New York: Routledge, 131–144.

Liu, J.C.E. (2015) 'Low-Carbon Plot: Climate Change Skepticism with Chinese Characteristics', *Environment Sociology* 1(4), 280–292.

Marlon, J., P. Howe, M. Mildenberger & A. Leiserowitz (2016) 'Yale Climate Opinion Maps – U.S. 2016'. Available at: http://climatecommunication.yale.edu/visualizations-data/ycom-us-2016/?est=consensus&type=value&geo=state.

Matthews, D. (2017) 'Donald Trump has Tweeted Climate Change Skepticism 115 Times. Here's All of It', *Vox*, 1 June. Available at: www.vox.com/policy-and-politics/2017/6/1/15726472/trump-tweets-global-warming-paris-climate-agreement.

Ministère de la Transition Ecologique et Solidaire (2019) 'The Multiannual Energy Plan'. Available at: www.gouvernement.fr/sites/default/files/locale/piece-jointe/2019/01/11_france_multiannual_energy_plan.pdf.

Nadin, R. & J. Painter (2011) 'China', in J. Painter (ed.), *Poles Apart: The International Reporting of Climate Scepticism*, University of Oxford, Reuters Institute for the Study of Journalism, 70–74.

Oberthür, S. & C. Dupont (eds.) (2015) *Decarbonizing in the European Union: Internal Policies and External Strategies*, Basingstoke: Palgrave Macmillan.

Oberthür, S. & L. Groen (2018) 'Explaining Goal Achievement in International Negotiations: The EU and the Paris Agreement on Climate Change', *Journal of European Public Policy* 25(5), 708–727.

Painter, J. (2011) *Poles Apart: The International Reporting of Climate Scepticism*, University of Oxford, Reuters Institute for the Study of Journalism.

Quitzow, R., S. Roehrkasten & M. Jaenicke (2016) *The German Energy Transition in International Perspective*, March. Potsdam: Institute for Advanced Sustainability Studies.

Ran, R. (2014) 'Perverse Incentive Structure and Policy Implementation Gap in China's Local Environmental Politics', in G. Kostka & A.P. Mol (eds.), *Local Environmental Politics in China: Challenges and Innovations*, New York: Routledge, 15–38.

Rayner, T. & A. Jordan (2017) 'The United Kingdom: A Record of Leadership Under Threat', in R.K.W. Wurzel, J. Connelly & D. Liefferink (eds.), *The European Union in International Climate Change Politics: Still Taking a Lead?* New York: Routledge, 173–188.

REN 21 Renewable Energy Policy Network for the 21st Century (2018) 'Renewables 2018: Global Status Report', Paris: REN21 Secretariat.

Ritchie, H. & M. Roser (2017) 'CO_2 and Other Greenhouse Gas Emissions', *Our World in Data*. Available at: https://ourworldindata.org/co2-and-other-greenhouse-gas-emissions.

Saad, L. (2017) 'Global Warming Concern at Three-Decade High in U.S.', *Gallup*, 14 March. Available at: https://news.gallup.com/poll/206030/global-warming-concern-three-decade-high.aspx?g_source=link_NEWSV9&g_medium=TOPIC&g_campaign=item_&g_content=Global%2520Warming%2520Concern%2520at%2520Three-Decade%2520High%2520in%2520U.S.

Sandalow, D. (2018) 'Guide to Chinese Climate Policy 2018', *Energy Policy*, Columbia University. Available at: https://energypolicy.columbia.edu/sites/default/files/pictures/Guide%20to%20Chinese%20Climate%20Policy%207-27-18.pdf.

Schreurs, M. (2010) 'Climate Change Politics in the United States: Melting of the Ice', *Analyse & Kritik* 1, 177–189.

——— (2016) 'The Paris Climate Agreement and the Three Largest Emitters: China, the United States, and the European Union', *Politics and Governance* 4(3): 219–223.

——— (2019a) 'Climate Change Denial in the United States and the European Union', in M.J. Peterson (ed.), *Contesting Global Environmental Knowledge, Norms, and Governance*, New York: Routledge, 89–109.

——— (2019b) 'Greening China's State-led Growth Regime', in K. Huebner (ed.), *National Pathways to Low Carbon Emission Economies*, New York: Routledge, 169–184.

Simon, F. (2019) 'Europe Ringfences 35% of Research Budget for Clean Tech', *Euractiv*, 20 March [updated 21 March]. Available at: www.euractiv.com/section/climate-strategy-2050/news/europe-ringfences-35-of-research-budget-for-clean-tech/.

Skjærseth, J.B., G. Bang & M.A. Schreurs (2013) 'Explaining Growing Climate Policy Differences between the European Union and the United States', *Global Environmental Politics* 13(4), 61–80.

Stanway, D. (2019) 'China's Population Set to Peak at 1.44 billion in 2029 – Government Report', *Reuters*, 5 January.

Timperley, J. (2018) 'In-depth: How the UK Plans to Adapt to Climate Change', *CarbonBrief*, 26 July. Available at: www.carbonbrief.org/in-depth-how-the-uk-plans-to-adapt-to-climate-change.

Union of Concerned Scientists (2004) 'Scientific Integrity in Policymaking: An Investigation into the Bush Administration's Misuse of Science', *Union of Concerned Scientists*, March. Available at: www.ucsusa.org/sites/default/files/legacy/assets/documents/scientific_integrity/rsi_final_fullreport_1.pdf.

United States Climate Alliance (2019) *States United For Climate Action*, Website, September. Available at: www.usclimatealliance.org/.

U.S. Environmental Protection Agency (2018). Inventory of U.S. Greenhouse Gas Emissions and Sinks, 1990–2016. EPA 430-R-18-003. Available at: www.epa.gov/sites/production/files/2018-01/documents/2018_complete_report.pdf.

Voïta, T. (2018) 'The Power of China's Energy Efficiency Policies', *Études de l'Ifre*, Ifre. Centre for Energy, September.

Wang, C., A. Engels & Z. Wang (2018) 'Overview of Research on China's Transition to Low Carbon-development: The Role of Cities, Technologies, Industries and the Energy System', *Renewable and Sustainable Energy Reviews* 81, 1350–1364.

Watts, J. (2010) 'Senior Chinese Climatologist Calls for Reform of IPCC', *The Guardian*, 9 February. Available at: www.theguardian.com/environment/2010/feb/09/chinese-climatologist-ipcc-reform.

Watts, J., J. Vidal, R. McKie & R. Helm (2009) 'China Blamed as Anger Mounts Over Climate Deal', *The Guardian*, 20 December. Available at: www.theguardian.com/environment/2009/dec/20/china-blamed-copenhagen-climate-failure.

World Coal Institute (2009) 'The Coal Resource: A Comprehensive Overview of Coal', London: World Coal Institution. Available at: www.worldcoal.org/file_validate.php?file=coal_resource_overview_of_coal_report(03_06_2009).pdf.

Wübbeke, J. & G. Ting (2017) 'Green Tech is China's "Gold Mine"', *Chinadialogue: China and the World Discuss the Environment*, 16 May.

Ye, Q. & J. Lu (2018) 'China's Coal Consumption has Peaked', *Brookings Institution*, 22 January. Available at: www.brookings.edu/2018/01/22/chinas-coal-consumption-has-peaked/.

Part V

Conclusion

12 Conclusion

Jing Men, Simon Schunz and Duncan Freeman

Introduction

The authors of this book address the role of three key actors in a changing global order. The complexity of the problem of the roles of the EU, China and US in an evolving global order is reflected in the chapters of each author focusing on different actors and policy areas. As the introduction notes, this volume offers no unified approach to its underlying subject, nor does it offer a unified analysis or model of the problems of an evolving global order and the role of the three actors. The diversity resulting from allowing the authors scope to approach the problem in an eclectic manner perhaps best permits a reflection of the complexity of the triangle that exists between the EU, China and US.

The following section provides an overview of the key findings of each chapter. These findings reflect the perspectives from the viewpoint of the actors and the lens of the policy areas that they focus on as well as the differing analytical approaches they adopt. This chapter concludes with reflections on unifying themes drawing on the chapters of this book and possible future developments.

Key findings

Foreign and security policy

In this book, three chapters discuss how China, the EU and the US interact in the field of foreign and security policy and how their discourses and policies have been evolving during the past few years. As the most important players in global and regional affairs, the interests of China, the EU and the US are increasingly intertwined, which requires coordination and cooperation between them. Yet, as Henrikson points out, until now, no trilateral institutional arrangement is envisaged. Research and analysis in the three chapters mainly focus on how China-EU, China-US and EU-US relations have been changing and why these changes occur. The US is regarded as the most powerful among the three and acts as the 'strongest upholder of the pre-existing international order but finding itself unable to resolve the problems without the cooperation of others', according to Henrikson. He argues that the US gives priority to its 'pivot' to Asia policy and Indo-Pacific strategy, While the EU lacks capacity for coercion in the region due to the fact that it does not have a military presence in the Asia-Pacific. However, since the European External Action Service, the institution to deal with security and foreign policy, was established, the EU is getting more active in designing new policies and involving itself in key international and regional affairs. The EU published its Global Strategy on foreign and security policy in June 2016, and since then presented annually updated reports on how the strategy has been implemented. When analysing the EU global strategy, Tocci – one of its main authors – contends that the principles embraced by the strategy, including engagement, responsibility, unity and partnership, are closely related to pragmatism. By introducing 'principled pragmatism' in its global strategy, the EU intends to 'remove its rose-tinted glasses and pragmatically look at the world as it is, and not as it would like to see it' (Tocci 2017: 64). This echoes the conclusion drawn by Montesano in his chapter, who argues that with the establishment of a stronger foreign and security policy institutional framework, the EU moves towards a fully fledged external actorness. At the same time, the EU develops a more pragmatic outlook and allows more strategic flexibility in practice.

According to Can and Soto, primarily addressing foreign and security policy matters from the Chinese perspective, China is an important global power and an emerging 'order-shaper'. Its purpose is to reform the current international order both from within and without, to reflect and reinforce not only the interests of the developed countries but also the interests of the developing world, 'to forge relationships based on mutual trust, mutual respect, and win-win cooperation' and 'to foster a more multipolar, just, equitable, and legitimate global order'. Can and Soto also stress in their chapter that to safeguard the existing arrangements of world order conforms to China's fundamental interests, therefore, China seeks close cooperation with both the US and the EU. Nevertheless, due to an increasing US unilateralism and protectionism, China and the EU may currently share more similar concerns in global governance. Their 2003 strategic partnership and the 2020 Strategic Agenda for Cooperation can be regarded as the foundation for China-EU partnership. For China, the partnership with the EU is an integral part of Chinese comprehensive foreign policy which serves the latter's purpose of fostering global peace, stability and development. Montesano draws similar conclusion in his chapter and demonstrates a noticeable inward-looking approach taken by the Trump administration, which 'prioritises the narrow, self-centred national interests and very sceptical towards the multilateral order'. In contrast, although China under Xi's leadership grows to be more assertive in its discourse and policy initiatives, it takes a pragmatic approach and behaves more proactively yet responsibly in the international arena. This is particularly visible in its engagement within the multilateral system.

While both the EU and China follow pragmatism in their foreign policy, one cannot ignore the differences in their approaches and ends. It is true that the EU is pursuing growing pragmatic adaptability and more flexibility in global governance. However, the EU, just like the US, feels increasingly challenged by China with its different political system and development path. Although China expresses on many occasions its support to the current international order, the Americans and the Europeans remain sceptical about China's intention, and it remains unclear how far China will go and what is the price that the West needs to pay to facilitate China's development. Blackwill and Tellis (2015: 4) stress that China's rise poses a 'threat to US primacy in Asia – and could result in a consequential challenge to American power globally' and argue that Washington needs to develop a new grand strategy towards China. With growing US dissatisfaction with China's rise at American expense, the Trump administration, in its National Security Strategy of December 2017 and the National Defense Strategy in January 2018, addressed China as a predatory rival. In the first half of 2019, the US government started to take measures to address the perceived and real challenges posed by China. On the other side of the Atlantic Ocean, the EU labels China as a 'systemic rival' in its most recent policy paper on China (European Commission 2019). The EU has also become more critical of China's behaviour and growing Chinese influence in Europe. While both the US and the EU are wary about China's policy of *Made in China 2025*, the EU is most concerned about cooperation between China and Central and Eastern European Countries.

The recent US and EU's antipathy to China is explained by Mearsheimer in his recent work on the liberal international order (2019). According to him, the liberal international order is closely related to the hegemonic position of the US and the unipolar world, but the order contains the seeds of its own ruin. Among many other reasons, hyperglobalisation produced significant economic costs for the West but created great opportunities for China to grow. Despite the commitment of the US and the EU to turning China into a liberal democracy, China successfully resisted such attempts and manages to adhere to its own road of development. The rise of China helped undercut unipolarity and undermine the liberal order. Instead, a multipolar world is in shape in which China and the US are competitors, and 'will be concerned principally with waging security competition against each other' (Mearsheimer 2019: 44). As a result, realism returns to the international system, as competition for power dominates.

One noticeable feature of foreign and security policy of China, the EU and the US is that realism and pragmatism coexist. On the one hand, China is a significant competitor for the US and the EU, for example, on the South China Sea; on the other hand, the US and the EU choose to cooperate with China when it is necessary – the EU cooperated with China on the Iran issue whereas the US cooperated with China on the North Korea issue. The contemporary international system is characterised by the interplay between cooperation and competition. The world is connected, contested and complex. Its future is, to a large degree, decided by the interaction between China, the EU and the US.

Economy, trade and investment

Economics occupy a prominent place in most theories of international order. In practice questions of economic policy have come to occupy a pre-eminent place in international relations (IR). Trade and investment are not the only elements to this, but they increasingly dominate international policy-making, especially in the specific case of the relationships between the EU, China and the US and their wider role in the global economy either through cooperative efforts to solve global problems or create global governance or attempts to secure national advantage through competitive policies. The recent tendency has been towards increased national competition in trade and investment policy, evidenced particularly by the policies of the Trump administration, although its policies are neither unique nor unprecedented in the history of economic policy-making. The Trump administration has nevertheless arguably brought about a significant shift in international policy compared to the recent past, although fundamental questions are to what extent and how the Trump administration represents a break with the past and any international order which may have existed. One of the questions underlying the chapters in this section of this book is whether recent developments, exemplified by conflicts over trade and investment at bilateral and global levels, represent a fundamental break with the past, or indeed a breakdown of the global economic order, or reconstitution of a new order.

In her chapter Gstöhl argues that there is a tripolar structure emerging between the EU, US and China. Considering the order from the point of view of the EU, she argues that its policy has been changing in recent decades in response to changes taking place in the relationship with the other major partners. She uses an eclectic approach based on IR theories of neorealism, neoliberal institutionalism and constructivism – and identifies changes in power constellations, institutions and ideas as potential explanatory factors, while downplaying domestic issues. According to Gstöhl there have been changes in EU policy on trade from managed globalisation to competitive liberalisation, and finally more recently a geoeconomic approach. She argues that there is a tripolar structure of trade between the EU, China and the US, but that the three have no common agenda, implying that while there may be a structure in the real world of trade flows, this may not be replicated in the order of the institutional world. Gstöhl points to the difficulty of change in an embedded order and sees the international structure as configured by power, institutions and ideas, based on mainstream IR theories.

Meunier in her chapter argues that the policies of the Trump administration denote major discontinuities with US post-war policy on trade and investment by challenging the multilateral trade order and the value of trade openness. The Trump administration has adopted a transactional and bilateral view of trade and threatens even to leave essential institutions such as the World Trade Organization (WTO). Meunier recognises that the policy of the US under Trump has proved difficult to analyse through the traditional political economy models, where for instance trade policy is determined by domestic economic interest groups. The chapter addresses the question of how US trade policy fits within a world which is more uncertain, where anti-globalisation is more significant, and which is more multipolar with the EU and China now almost equal actors with the US. Like Gstöhl for the EU, Meunier considers the structural power of the US based on factors such as gross domestic product (GDP), trade and investment flows. Perhaps inevitably in the case of the US and the Trump administration, Meunier also takes into account domestic political factors, which Gstöhl does not consider in her discussion of the EU. Meunier argues that globalisation was promoted by previous administrations, but without adoption of domestic policies to compensate for negative impacts within the US, leading to dissatisfaction among sections of the population which was exploited by Trump in his election campaign. The retreat of the US from global governance is demonstrated in Trump administration policies that have implications for the international trade and investment system. Meunier raises the question of whether the EU or China, or a combination of them, can take over from the US. She argues that the post-war order was largely a US creation and suggests that the order's success carried the seeds of its own decline as it allowed the rise of the EU and other powers. While there has been a decline of US structural power, previous administrations were willing to work to sustain global governance whereas President Trump has abandoned this policy. However, echoing Gstöhl on the difficulty of a transition to a new order, Meunier questions whether either the EU or China can replace the US in its role, despite their increased structural power relative to the US.

Ding in his chapter focuses on trade, including both goods and services, and direct investment flows between China, the EU and US. These flows reflect similar developments to those highlighted by Gstöhl and Meunier in their discussion of the structural economic power of the China, the EU and US, most importantly the emergence of China as a major global economic actor. According to Ding, the US is the most advanced economy in the world, the EU is the largest and most successful economic union in the world and China is the largest developing country in the world. Unlike Gstöhl and Meunier, Ding provides an economic analysis of the underlying economic relationships between the three, arguing that they exhibit a high degree of complementarity. Imbalances in goods trade, which have been the target of policies adopted in the EU and US, are based on comparative advantage resulting in shifts in industrial production to China, although other factors such as the contribution of policies adopted in the US and EU like export controls have also played a role. Ding argues that the underlying differences in development stage and in economic structure and comparative advantage are the causes of trade and investment frictions between China on the one hand and the EU and US on the other. He points to several areas of contention that result from this that have led to increased conflict with China, notably increased protectionism by both the EU and China. This has been reinforced by policies adopted by the EU and US in negotiation of bilateral and multilateral agreements designed to isolate China. The policy of the US since the election of President Trump has intensified conflict with China despite the efforts of Xi Jinping to promote cooperation. However, Ding argues that despite this the underlying factors of cooperation in the mode of production brought about by globalisation will continue, and that this will be the ultimate basis for cooperation between the three. In this sense, he implies that the fundamental economic order will persist.

The three chapters on economics point to similar facts in terms of trade and investment flows. However, these facts are open to varying explanations and interpretations. The chapters offer different interpretations of the possible future direction of development of the relationship between the three actors and the constitution of the global system. In part this could be said to reflect well-known long-standing debates over fundamental differences in the consequences of international trade and investment flows. Do they increase the likelihood of conflict or cooperation? The chapters indicate that like the relationship of the EU, China and the US and their role in the future global order, the analysis of the changes will continue to raise unresolved questions.

Climate change and energy

Climate change and the low-carbon energy transition that it entails figure among the major political challenges of the 21st century. As issues of a truly global nature, their successful tackling requires inter- and transnationally concerted action. Key to the effectiveness of that action are the contributions of major emitting countries. Whereas during the 1990s these key emitters had been from the group of Organization for Economic Cooperation and Development (OECD) countries, with the US, the EU and its members and Japan at the forefront, since the middle of the 2000s the geopolitics of climate change has profoundly evolved. China became the world's top emitter in 2006, turning the country into a central player in the global climate regime alongside the US, while the EU's (and Japan's) significance has been in relative decline. Given the importance of the climate challenge as well as the three players' relevance for solving it, Part IV of this volume considered the bi- and trilateral relations, embedded into the multilateral context, between China, the US and the EU in the global politics of climate change and energy.

In her chapter on the relations between the three players from a predominantly Chinese perspective, Bo Yan draws on concepts derived from IR theory related to major powers, interactions to argue that the three parties' generally 'co-opetitive international relationship with high fluidity' has gone through different phases across time. During the negotiations of the 1997 Kyoto Protocol, the pattern of interaction between the three players could be characterised as a 'romantic triangle', based on cooperative China-EU and EU-US relations and antagonistic China-US relations. This initially changed during the period after Kyoto to a pattern of 'marriage', with a cooperative China-EU relationship, and more challenging China-US and EU-US relations. The run-up to the 2009 Copenhagen summit was characterised by a high degree of volatility, with signs of a status quo-oriented 'marriage' between China and the US, and negative relations of these two with the EU. This changed notably around the 2015 Paris summit when the scenario of a 'ménage à trois' set in, with productive bilateral relations between all three actors.

This positive 'multiple bilateralism', involving the three players and India, arguably enabled the adoption and ratification of the Paris Agreement (Belis et al. 2018). However, the election of Donald Trump brought a sudden halt to this scenario, bringing it back to a 'marriage', that is, co-leadership between China and the EU alongside antagonistic relations of these two with the US ever since late 2016. Despite the antagonism in transatlantic and transpacific relations at the government-to-government level, cooperation with the US does still exist, however, as China and the EU interact with many sub-federal players (states, cities) as well as with civil society actors in the US. This may point to a new form of transnational 'ménage à trois', which Bo Yan considers as key to the future global climate order.

In her discussion of the three players' interrelations from the US perspective, Miranda Schreurs adopts a constructivist foreign policy analysis perspective by analysing how the ideas and framing held and advanced by policy-makers from the US, China and the EU domestically about (i) climate science and (ii) whether climate change is to be considered as an economic opportunity, determine their foreign policy positions. This allows her to discuss the scope conditions for their potential cooperation on climate change and the energy transition and thus explore the prospects for a global climate order involving these key emitters.

In the US, climate science has been met with scepticism by political leaders, notably among Republicans. The most sceptical of all US Presidents, Donald Trump, has acted upon his stance by reversing federal-level climate activities initiated by his predecessor, spurring reinvestments into fossil fuels and disengaging from global climate politics. The US position on the science of climate change stands in stark contrast to that of the EU, which has for a long time tied its internal and external climate policies to the climate science as synthesised by the Intergovernmental Panel on Climate Change (IPCC), and notably to the 2°C scenario developed by the IPCC in its consecutive assessment reports. China's leadership, while more sceptical in the past, has more recently fully embraced IPCC-reported climate science and vowed to act upon it in its domestic climate and energy policies and climate diplomacy. This has enabled it to more closely collaborate with the EU, whereas both China and the EU have difficulties in finding common ground with key US policy-makers at the federal level.

A similar pattern emerges on the framing of climate change and the energy transition by the three parties. Whereas in the EU, the issue has since the late 1990s been framed – in line with the narrative of 'ecological modernization' – as an opportunity to develop a modern, climate-neutral economy, China's leadership has more recently embraced the idea of becoming a global leader in renewable energy technologies, thus equally framing the transition to a low-carbon economy as a major opportunity. Attempts to do likewise in the United States have repeatedly met with resistance. Obama's administration came closest to achieving such a framing, but ultimately had to resort to imposing climate measures through executive rather than legislative initiatives – testifying to the fact that a framing in terms of 'opportunity' had insufficiently caught on among portions of the political establishment and the public. This observation is certainly confirmed by the election and actions of his successor in the White House.

For Schreurs, the domestic ideational context in the US – at least at the federal level – is thus not prone for producing foreign policy positions that enable durable cooperation with China and the EU. These latter two find themselves however increasingly in agreement about climate science and the need to tackle it by seizing the opportunity that it entails to modernise societies. For China and the EU, it seems that a shared understanding has set in that it is now 'appropriate' to domestically and globally act on climate change. This lays the grounds for co-leadership, signs of which are clearly detectable in the discussions about the Paris Agreement implementation.

This optimism with regard to the durable prospects of China-EU cooperation under the Paris Agreement umbrella is not shared by Duncan Freeman. In his political economy account of EU-China-US relations on climate change and energy from a European perspective, he argues that the Paris Agreement climate objectives – even when they are framed in economic opportunity terms, and even if this framing is accepted by policy-makers and private sector actors across major emitters – can only be achieved within a broader global economic order that is favourable for decarbonisation. Instead of pointing into the direction of increased trade and investment flows to support this decarbonisation, the economic policies of the three players exhibit, however, tendencies of increased national interest protection. This implies that the global climate order created by the Paris Agreement and relying on mutual trust, cooperation and ultimately to a large extent on the shared belief that climate mitigation is not only necessary but also a real economic opportunity, might collide with a global economic order whose multilateral features are – as argued also in Part III of this volume – themselves under increased pressure. An obvious source of this pressure is the Trump administration's 'America First' doctrine. However, as Freeman argues, it does not stop there. China's industrial policies aimed at a low-energy transition are also seen with suspicion by the EU, as frequent recourse to trade defence measures indicates. A major – and currently seemingly very difficult – challenge for China, the EU and the US (and other players) is thus to converge around a globally 're-embedded economic liberalism' that complements the Paris Agreement-based climate order to enable the necessary global low-carbon transition.

All three chapters underscore the importance of the three major emitters and an entente between them – if not at the fundamental level of beliefs about climate change, then at least in the form of interest convergence – for the success of the global climate order created with the Paris Agreement. Where major structural obstacles at the global and domestic levels, notably in the US, are highlighted, the three chapters converge on the idea that agency is central for a durable low-carbon transition. Pragmatically, this agency is seen as coming not just from the central governmental level but also from subnational entities such as states and cities, as well as from transnational activities, and notably the activities of the private sector and civil society. Increasingly in the area of climate change and energy, it becomes thus necessary to think global order by factoring in the trilateral transnational dynamics at play.

Conclusion

As noted in the introduction, one of the underlying questions this book seeks to address is the role of the EU, China and the US in an evolving global order. This volume assumes that the EU, China and US are important, not just in themselves and via their direct bilateral relationships but also more widely in global affairs. All the authors in this book follow this assumption, thus there is general agreement that the EU, China and the US and their relationships are globally important in each of the three policy areas addressed in the separate chapters. Implicit in this is the assumption that the triangle that they constitute is not only more than just three significant bilateral relationships but also per se important to the structure of global order in each of the three policy areas this volume addresses. That the EU, China and the US are changing and the relationships between them and their global impact are consequently evolving is also examined in one way or another by all the authors. However, as the chapters demonstrate, not all the authors agree on the precise nature of the triangle of relationships and the changes that are taking place nor the possible outcomes of their global impact.

As the introduction notes, this volume adopts a decentred approach to the relationship between the EU, China and US. The authors address the subject from the point of view of different actors and policy areas and adopt different intellectual frameworks. The eclectic approaches adopted by the authors have the advantage of providing varying perspectives to the complexities of the matrix of the changing relationships between the EU, China and the US across the three policy areas of foreign policy, trade and climate change and energy. But this approach in the book as a whole almost inevitably leads to a lack of unified analyses across all the chapters and consequently of their conclusions. One of the implicit agreements of the authors is that the previously existing relationships and global order are changing, or being replaced. Yet, the authors in some chapters addressing the standpoint of different actors come to differing conclusions on questions as to how the relationships are changing, and what the outcomes may be. This in itself underscores the complexities of the role of the actors on which they focus, and the nature of their relationship to the other elements in the triangle and the global order. However, this reflects not just the complexities as a set of facts in the real world but also how they are constructed by the different actors. In some cases, it is not just that the same facts are perceived or analysed differently but also the underlying facts referred to in the chapters are not necessarily the same. Of course, this is hardly surprising when actors such as the EU, China and the US justify their actions. In academic debate this may be equally the case. Each actor has its own view and perspective on the relationships with the others as they construct the world differently. In itself this may be a unifying theme of this book. In a time of change, how that transformation is perceived by the actors who themselves are creating it is an important factor in how the change is worked out. Furthermore, the varying conclusions of the authors on key questions such as the likely future relationships of the EU, China and the US and their global impact is the result of more than just the standpoints of the actors. They may also reflect the differences in the various policy areas addressed by the authors. Viewed through the lens of foreign policy and security, economics and climate change, the actors and their relationships in the triangle and how they develop do not necessarily look the same.

That the authors have differing views may also in part depend on their chosen intellectual framework, whether it be historical, IR, economics, political economy or any other. Adopting eclectic approaches, without a unifying model, the chapters lay their emphasis on different factors in the relationships among the EU, China and the US and almost by definition lead the authors to different conclusions. The eclectic approach allows a reflection of the complexity of the actors and the relationship between them – the complexity of the evolution which is occurring in the triangle and the role it plays in the world. Allied to this complexity, the diversity of the chapters brings to the fore the degree of uncertainty related to the current evolution of the triangle and its future development.

One of the main points of agreement among the authors is that the changing relationship among the EU, China and the US and the wider implications for the world in which they are the major international actors is caused, to a certain degree, by the rise of China. This is most evident in the case of economics but is also in other areas. As noted in the introduction, the decline of the hegemonic US and the increasing global importance of China relative to the other actors and its global implications is a question that has impacts in all the policy areas discussed in this book, whether foreign policy and security, trade and investment or climate change and energy. This in itself is hardly novel, however, whereas addressing the specific question of the triangular relationship between the EU, China and the US provides a set of parameters that go beyond common approaches based on bilateral, regional or global analysis.

The rise of China is examined, in one way or another, by all the authors in this book. In recent years in particular, the rise of China points to a different development model, based on a totally different political system, which leads to questions on the uncertainty of future global order. Some even maintain that a new Cold War may be coming (Kaplan 2019). The central concern in the EU and the US is: how far will China challenge the existing international economic and political system? And how much will the EU and the US tolerate China's further development? China benefits significantly from the liberal economic order based on free trade, but its adherence to national sovereignty leaves no space for political integration and norm-setting that was once expected by the EU and the US. Martin Wolf warns that 'unbridled strategic competition between China and the west would be a disaster' (2019). Chinese scholar Yan Xuetong explains that China will act very cautiously to avoid direct confrontation with the US and manage its relationship with the latter pragmatically unless its core interests are jeopardised (2019). John Keane and Kerry Brown (2018) call for 'an opening of minds' and stress that 'the irreversible entanglement and co-operation' between China and the US should not be underestimated. It is too early to clearly articulate how the global system will evolve and how the international order will be further shaped by the interaction between China, the EU and the US. The research in our book indicates multiple paths to future research on what will continue to be one of the central questions related to the future global order.

References

Belis, D., S. Schunz, T. Wang & D. Jayaram (2018) 'Climate Diplomacy and the Rise of 'Multiple Bilateralism' between China, India and the EU', *Carbon & Climate Law Review* 12(2), 85–97.

Blackwill, R.D. & A. J. Tellis (2015) *Revising U.S. Grand Strategy Toward China*, Washington: Council on Foreign Relations Press.

European Commission (2019) *EU-China – A Strategic Outlook*, Strasbourg, March 12, JOIN (2019) 5 final.

European External Action Service (2016) 'Mogherini Sets Out Core Aims of EU Global Strategy', 22 April, Brussels.

Kaplan, R.D. (2019) 'A New Cold War Has Begun', *Foreign Policy*, January 7.

Keane, J. & K. Brown (2018) 'One World, Two Empires: Is China-US Conflict Inevitable?' *South China Morning Post*, March 17.

Mearsheimer, J.J. (2019) 'Bound to Fail: The Rise and Fall of the Liberal International Order', *International Security* 43(4), 7–50.
Tocci, N. (2017) *Framing the EU Global Strategy: A Stronger Europe in a Fragile World*, Basingstoke: Palgrave Macmillan.
Wolf, M. (2019) 'The Challenge of One World, Two Systems', *Financial Times*, January 29.
Yan, X. (2019) 'The Age of Uneasy Peace', *Foreign Affairs* 98(1), 40–46.

Index

Note: Page numbers followed by "n" denote endnotes.